C000264513

PRAISE FOR *GAME*
GAMIFICATION IN
RESEARCH

'Incredibly well-written and insightful. Whether you're a lifelong or aspiring researcher, think of *Games and Gamification in Market Research* as the only guide you need to create engaging game-based surveys that deliver more reliable data. From debunking misconceptions about game-based research methods to providing easy-to-understand guidelines for designing and making game-based surveys, Adamou envisions a new and improved research landscape, driven by gamification. Side benefit... respondents will actually enjoy participating in your research!' **Kristin Luck, Growth Strategist/Adviser, Luck Collective**

'Market researchers, who have been in the industry for long, know that their work is to better understand people, as opposed to "consumers". Unfortunately, over the years, getting people to answer questions has become a case of diminishing returns in terms of engagement. Surveys have become boring! Betty Adamou took the huge responsibility of finding a way out. Tapping on human psychology and behaviour, she has worked hard on the concept of game-based research methods. It's a huge game changer! One needs to read the book to believe. I can't thank Betty enough for making research more exciting and useful.' **Nasir Khan PhD CMRS, Principal Researcher and CEO, Somra-MBL Limited**

'*Games and Gamification in Market Research* is a labour of love and I thank Betty Adamou for making market research interesting again. This book arms the reader with a 360-degree insight into effective, engaging market research techniques. I already have favourite chapters I'll refer to time and again.' **Ade Onilude, Founder and CEO, Women in Marketing CIC**

'Betty Adamou manages to blend passion and practicality – drawing on her love of gaming and her hard-won experience earned through pioneering the use of games in the context of market research. This book has something for anybody interested in the application of games and gamification, from the seasoned professional to the newcomer.' **Ray Poynter, Co-founder, NewMR**

'Essential reading for the researcher seeking to use the engagement techniques of gaming to maximize survey participation and consumer insights.' **Mike Cooke, Legal Affairs Committee Chairman, ESOMAR**

'Betty Adamou is the absolute expert when it comes to games and gamification in market research. Her book is steeped in practical advice and is written in such an engaging way that you won't be able to help yourself in sharing her knowledge with others. Don't expect a dry manual. This is a great read with lots of activities to get you involved.' **Fiona Blades, President and Chief Experience Officer, MESH Experience**

'An interesting, informative read without the bulk. Betty Adamou is a master of her craft and this book is a gift to all who venture into the realm of games and gamification for market research. Betty takes a step back to help you focus on the psychology behind why these methods will help you succeed. A must-read for all people interested in the field.' **Laura Fagan, CEO and Founder, *The Pain Journal***

'Gamification has become one of research's verifiably worthwhile new tools to improve surveys in a variety of ways, benefiting the respondent, research agency and client. Who knows more about this subject than Betty Adamou? There's no expert out there who I respect as much on the subject as Betty, which is why I can't wait to get my copy of *Games and Gamification in Market Research*.' **Bob Lederer, Editor, Publisher and Producer, RFL Communications**

'Market research is going through a state of disruption on many fronts. We have big problems to solve, including respondent engagement, data quality and client belief in the powers of great consumer insight. Game-based research provides many of the answers to these problems and in this book Betty Adamou demonstrates how we can all benefit from more gamification.' **Stephen Phillips, CEO, ZappiStore**

'Betty Adamou has expertly developed an essential guide, providing the reader with a range of tools that will enhance the experience of participants and researchers alike, while improving the quality of data collected. This is a well-thought-out and insightful integration of the engaging nature of video games with market research.' **Jon Harrison MBA ODCC, Director of Learning and Organizational Development, Nova Southeastern University, and author, *Mastering the Game: What video games can teach us about success in life***

'*Games and Gamification in Market Research* is the book you hope to discover. A product of personal passion, developed through study of the academic principles underpinning our understanding of human behaviour and refined through commercial experimentation, it offers us a refreshing perspective on how to evolve our bread and butter. Betty Adamou invites us to collectively progress our approaches, blending in better understanding of what makes humans tick, to elicit more accurate data and insight. If you want to learn how to elevate what you do in your day-to-day from one of our industry's brightest and most innovative, this book is for you.' **Danielle Todd, Account Director, Relish Research**

'This book is destined to become the standard text on the subject of gamifcation and games to collect consumer data. It is a defining event in the development of gamification of data collection and will be a reference for years to come.'
Andrew Jeavons, Co-founder and Director of Analytics, Signoi

'Working with Betty Adamou while this book was being developed not only ignited my interest in gamification as a methodology, but also in market research as a career path. Insightful and interesting, *Games and Gamification in Market Research* sheds light on narrative surveys, and how they can be used to reach significant levels of engagement, putting the person before the respondent.'
David Wiszniowski, Senior Consumer Research Analyst, SkipTheDishes

'Betty Adamou is quite simply the authority on insights and gamification. Her book is a compelling and actionable guide that will help you to uncover deep consumer insight in more creative ways.' **KaRene Smith, Founder, Shine Insight**

Games and Gamification in Market Research

Increasing consumer engagement in research for business success

Betty Adamou

KoganPage

Publisher's note

Every possible effort has been made to ensure that the information contained in this book is accurate at the time of going to press, and the publisher and authors cannot accept responsibility for any errors or omissions, however caused. No responsibility for loss or damage occasioned to any person acting, or refraining from action, as a result of the material in this publication can be accepted by the editor, the publisher or any of the authors.

First published in Great Britain and the United States in 2019 by Kogan Page Limited

Apart from any fair dealing for the purposes of research or private study, or criticism or review, as permitted under the Copyright, Designs and Patents Act 1988, this publication may only be reproduced, stored or transmitted, in any form or by any means, with the prior permission in writing of the publishers, or in the case of reprographic reproduction in accordance with the terms and licences issued by the CLA. Enquiries concerning reproduction outside these terms should be sent to the publishers at the undermentioned addresses:

2nd Floor, 45 Gee Street	c/o Martin P Hill Consulting	4737/23 Ansari Road
London EC1V 3RS	122 W 27th St, 10th Floor	Daryaganj
United Kingdom	New York NY 10001	New Delhi 110002
www.koganpage.com	USA	India

© Betty Adamou, 2019

The right of Betty Adamou to be identified as the author of this work has been asserted by her in accordance with the Copyright, Designs and Patents Act 1988.

ISBN   978 0 7494 8335 7
E-ISBN   978 0 7494 8336 4

British Library Cataloguing-in-Publication Data

A CIP record for this book is available from the British Library.

Library of Congress Control Number: 2018038335

Typeset by Integra Software Services, Pondicherry
Print production managed by Jellyfish
Printed and bound by CPI Group (UK) Ltd, Croydon, CR0 4YY

For Dad, the most playful person I ever knew.
And for Paul, my husband and best friend in life's adventure.

CONTENTS

Don't miss the supporting companion website for this book which can be accessed via **www.koganpage.com/gamesandgamification**

FOREWORD

I've spent 25 years of my life carefully and mindfully crafting my questionnaire design skills for the marketing research industry. I've always enjoyed writing questionnaires, and get a big kick out of analysing and reporting on the data. But the research industry has a big problem and it pains me to say this: most of the questionnaires we write are really, really boring.

Throughout my undergraduate and graduate studies, I took advanced classes in research methods, questionnaire design, statistics and psychometrics. Looking back at those classes now, I realize they were missing a fundamental component. None of them, and none of the associated textbooks, focused on treating research participants as human beings, as real people who like and need to play. My formal education taught me about leading questions and double-barrelled questions but it never taught me to create a research experience that was fun and engaging, one that people would look forward to and seek out for enjoyment.

The consequence has been unmistakable. Researchers have taught people that questionnaires, and research in general, are boring and people have responded in kind. Survey response rates have declined drastically over the years and the cost to recruit participants has risen as a result. Even when we manage to convince people to at least begin answering questionnaires, completion rates are low because, as we all know, most questionnaires are boring, complicated, and not respectful of the human being volunteering their time for the researcher's benefit.

Is there a solution? Fortunately, you've got it in your hands right now. *Games and Gamification in Market Research* is a unique and timely contribution to the marketing research knowledge base.

More than five years ago, I met Betty Adamou in Venezuela, a peculiar meeting place when one person hails from Britain and the other from Canada. We had both been invited as expert speakers to a Best of Esomar conference. After finishing my talk, I took to my seat ready to find out who this Betty person was. I'd never heard of games and gamification in research before and, frankly, was quite puzzled by the concept.

To my delight, she too was passionate about creating a more positive, engaging research experience for participants. She too was dissatisfied with the status quo of continuing to write boring questionnaires because we've always written boring questionnaires. She had a plan to turn around response rates and show participants that research was something to look forward to. She had a solution and was going to bring it to market.

With that shared passion, I've watched Betty build her business and her clientele with one thing in mind – to make the research experience engaging by using games. As Founder and President of Research Through Gaming, Betty has tirelessly and freely shared her wisdom and her passion with students and practitioners in hundreds of webinars, workshops, guest university lectures, and conference presentations around the world including North America, South America, APAC and Europe. She's worked with numerous Fortune 500 companies to teach and help them conduct more engaging research with the use of games. She has become a master of game-based research.

And now it's your turn. Throughout this book, you'll find something you can get nowhere else. A renewed sense of what research should be like, a new sense of applying discovery and play to the research experience. You'll learn how games can be an important part of the market research process and, in fact, you'll see that digital games aren't all that different from online surveys. In the simplest of terms, a questionnaire is just a game that hasn't been brought to fruition yet. And questionnaires aren't the only research tools that can benefit from games and gamification. This book will undoubtedly provide ideas to make focus groups, online communities and other qualitative research projects more engaging for participants. Your toolbox of skills and tools is about to grow exponentially!

The game-based research mindset has impact for you as a researcher as well. Psychologists will tell you that intrinsic motivators like personal joy and engagement are far more effective than extrinsic motivators like cash. We know how expensive it is to financially incentivize participants so if that alone is your motivator, you'll benefit from internalizing the concepts in this book. Similarly, you'll also personally benefit from this book in that it will help you increase your empathy for participants, build better relationships with them, and consequently help to improve layperson perceptions of our industry. It's simply a 'win win win' situation.

I wish you great fun on your new journey. May you experience joy and passion as you learn a new approach for making research more engaging through gaming.

Annie Pettit, PhD CMRP FMRIA
Research Methods Consultant
Author of *The Listen Lady, People Aren't Robots: A practical guide to the psychology and design of questionnaires,* and *7 Strategies and 10 Tactics to Become a Thought Leader*

PREFACE

Everywhere I go, people are engaged in some form of play. On trains, people in suits, sportswear and overalls pass the time engrossed in *Candy Crush*. On the street, people hand over loyalty cards to cashiers to gain points for coffee and other goods, and people jogging by come fitted with contraptions like Fitbit's, counting their steps to let them know if they've achieved today's goal. When you understand more about play, games and gamification, you realize it's all around us. As one of my students put it 'I can't unsee gamification – it's everywhere!'. Indeed, play is so central to our lives that everyone is absorbed in games and gamification in some form or another, multiple times per day. But why?

Academics studying games and play have discovered that these innocent point systems and virtual badges tap into our psychological needs for mastery, autonomy, relatedness and purpose. It's the reason that Fortune 500 brands and start-ups have introduced more play culture and games in their day-to-day work and work environments, and why gamification is so pronounced in education, healthcare, training, engineering, and yes, research. Play (and playing games) has proven to increase creativity, productivity, problem-solving, motivation, and helps to bring about innovative ideas. Play also cures boredom and aids the passing of time. Play generates continuity and completion desires, among many other benefits. Playing games has equated to success in many industries, and playing games delivers success for market research. Game-based research has increased research efficiency with response rates of over 70 per cent, completion rates of over 90 per cent, continuation rates of over 80 per cent, and self-reported participant enjoyment of over 90 per cent. It has also delivered better nationally representative samples, richer insight that has improved marketing, communications and new product development – just a handful of the benefits and real-world results.

Game-based research (which includes games and gamification) is the most effective technique I've seen or used in 12 years working in market research, and this is partly because it can be applied with literally any other research methodology, making it widely accessible.

The philosophy of this book, and at the heart of Game-based Research Methods (GbRM) is the 'playspondent mindset'. Game-based research methods is a term encompassing any research approach that uses games and/or gamification techniques. The portmanteau is the marriage of 'player' and 'respondent'; hence 'playspondent'. This mindset starts every researcher on a quest to approach their relationships with participants as a game designer does with his or her players. Where efforts are made to provide *intrinsically* engaging and even emotive experiences. Where design is approached with empathy. Where play is encouraged. This approach creates a cocktail of benefits that aid the commercial success of research suppliers and buyers, not just in improved richness and detail of responses, but even gaining *untapped* insight unavailable through traditional online surveys. By adopting and learning about the relationships and processes inherent in games and gamification, researchers will also evolve trust and build two-way relationships with participants. This will improve the reputation of the market research industry (or whatever market research might become in the future), and attract new and divergent talent with the many careers that GbRM has to offer.

For some readers, the world of games may be unknown. As market researchers, you're not expected to be game players or game experts. That's why *Games and Gamification in Market Research* provides an overview of key developments in the games and gamification industry, along with how-to guides on designing your own game-based surveys.

With more people using research-games and gamified surveys, together we will grow a community of 'research artists': academics, designers and developers who are specialized in these methods and can shape what game-based research can *really* become.

We are at the precipice of huge developments; we don't know everything there is to know about GbRM yet, but the journey will be thrilling, especially as we use games as simulations and harness technologies like augmented reality and virtual reality. Through 'learning by doing' activities in this book, you'll hone the craft of designing game-based surveys, learn how to appropriately execute them, and be inspired by games to create emotive, experiential research-games and gamified surveys.

In many ways, I have been writing this book for almost eight years; studying, designing, playing, making, thinking and experimenting with games as a research instrument, and throughout this process, links between games and market research have continually been uncovered. This book is the translation of that study and development. And now it's your turn. Play games, study games, make games, and start to see the transformation of your research results and participant relationships. In the spirit of the mastery and collaboration of games, readers can visit the companion website and LinkedIn group to share your experiences with GbRM applications, your ideas, and together we can grow a community of experts.

Join the community via **www.koganpage.com/gamesandgamification**
Now let's PRESS START.

Betty Adamou

ACKNOWLEDGEMENTS

There are so many people to thank in helping bring this book to life.

Thanks to Jenny Volich and Charlotte Owen from Kogan Page for their support, enthusiasm and the incredible invitation to write this book.

A huge thanks to brilliant industry peers who took time to review this book and give feedback: Stephen Philips, KaRene Smith, Laura Fagan, Fiona Blades and Mike Cooke. With special thanks to three more people:

Annie Pettit, a brilliant mentor and friend who never let up on making me write and contributed many hours of reviewing and editing. Thank you for everything.

And Ray Poynter, another mentor and friend who also spent time providing instrumental reviews.

Thank you to Pamela Schindler for your encouragement, kind words, great advice, and being such an inspiration.

Thank you to others who took the time to review and give feedback of specific chapters: Jane Frost of the *Market Research Society*; David Wizsniowski; and the mysterious anonymous reviewer.

Thank you to Andrew Jeavons, who was *the* person who made me quit my job and start Research Through Gaming. Thank you for your friendship, support and guidance.

Thanks to the PhD dream team: Dr David Birks, Dr Anca Yallop and Dr Martina Hutton. Although we only had each other's company for a year, that time was pivotal and will never be forgotten. I hope this book does you proud.

Thank you to all Research Through Gaming clients, whose resolve to do research differently has been incredibly refreshing. Thank you for the opportunities to work with you and the kind permissions to share our work.

Thank you to all RTG participants, who took part in their first ever ResearchGames with us. Thank you for your participation, feedback and support. The case-studies in this book would be nothing without you.

Thank you to Marco Schmidt at Nebu, the first person I spoke with about 'how cool it would be if surveys were games'. Our ideas will change the world.

Thank you to the talented programmers who have worked on our ResearchGames, making it possible to bring my ideas to life: Vadim Gnadishev and Vitaliy Moskvin from the AlphaWeb Group; and Oscar North, Will Poynter and Arne Seib.

Thank you to the team at Askia for your support and collaboration, and letting me see what I could push or break.

Thank you to the experts who gave their time to provide one-to-one interviews, and to the equally talented game designers, cosplayers and game developers who granted kind permission to use examples of their work.

Thanks to RTG 'fans', including my industry peers and students, who have been following my work and have sent kind messages over the years and words of encouragement for writing this. Your messages were always appreciated more than you'll know (special shout out to Anije Lambert).

Thank you to my mum, for all her love, prayers, olives and support. To my brother Raphael, the biggest gamer I know, for teaching me so much about the variety of ways players can be engrossed in games.

Thank you to my life-long friend Maria Louca. Without her support, I don't know if I would even be in the mental or physical space to write this book. Thank you for being there.

Last, but certainly not least, thank you to my wonderful husband Paul. Could not have done this without your support, love and kindness, or without all the tea.

TRADEMARKS AND USAGE

The terms 'ResearchGame' and 'Playspondent', and their plurals, 'Research-Games' and 'Playspondents' are trademarked terms by Research Through Gaming Limited.

The term 'ResearchGame', stylized with a capital R and G, with no gap between the words, is not allowed for commercial use. Readers are welcome to use 'ResearchGame' in educational contexts where Research Through Gaming products are described as illustrative cases. The term 'Playspondents' is also permitted for educational use, but not for commercial use.

Wherever the term 'ResearchGame' is mentioned, this will refer specifically to products made by Research Through Gaming Limited.

Readers are welcome to use the term 'research-game' or 'research-games', as noted in this book.

Introduction

One of the reasons I was inspired to use games as an instrument to conduct research (and develop a company from it) was from reading a single line in the book *Reality is Broken* by Jane McGonigal: '[games] … can teach you about your true self: what your core strengths are, what really motivates you, and what makes you happiest'.[1] Where more so than in market research do we want to know what motivates people (to buy things, to desire things) and what makes them happier?

Through four parts, *Games and Gamification in Market Research* explores the theory, concepts and evidence for using games, gamification and playful approaches in online research, and encourages independent experimentation in game-based research design. Design guidelines have been developed to provide structure in what can be an abstract process. In the final words, we understand the technical requirements to make game-based research designs 'come to life', and predict how the future will unfold for game-based research methods (GbRM) with technologies like artificial intelligence (AI), virtual reality (VR) and augmented reality (AR).

In a day and age where engagement is king, games and gamification has become synonymous with engagement and data collection. When game-based approaches are applied in market research, researchers can create more engaging research experiences, generate valuable insight and future-proof commercial research endeavours. This is especially important as the pressure on researchers is more demanding than ever. While lots of people use games and gamification to create user/customer engagement, game-based research methods asks researchers to do those things *and* collect quality data that can then be translated to insight, of which businesses will make decisions that will have real-world impact. Researchers designing game-based surveys have one of the most complex and most unique tasks of all.

Customer data are required at a higher frequency now than ever before in history, and intrinsically engaging people to share information is key. But data requirements have evolved; we want to understand people on an emotional and experiential level. What better way to simulate emotion and experience while collecting data than through games? We also want to know not just what people liked and didn't like about our products and services yesterday; we want to know what they are *likely to do in the future*. Games are the perfect platform for future simulations to understand decisions and behaviours in context. As such, this book is not just about what has been, and what is now, but helps to shape what is yet to come.

You may wonder if a game designer would be better suited to designing research-games and gamified surveys, but that isn't necessarily the case. As a researcher, your experiences mean that you are already halfway to becoming a GbRM practitioner, because you understand the fundamental research principles that will *drive* the game-based research design. If you are a game designer interested in GbRM, consider learning about market research from the many market research webinars, workshops and conferences. Get in touch with the professional market research bodies in your area and see what learning platforms are available.

Using GbRM is about understanding the existing connections between games and research *and* excavating the connections that haven't been investigated yet. Some of the connections are obvious; play is exploratory and so is research. Both the game and the survey are interactive mediums. Both researchers and game designers want to engage participants. Both the survey participant and the game player are tasked to complete rudimentary and sometimes more taxing or creative cognitive tasks. Both the game and the survey should be platforms to make people think. But surveys are boring because they don't tap into our psychological needs, they don't intrinsically engage us and they don't encourage play like games do, but they could. The foundations are already there.

Using games as a research instrument is a powerful tool, going beyond quantitative research into what is often described as 'online qualitative', even online ethnography. Projective techniques can be used in game-based research, as well as making use of in-context observations of how participants behave. In this sense, research-games and gamified surveys are fluid methodologies – they can be used to simply create intrinsic engagement among participants and/or go *beyond* that to become online qualitative tools in which we begin to explore aspects like heuristics, implicit associations, as well as observing behaviours through simulations in 2D, 3D or even virtual reality environments. This is where the opportunities of GbRM get juicier in terms of the types of data researchers can collect and the insight that can be captured.

Interaction with a research-game goes beyond mere 'taking part' – participants *play* research-games, and to play has function. As we explore in this book, play boosts our problem-solving skills, creativity and collaboration (among other benefits); these are desirable behaviours for researchers to harness. We learn through play but through *observing* play, the observer can also harness information and learn. **In this book, I look at play through a different lens: 'play as data generator'.**

Play has been described as the opposite of seriousness;[2] however, play in a research context has 'serious' outcomes, like data and insight for commercial endeavours. As such, through game-based research, we encourage participants to engage in serious play and research-games become part of the genre of Serious Games.

Serious Games consider stakeholders and end-users, and have been used in a variety of industries, with varying degrees of success. They have been used to help people understand more about their medical conditions, for employee training and recruitment, to overcome psychical or mental setbacks, to raise awareness and explore issues like racism, sexism and homophobia, and for commercial gain to promote a product or service. Why have there been varying degrees of success? Often because of the quality of design, which is integral to everything from the onboarding process to the long-term relationships built with users. That's why design, and understanding the design process, is so fundamental to game-based surveys; they too need attention to design so that researchers can appropriately engage audiences and uncover the truth about what people think and feel, and what they will do.

The power of game-based research is not at its zenith yet, and that's why we need the following:

- more research-game designers;
- more research into game-based survey design;
- game-based research methods taught as part of research modules in schools and universities as part of market research studies;
- for game-based research to evolve.

In the final part of this book, I discuss the possibilities for game-based research with other technologies. I hope the students and graduates of today will take these techniques by the horns and evolve them in directions that we haven't even envisaged yet. It really is only our imagination that holds us back when it comes to game-based research.

In the latter 'worlds' of this book, we will also see how games and gamification don't just help us solve our research problems for today, but help us go *beyond* the immediate rescue mission to actually improve the way our industry works for tomorrow. We will see that by improving our survey designs through using game-based methods, we open our doors to new talent and evolve as an industry with exciting careers and new opportunities for research users.

Who should read this book?

Games and Gamification in Market Research is for people who work in the multitude of fields that make up market research and insight industries, who are interested in increased participant engagement, improved data quality and innovation. If you are an insights innovation manager, project manager, client success manager, research lecturer or a programmer, then this book is also for you as within these pages there are ideas to inspire new research designs and technological approaches.

But you may have none of those job titles; you may be a student, sitting in your library at university, poised over this book with a highlighter in hand. Or you may be working at your very first research job. If so, I want you to see the variety of opportunities you have at your fingertips and shape the future of research (not to shun the seasoned market researchers, of course). YOU are going to be the thought-leaders and game changers (pun intended) when we are all old and retired. You will evolve our industry, and I am intrigued to see how you use and mature GbRM in the years to come. No matter your breadth of experience; from a veteran researcher to shiny new student, or whether your background is in psychology or linguistics, behavioural economics, narratology or anthropology, you will find something that resonates with you and your research practices in these pages because GbRM is at the intersection of at least a dozen disciplines.

How to read this book

Games and Gamification in Market Research is structured in four parts to reflect the workflow process of the research practitioner: from understanding to making and launching. There are aspects of this process that are the same or similar to working with other methodologies. Only the aspects of the research processes that are different from or particular to game-based research will be discussed in this book. For instance, the processes of finding insight in research results is the same process when using game-based methods as it is with any other methodology. As such, this book won't delve into how to find insight in your data – the difference will be in the *quality* of data you will be working with when using game-based methods. There is a wealth of books and other publications that discuss how to find insight in research data – these are listed in the 'Recommended reading' section below.

At first glance, the process of understanding, designing and executing game-based research may seem linear:

Step 1: understand the methodologies of GbRM.

Step 2: apply that knowledge to develop your game-based research design.

Step 3: develop the design as a 'live' survey.

Step 4: launch the game-based survey and collect research results.

Step 5: analyse the research results and find insight in the data.

Step 6: present the research results and insight to the research buyer.

However, when it comes to game-based research, the process should be considered as a process that keeps on giving, where the knowledge you gain in every GbRM study contributes to the theory and design knowledge about these techniques, which will then help to improve your next game-based research study. As such, the process is perpetuating; even when things might not go right, you can learn from mistakes and this will make future research-games or gamified surveys more effective.

Recommended reading

Harrison, M *et al* (2016) *Market Research in Practice: An introduction to gaining greater market insight*, Kogan Page, London

Poynter, R (2010) *Handbook of Online and Social Media Research: Tools and techniques for market researchers*, Wiley, Chichester

Schindler, PS (2018) *Business Research Methods* 13th Edition, McGraw Hill Education, New York

Take a look through the NewMR.org online archive, where many years worth of recorded webinars by some of the industry's leading figures discuss a variety of research methodologies and technologies.

Notes

1 McGonigal, J (2011) *Reality Is Broken: Why games make us better and how they can change the world*, Penguin Press, New York

2 Huizinga, J (2016) *Homo Ludens: A study*, Angelico Press. 1st edition published in 1949 by Routledge and Kegan Paul Ltd

PART ONE
World of Understanding – overview

Online market research as it is in the majority, is unsustainable. More than that, it's not working to its full powerful potential. Yet.

Through issues like low participant engagement, depleting data quality and facing increasing competition through other forms of data collection, many research providers wonder how they will survive using the same traditional online research methodologies in the future. But change is afoot.

Using games and gamification in market research is not just a rescue mission, it's a call to completely reinvent the way researchers work, how data are collected, the types of data that can be collected, and how participants interact with researchers and data collection systems. Game-based research methods (or GbRM – an umbrella term describing research that uses games and/or gamification) are about the survival of market research and making it thrive.

GbRM will help researchers improve participant engagement and nudge desired participant behaviours by turning the dial away from extrinsic motivators to *intrinsic* motivation and encouraging play, which, through the increased collaboration, creativity, engagement and problem-solving skills that come with intrinsic engagement and play, will help improve data quality, harness untapped insights, and even re-engage suppliers and buyers in the research process. GbRM could even shape the way we design data collection software or hardware in the future.

But this process of change must begin at the beginning: drastically improving participant engagement. And what better medium to be inspired by than the most engaging medium of all time: the game.

Gamifying a survey, or creating one as a fully-fledged game, is not a 'lipstick on a pig' approach: far from it. While games may seem frivolous to some, and by proxy game-based research may be viewed in the same light, this world introduces games through a lens you might not have considered before, showing how we can harness the capabilities and structures inherent within games to solve real issues faced by the market research industry. This world illustrates where those issues lie to pinpoint how and where game-based research methods can provide solutions.

At the most basic level, GbRM will intrinsically engage participants in a way never done before. This in itself has many benefits. You will be surprised how many people are simply grateful that somebody, *anybody,* is making an effort to develop more engaging surveys. Of all the frequently used terms participants provide in their feedback about Research Through Gaming ResearchGames, 'thank you' is the most frequent, followed by terms like 'fun', 'cool', 'interesting' and other similar sentiment. When I look through the feedback and see the comments... 'that was great, thanks so much!', 'thanks for letting me be part of this!', 'I love this idea THANK YOU',[1] I think 'no, thank YOU'. But these participants thank the invisible person behind the ResearchGame design, who they don't know, because they're so plain delighted it's not yet another boring market research questionnaire.

But at the more powerful, advanced levels of using GbRM, it is at this point quantitative research transcends to become online qualitative. We can place participants in situations and simulations to understand how context drives behaviours and choices – all happening while we observe rather than ask questions. Through that observation, we will use game-based research to understand what people think and feel, yes, but also what they will *do.* In turn, this will help businesses develop predictive models to anticipate the behaviours and outcomes of a thousand marketing approaches, product developments, social service processes and so on.

At this level, we're taking more advantage of the implicit and beginning to shape research experiences around the ways our memory actually works and how people live their lives. Through GbRM, we will use state-dependent recall but also future-gaze through designing state and context induced simulations to understand behaviours and choices. Research-as-game will finally be reflective of (and understand) the many complexities of human emotion and pinpoint key drivers to help businesses make decisions.

The good news is that all of this is already at our fingertips.

This world highlights how actually online surveys and games have many similarities, making GbRM more accessible than we might think. This section also shows us how much we can learn from the games industry to intrinsically engage our own participants and encourage their creativity, problem-solving and collaborative skills. We will do away with existing misconceptions about games and gamification to make room for understanding the benefits of these methodologies and what it is that makes games so engaging. We will look at the multiple facets inherent in games: a cocktail of narratology, positive reinforcement, heuristics, semiotics, linguistics, cognitive psychology and more.

And we will even look at how games, data and insight are already working harmoniously. This journey is just the beginning.

The impact of low participant engagement in market research

01

This chapter will cover:

- the eight side effects of low participant engagement;
- how these eight side effects negatively impact the market research industry at large;
- how the game, the most engaging medium of all time, is the perfect antidote to low engagement.

If we are to look at game-based research methods (GbRM) as tools for both prevention and cure of low participant engagement, then we must first understand the full picture of the issues taking place.

According to the 2017 GreenBook Research Industry Trends (GRIT) Report, 70 per cent of the market research industry relies on traditional surveys[1] to collect opinion data[2] and other forms of information. Other reports and market research experts predict that the use of traditional online surveys in market research is actually higher, at 80–90 per cent. Alarmingly, these high numbers do not negate (but perhaps even exacerbate) one universal problem: low participant engagement. Low participant engagement negatively impacts *every* aspect of the research process and every person involved. The drawbacks have been vocalized online[3, 4] – highlighting the problems and spreading mistrust of market research. Consider these eight domino-effect issues.

Eight side effects of low participant engagement

1 **Low response rates.** Response rates describe the quantities of people who respond to a survey – that is, how many people actually begin a survey. Low response rates could be caused by several factors: there are other online distractions, or participants have so many emails that they miss your survey invitation. Participants who have been previously bored by online surveys may be reluctant to begin new ones, resulting in low response rates for *all* online studies, not just yours. This shows how one participant's bad research experience can impact other projects, making the process more difficult for everyone involved. Low response rates lead to ...

2 **Low completion rates.** Participants can't complete surveys they don't start. Just because someone might begin answering an online survey, it doesn't mean he or she will finish it. Often surveys can be long and cumbersome, so people drop out during the course of taking part. People can drop out of a survey for other reasons: they might be experiencing an emergency, or simply want to stop and make a snack. The games industry shows us a different picture – that players can be so intrinsically engaged that they play games for hours on end, even ignoring hunger pangs.

3 **Declining panel response rates and panel sizes.** A panel refers to a pool of people who have signed up to participate in online surveys from different research buyers. Low engagement doesn't just impact response and completion rates for individual research projects, it can even lower the collective response and completion rates for online panels. This affects dozens if not hundreds of research projects. People who once signed up to receive surveys from panel companies and loyally completed them, may have become bored over time and take part less and less. Eventually, such participants are labelled as 'inactive' panellists. Panel sizes then decrease. This leads to ...

4 **Longer field durations.** When surveys are so cumbersome and/or boring that people don't want to start or complete them, 'field times' (the length of time surveys are active online) are often lengthened to accommodate low completion rates. For instance, if research providers can't achieve a target of 500 completed surveys in two weeks, they can (budget and time permitting) increase the timeline in the hope of making up the required numbers. This leads to ...

5 **More money spent – higher costs per project.** Extending field time requires further human and digital resources. This costs money. Even if field times are lengthened by just a few days (although field times can be extended by extra weeks or months in some cases) this might increase costs for a given project from a few hundred dollars to thousands of dollars. As well as these sorts of costs to consider, research providers try to increase their chances in gaining the quantity of required completed surveys by spending elsewhere. They may do one or all of these three things:

   – **Award higher incentives**: this can be an increase of how much money participants are paid as a reward for completing surveys, or giving them higher value vouchers and so on. However, even an increase of the incentive value doesn't always work (if it did, we might not see low response and completion rates). By contrast, people play games *without* payment. While there are in-game rewards that keep players engaged, they spend money *to play* games; a completely different dynamic compared to participant interaction with market research.

   – **Recruit even *more* panellists**: in efforts to increase the probability that research providers capture the required quantities of completed surveys, they may spend more money on advertising to try to get more people to sign up to their panel company to take part in surveys.

   – **Send out more email invitations** to participants so that they can take part in surveys, but this often results in participants feeling 'spammed' and again, isn't necessarily effective.

6 **Unreliable data and/or poor data quality.** With the above issues at hand, data quality is questioned. Indeed, continued inaccuracies in data findings have led to a well-documented research buyer confidence crisis.[5] Two factors may lead us to question data quality:

   – **Straightlining**: or speedrunning, is when a participant selects survey answers quickly just to complete the survey faster, often not thinking about his or her responses at all. This is certainly not the case with every participant, but it does happen. And if people are speeding through your survey, how much can you rely on their responses as thought-out and truly reflective of their opinions and experiences? Could you trust that data enough to make multimillion dollar business decisions? Probably not.

   – **Confusion**: even participants who *want* to respond to surveys in an attentive way might not always provide 'correct data' because of badly written questions and/or poor survey design. Again, this is not the case with every survey, but it is well documented that better question design (as well as improvements in overall survey design and accessibility) are needed in market research.

7 Homogeneity among panel companies. When many market research companies design the same boring questionnaires, often adopting the same aesthetic, nothing sets them apart. This leads to homogeneity among research providers. Jonathan Clough, co-founder and director of ResearchBods, writing in MRIA's *VUE* magazine in 2014, captured this issue well: 'the emergence of technology, in particular the internet, has brought about the commoditization of research panels. This has all but diminished the USPs of many of the companies out there, with most having to significantly reduce prices in order to remain competitive and relevant.'[6] This is likely because many research companies use the same survey software from the same eight or so survey software providers. Many of those providers offer customization capabilities, so that researchers can change up the design and differentiate their 'look and feel'. The quantity of researchers who take advantage of such customization capabilities is unknown. By contrast, there's an unlimited list of games made using the same software (Unreal and Unity are two of many examples of game engines) but through differences in design, they offer *completely* different game products.

8 Unengaged staff and clients. Your clients don't get the data and insight they need and question if they can trust it. Your participants are unengaged. Who wants to be the person in the middle of that? Who wants to write boring surveys? Unengaged participants, researchers and research buyers means everyone loses out.

This list of the eight effects of low participant engagement definitely captures the worst of the situation. You may be reading this feeling fairly satisfied that participants love your surveys, or you're safe in the knowledge that you have happy clients. While this is true for many a researcher, my question is this: as technology moves on, as we evolve our expectations of digital experiences, and as new methods of data collection pop up every day, will you feel as comfortable in five years' time? Or 10 years' time? Are disengaging modes of carrying out online research sustainable? No.

Surely it is better to take the money that is currently spent on patching over the issues and instead invest those funds on improving the survey design and increasing participant engagement. In my view, prevention and change is always better than cure.

And change is happening, for some. Market research is beefing up with technology companies and innovative new start-ups. The many conferences that make up a researcher's busy social calendar are great at giving audiences a chance to see under the hood. As an industry, we are currently obsessed with the new and with technology. While such change is whole-heartedly welcomed, refreshing and exciting, what kind of position will your business be in if you're not a fancy new tech start-up? What can these sorts of companies do to solve the commercially crippling issues in our list, improve participant engagement and elevate data quality? Game-based research is the answer.

The key difference between digital games and online surveys is that while online surveys are unengaging and rely on extrinsic motivators, games are the most engaging medium of all time. Mobile games accounted for more revenue than any other form of entertainment in 2017, generating US $40.6 billion worldwide[7] and people spend more money on games than they do on movies and music combined (at an estimated revenue of US $92 billion in 2017).[8] Not only do they inspire intrinsic engagement, but play. Both outputs have significant benefits in market research and as such, games are the perfect antidote to all eight of these issues. But digital games and online surveys have many similarities, as we explore in Chapter 2.

Notes

1 Traditional surveys are considered to be surveys that, in the majority, have one question per screen, use grids, Likert scales, drag and drop functions, have a block-colour background and have a similar layout and general aesthetic as paper surveys, but online. Traditional online surveys may also include images, video and some basic dynamic interface, but would still be considered 'traditional' in their aesthetic and interactivity.

2 *Dominant Data Collection Methods* where 56 per cent of dominant data collection methods are reported to be online surveys, and 14 per cent reported to be mobile surveys. GRIT Report Q3–Q4 2017 published by GreenBook (available online and in print).

3 Dooley, Roger (2012) [accessed 9 May 2018] Why so much market research sucks, *Forbes Magazine* [Online] www.forbes.com/sites/rogerdooley/2012/10/04/market-research/#31c994627394

4 Silva, Pia (2017) [accessed 9 May 2018] Forget market research. Do your thing. *Forbes Magazine* [Online] www.forbes.com/sites/piasilva/2017/10/04/forget-market-research-do-your-thing/#22c627834278

5 RFL online (2018) [accessed 4 June 2018] Inaccurate polls draining UK research revenues, RBDR [Online video report] https://youtu.be/_PdDv6t0BdI

6 Clough, Jonathan (2014) [accessed 20 May 2018] Community rewarded research: A new approach to respondent recruitment ad incentivization for children, young people and families, *VUE magazine* [Online] http://mria-arim. ca/vueonline/PDF/VUE-June-2014.pdf

7 Statista (date and author unknown) [accessed 20 May 2018] [Online] www. statista.com/topics/1906/mobile-gaming/

8 Taylor, George (2016) [accessed 28 May 2018] Why is gaming more popular than music and film? *Huffington Post* [Online] www.huffingtonpost.co.uk/ george-taylor/why-is-gaming-more-popular-than-music-and-film_b_10095376. html

The surprising similarities between digital games and online surveys

02

This chapter will explore:

- similarities between digital games and online surveys, from the challenges faced to user interaction;
- rethinking online surveys as productive 'entertainment snacks'.

People can be cautious towards things that are different from what they know. Unsurprisingly, some researchers have reservations about games and gamification as tools for data collection. This chapter illustrates that there are more similarities between digital games and online surveys than one might think. These similarities are useful to understand as they can help promote confidence in researchers who are thinking of using game-based research methods, and we can begin to evidence that common ground exists for a natural merger of both disciplines.

If we think of both platforms simply as digital products, the parallels can be drawn easily:

1 **Finish line**: both digital games and online surveys are made to be completed.

2 **Measuring engagement**: people working in game companies and in research companies evaluate engagement in similar ways. For example, measuring the duration of participation, completion rates, additional voluntary actions and so on.

3 **Paradata and metadata** are collected from player interactions with games and participant interactions with surveys.

4 **Audience engagement** is crucial for the survival and growth of both the game and research industries. Both are saturated and competitive markets and are equally 'overcrowded'. As such, how to engage audiences in effective and innovative ways is top of the agenda for both industries.

5 **Pricing and free models**: as both markets are saturated, this drives how games and surveys are priced, if priced at all. 'Freemium' models in gaming are popular, and in research many DIY survey tools and data analysis tools can also be used for free.

6 **Online communities:** online research panels and game communities are relied upon in both industries for creating and perpetuating user engagement. Many market research organizations have developed panels of participants into the hundreds of thousands, ready to take part in research. Market research online communities (MROCs) may have smaller numbers but are one of the most popular types of online research today.[1] Equally, game companies have their own 'panels' – communities they tap into in order to troubleshoot issues, for insight and to promote new products to people ready to play games. What is the PlayStation Network (PSN) if not a massive online community?

No other medium is as similar to digital games as online research. Even the challenges that both industries face are comparable.

Technological challenges

Both digital games and online surveys rely on technology (as well as design) to develop products for maximum user accessibility and engagement. Game designers and survey designers must consider the quantity and types of devices on which their products will be made available/playable. But the decision-making process isn't just about 'should this work on the latest iPad?' The programming languages used to develop the software in the first place also need consideration. For example, use Flash and the survey/game won't work on most mobile devices.

As it's impossible to test a survey or game on every device configuration, for every browser, for every browser version and to prepare for every browser update, or anticipate every new mobile phone release, real trade-offs have to be made. For both game and survey developers, making decisions regarding the devices used for playability/accessibility has direct economic consequences. More devices means more playtesting and human resources. On the flip side, limited accessibility can be equally disadvantageous from a financial point of view. For both surveys and games, a balance must be struck and the cost/benefit analysis considered.

Economic challenges

How much will it cost to deploy an online survey or digital game if made available on 15 mobile devices versus 35 mobile devices? How much money can be spent on design to ensure user engagement? Will better design or increased accessibility provide a better return on investment? These are economic challenges that game designers and research designers must overcome.

Creative challenges

Game and survey designers must satisfy stakeholders. In the game industry, stakeholders include people who have a vested financial interest in a game being successful. In the research industry, the stakeholder is the research client. It's a balancing act when trying to satisfy game players and/or research participants with a creative and engaging platform while satisfying stakeholders who need a return on their investment. Design efforts versus successful engagement is another balancing act.

Time challenges

The inside joke among researchers is that survey results are needed 'yesterday', such are the time constraints faced by the market research industry. Although the game industry undoubtedly has longer development times for designing and launching their products, their time constraints are just as real, representing other challenges around creative input. For both online surveys and digital games, creative sacrifices are often made to get things done on time.

Innovation challenges (and obsession)

Market researchers talk about innovation *a lot*. While many innovations in market research are certainly a breath of fresh air, such innovations are often 'a day late and a dollar short' compared to the innovations and outright inventions from the game industry. Both digital games and online research need innovation to engage people, gain competitive advantage, and grow as businesses.

While the application of 'innovation' differs in online surveys and digital games, we can't deny that both industries are obsessed and challenged by it; obsessed because innovation is one of the ways the game and survey can gain audience engagement – there is no denying the power of the novel. Innovation is also a way to stand out from competitors. If research supplier X has an innovative take on their surveys, this can engage participants *as well as* research buyers. In the games industry, innovation can help get funding and make sales.

The challenge is that innovation can require large investments of time and money. The digital game industry has invested heavily in many innovations: from augmented reality to virtual reality and beyond. Indeed, fully-fledged inventions have been born from this industry. Kinect, the motion sensing input device, is one of two inventions for games created by software engineer Alex Kipman for Microsoft. The Kinect, used for the Xbox game console and Windows PC, 'revolutionized personal entertainment with its ability to fully recognize and adapt a human's form and gestures into video game and other entertainment experiences.'[2] Such inventions have benefited other industries. Kinect technology has been used in drone flight, 3D scanning, and even being able remotely to pet a cat.[3]

But even when we get passed the hurdle of financial and time investments, innovation represents other difficulties; on one hand, innovation is key but on the flipside, excessive developments can result in a 'newness' overload, in which every innovation is less impressive and soon forgotten when the 'next big thing' comes along.

Looking at these similarities, we see digital games and online surveys have much common ground.

How users control and manipulate worlds

We will now explore similarities between player and participant interaction, and what game designers and survey designers expect audiences to do.

When we play games, there's a sense of purpose and control amid the chaos, and chaos it truly is. Game designers have come up with a myriad of imaginative ways to obscure the path of the player and cause problems. Where else do we voluntarily face a maelstrom of such troubles and obstacles and call it 'entertainment'? Where else in our digital lives do we place ourselves in situations where even the tiniest action has (sometimes massive) repercussions? The answer is actually the online survey, but we'll come back to this in a moment.

In no other place in our lives is our control more immediate, where our action (or inaction) has a direct effect on something or someone, than in games. In that sense alone, games are more powerful than any other media. Experiencing how we shape our game worlds is thrilling. In the game world, you can successfully overcome obstacles and level up. You are in control because you've manipulated the game world to clear your path and reach your goal.

It may seem far-fetched to draw parallels from this sense of control and changing virtual worlds in games to comparisons with online research, but scratch the surface a little and the similarities are unmistakeable. Let's think about the level of control we give to survey participants; we ask them what they think, or what they will do, and observe their actions. That data, that insight, helps to shape everything around us, from the products on sale to our social services. The consumer, as they say, is king. Thus, the control given to participants has consequence, just as the decisions of a game player has consequence in their (virtual) world. The opinions and feelings of participants – their data – have control and weight in shaping the *real* world.

Some of the ways that control is exercised has some conceptual constructs. In a blog by Mustard Research, they list 10 projective techniques to use with research participants. These techniques range from tasking participants to imagine and shape entire planets, or imagine the future via a 'time-machine' activity.[4] In games, harnessing the human imagination in these ways has been part and parcel of gaming since it began.

We give participants such control because, like in games, obstacles (albeit commercial, real-world obstacles) need to be overcome. Whether it's a videogame or whether it's a survey, there is a problem to solve; we're seeking an ideal result, a utopia in the face of multi-layered business issues. And to overcome obstacles means researchers ask participants to problem-solve, just as game players are tasked to problem-solve. Digital games ask people to complete repetitive, rudimentary and sometimes more advanced cognitive tasks. So do online surveys. When researchers restyle these parallels in control, shaping worlds and problem-solving with a game-designer mindset, they will transmogrify their surveys to generate the kinds of intrinsic engagement that games create. Research-games can become forms of creative expression.

Projective techniques, characters and avatars

Through projective techniques, researchers also encourage participants to place themselves in other people's shoes, to effectively become a character. Herein lies another likeness with digital games: the use of characters and role-play is as common in games as point systems.

Projective techniques can include things like 'which product would you launch if you were the president of this brand?' or 'if you were head of marketing, which campaign would you use?' – these are personification techniques in which users 'project' their feelings, opinions and desires through the lens of another role.

I have used these techniques in my own ResearchGames, but have gone further to allow participants to create their own avatars, thus building the emotional connection between participant and their character further. I have tasked participants to dress their avatar as if they were living in the year 2030 (with a choice of futuristic clothing and gadgetry) through to making their avatar as if they were the head of a food company's marketing department.

Some market researchers have asked me if participants make 'realistic' or 'fantastical' avatars of themselves. This question is really about research validity. The answer is: it doesn't matter whether the avatars are created in a true likeness of the participants or not. What matters is the *insight*. What matters is the level of connection that the participant has with the research content. Can the designer make the participant understand the mindset of another person/character (or something more conceptual) and then make choices based on being 'in that role'?

The role of the designer is crucial here. If the software for creating visual anthropomorphic avatars is designed with a choice of what would be seen as fairly 'everyday' hairstyles, hair colours, clothes, accessories and so on, then the designer limits how atypical a participant can make his or her avatar. On the flipside, if the designer introduces an array of fantastical items, such as a 10-foot high mohawk or Rapunzel-length hair, then this gives participants licence to go off-kilter in how they style their virtual selves.

Fantastical items, however, can also be useful in terms of semiotics and insight. Let's say I introduce a pair of angel wings and devil horns to my standard 'Avatar Creator Tool' accessories section. The horns and wings are displayed among everyday items like hats, glasses, earrings, religious accessories and so on. I ask the participant something like 'If Brand X was a person, what would he or she look like?'

The participant may create the avatar in a fairly regular fashion but see the wings and horns and make a choice based on semiotics – the horns are chosen. The participant is saying something about what they think of the brand using that visual metaphor. The visual metaphor is useful to researchers. In this oversimplified example, we can see that not only is it nonsensical to determine the legitimacy of participant-made avatars by whether or not they are realistic or fantastical, but actually researchers can, by offering conceptual visual cues, gain useful insight that would be unavailable through traditional surveying methods.

Avatars are, in some form or another, in almost every digital game. Whether the player embodies a character, selects from a predetermined line-up of characters, or creates his or her own avatar from scratch, game 'characters' exist in some form or another. As players control their avatars, they are not necessarily behaving as their character, but making choices and behaving as themselves channelled through a virtual prosopopoeia, albeit with the strengths and/or limitations that come with using specific game characters: for example, if their character has a specific skill or weakness.

Researchers should view digital avatars as a vehicle for participant expression; to see avatars as giving participants freedom of movement, instead of viewing avatars in the more literal fashion of 'but did the participant dress his or her avatar as they dress in real life?'. Unless a research study is specifically about the brands people wear, it's a little redundant – especially as research buyers increasingly want to learn more about what people *aspire* to wear/buy/do in the future so they can cater for their desires. (Avatars are discussed further in Chapter 4, and again in Part Two: World of Design.)

There are many effective projective techniques recommended for market research: 'word associations, imagery associations, grouping and choice ordering techniques, imagery associations with consumer personalities'[5] through to 'brand eulogy' exercises[6] and other imaginative practices. These examples show that the projective techniques in research use the playful principles often seen in games. In games, players conduct similar exercises – they embody characters and are immersed in conceptual narratives, they make decisions based on a plethora of stimuli or based on a variety of contexts, all day long. They also harness characterization to problem-solve via empathy and to uncover deeper motivations.

As Kirsty Nunez, the President and Chief Research Strategist at Q2 Insights Inc. writes in the American Marketing Association (SDAMA): '[Projective] techniques allow researchers to tap into consumers' deep motivations, beliefs, attitudes and values. This is important because psychology has told us for a long time that much of what drives behaviour is emotional and irrational in nature. To some extent, these emotional drivers of behaviour lie below conscious awareness.'[7] In games, players often behave via emotional and context-based drivers. The emotional connections between game and player are what makes games so engaging and explains why millions of people spend millions of hours immersed in game worlds.

Using the similarities to rethink research participation: research-games as 'entertainment snacks'

Playing a game on your mobile device when waiting for a train or just to while away time on a lunch break is dubbed 'entertainment snacking' and is *very* common. According to a research study by entertainment company Mind Candy, half of us play app games while in the lavatory.[8] I've lost count of the number of people I see on trains playing *Candy Crush* – a mobile app game played by 93 million people every day.[9] Are 93 million people taking part in surveys every day? Unlikely. Are people using an opportunity to take part in research to while away time? Not really.

What is more fascinating than the frequency of playing games is the time that people dedicate to it. In a research study I conducted with my team at Research Through Gaming in 2010 in collaboration with Survey Sampling International (SSI) in the United Kingdom, findings showed that people play games for up to 30 minutes at a time on a mobile phone.[10] Another study shows that people play games for up to 45 minutes on their phones.[11] By contrast, researchers struggle to engage participants for those durations on mobile devices. In fact, researchers are encouraged to make mobile-based surveys as short as possible – even as short as 5 minutes[12] despite studies showing that 30 minutes and even 45 minutes of mobile phone interaction is entirely possible. It makes sense then for researchers, who require more than just 5 minutes from participants, to nudge them to 'entertainment snack' on surveys, or 'research snack' as the case may be.

Making research-games (and optimizing them for mobile devices) is an ideal way for participants to do something productive and gain value from their participation during their downtime. By explicitly promoting research studies as 'something to do in your downtime' or when bored, researchers can use 'downtime' and 'boredom' as triggers to make people think about survey participation. If the market research community were to promote surveys in this way, we could see higher response rates as a result of a new mindset. Got time to kill? Play a research-game!

This change of mindset in combination with promoting surveys for their transcendent purpose – as an integral part making the world we live in a better place – is a win-win situation. But the platform has to be intrinsically engaging to encourage those desirable types of interaction.

Throughout this book, further similarities between digital games and online surveys will be highlighted. Where there are differences, we will look to games as inspiration to bridge gaps and improve market research performance. Before doing so, there are some common misconceptions about games and gamification to demystify in and outside of market research, as we come to in the next chapter.

Notes

1 *Adoption of Emerging Methods* (pages 12 and 13) where 60 per cent of research suppliers and research buyers reported to currently use online communities. GRIT Report Q3–Q4 (available online and in print). **Note:** The authors of the GRIT Report note that figures will tend to be higher in the GRIT Report results compared to the market research population at large, as the responders to the GRIT survey (which helps to produce the report) are 'more engaged with the future of research'. As such, the sample is not representative, but the general consensus in the market research community is that MROCs are one of the most, if not the most, popular methods in market research today.

2 Quinn, Gene (2012) [accessed 20 May 2018] IPO to award National Inventor of the Year to Kinect Inventor, *IP Watchdog* [Online] www.ipwatchdog.com/ 2012/12/07/ipo-to-award-national-inventor-of-the-year-to-kinect-inventor/ id=31088

3 Walker, Rob (2012) [accessed 20 May 2018] Freaks, geeks and Microsoft: How Kinect spawned a commercial ecosystem, *The New York Times Magazine* [Online] www.nytimes.com/2012/06/03/magazine/how-kinect-spawned-a-commercial-ecosystem.html

4 Mustard Research (2016) [accessed 20 May 2018] Top 10 projective techniques [Blog] *Mustard Research* [Online] www.mustard-research.com/ blog/16/03/top-10-projective-techniques

5 Nunez, Kirsty (2015) [accessed 20 May 2018] Projective techniques in qualitative market research [Blog] *American Marketing Association* [Online] www.sdama.org/knowledge/projective-techniques-qualitative-market-research/

6 Mustard Research (2016) [accessed 20 May 2018] Top 10 projective techniques [Blog] *Mustard Research* [Online] www.mustard-research.com/ blog/16/03/top-10-projective-techniques

7 Nunez, Kirsty (2015) [accessed 20 May 2018] Projective techniques in qualitative market research [Blog] *American Marketing Association* [Online] www.sdama.org/knowledge/projective-techniques-qualitative-market-research/

8 Zolfagharifard, Ellie (2014) [accessed 20 May 2018] Candy FLUSH: Half of us play mobile games sitting on the toilet – and 10% of men prefer it to spending time with their partner, *Mail Online* [Online] www.dailymail.co.uk/sciencetech/article-2710894/Candy-FLUSH-Half-play-mobile-games-toilet-10-men-prefer-spending-time-partner.html

9 Smith, Dana (2014) [accessed 20 May 2018] This is what Candy Crush Saga does to your brain, *The Guardian* [Online] www.theguardian.com/science/blog/2014/apr/01/candy-crush-saga-app-brain

10 Results included as part of the paper and conference presentation by Adamou, B (2011) [accessed 27 May 2018] The Future of Research Through Gaming, Proceedings of the CASRO conference, Las Vegas [Online] www.academia.edu/9487174/The_Future_of_Research_Through_Gaming

11 Zolfagharifard, Ellie (2014) [accessed 20 May 2018] Candy FLUSH: Half of us play mobile games sitting on the toilet – and 10% of men prefer it to spending time with their partner, *Mail Online* [Online] www.dailymail.co.uk/sciencetech/article-2710894/Candy-FLUSH-Half-play-mobile-games-toilet-10-men-prefer-spending-time-partner.html

12 Hopper, Joe (2012) [accessed 20 May 2018] Rules of thumb for survey length [Blog] *Versta Research* [Online] https://verstaresearch.com/blog/rules-of-thumb-for-survey-length

Debunking common misconceptions in market research about games and gamification

03

This chapter will:

- debunk 16 of the most misunderstood aspects about games and gamification as mediums in their own right, and therefore as two different techniques used for market research;
- change the perceptions and approaches to using game-based research methods (GbRM).

Misconceptions hinder market researchers from embracing game-based research to its full potential. By demystifying these untruths, we can explore how research-games and gamified surveys can benefit research suppliers and buyers.

The most common misconceptions are listed below with explanations of why those misconceptions may have come to light, and evidence of why they are incorrect.

Misconception 1: changing the wording of questions alone gamifies a survey

Books are engaging, as are news articles. But are they games? No. For the same reason, survey questions that are reworded to sound more fun are also not games. Writing engaging questions is certainly crucial for research but changing question wording alone does not make your survey gamified or into a game.

Below is an example of what could be misunderstood as gamifying a survey. Let's imagine a research buyer wants to assess competition among laundry detergent brands. They create a survey to gather customer feedback. A typical way of writing a question on this topic might be:

> Please let us know which of these laundry detergents is the most effective for cleaning whites and other light coloured clothing.

The participant could then choose from a list of different laundry detergents with an 'other' option, or might just have an open text field (for an 'open verbatim' response).

The misconception is that rewording the same question in a style like the one below is making it 'gamified':

> Tomorrow, you have to provide six super-white, clean fairy costumes for your child's school production, but all the costumes have stains! What would you use to ensure that the fairy costumes impress the teachers and parents?

We can certainly see how this new wording is more interesting than the typical approach; we now have a situation-based narrative with added elements of social and time pressure. The tone is also now much more colloquial and there is a sense of challenge.

Case studies presented at market research conferences have shown that rewording questions in this fashion *does* reap benefits such as increased participant engagement and a greater number of participants reporting to have enjoyed the experience more (Chapter 11 explores existing case studies).

While there is value in these outcomes, the situational approach does not harness the constructs that make a game a game. These constructs are four 'ingredients': goal(s), autonomy opportunities, rules and feedback – they must work *together* to constitute a game (this is further explored in Chapter 4).

The reworded, situational question approach can be compared to text-based games (commonly known as text-adventures or CRPGs – computer role-playing games). While these types of games are pretty basic, they are a successful genre of games, currently seeing a revival as apps. But the difference is that text-adventure games, which like surveys are just text on a screen, include the four game ingredients. These reworded surveys do *not*.

It is possible to think of text-adventure games like *Zork*[1] as old fashioned, but there is much researchers can learn from these types of text-adventure games. They illustrate how we can create intrinsic engagement and encourage play with just text-on-a-screen. In recent years there has been a resurgence of entirely or largely text-based games. If you search (and I encourage you to play) app games like *Reigns* (Devolver Digital, 2016), *Choice of the Dragon* (Dan Fabulich and Adam Morse, 2010), *Blackbar* (Mrgan LLC, 2013), *Grayout* (also by Mrgan LLC, 2015) and *Choices* (Pixelberry Studios, 2016), you are likely to find them engaging and read rave reviews. You are also likely to see the diverse and unusual ways that these text-adventures have been approached. Some of these games are evolving stories that players can contribute to by making decisions; others work like puzzles to help reveal a mystery. But each type is engaging because it uses the game ingredients and combines that with great design. Without those game ingredients, we're just reading a book, an article or a shopping list.

Misconception 2: games and gamification for research are just for children

The average gamer is 35 years old.[2] If this demographic in itself isn't enough to convince you that games are not solely for teenagers and children, then think about the rise in social and casual games, such as those produced by Zynga (like *FarmVille*) and PopCap Games (like *Bejeweled Blitz*), and who is playing them; in the United States in 2010, the average social gamer was 43 years old.[3]

Games are designed and marketed for all ages. Just as games are designed for a specific age group, you can design an engaging game-based survey for an audience of *any* age. In my career as a ResearchGame designer I have been commissioned to design far more ResearchGames for adult participants, with the eldest participant to date aged 89.

Misconception 3: games are about using bright colours

Your research-game or gamified survey doesn't need to look like a cartoon, and neither do lots of digital games. I once heard a researcher say 'games [and hence, gamified surveys] are about using bright colours'. This is incorrect.

To illustrate this point, here is a list of several extremely successful games which don't use bright colours:

- *Pong* (Atari, 1972);

- *Zork 1* (and later versions, Personal Software, 1980);

- *Tetris* (the original by Elektronika 60, 1984, has since been created in many new versions);

- *Snake* (a game whose origins begin as far back as 1976, but was made famous on Nokia mobile phones in 1997. The game has been through dozens of iterations on other devices, including smartphone apps);

- *Canabalt* (Semi Secret Software, 2009);

- *Limbo* (Playdead, 2010);

- *Grimm: Ride of the Perambulator* (ROBOX Studios, 2011);

- *Call of Duty* (first released in 2003 by Activision).

Games like *Snake* and *Tetris* are so engaging, they are still being played in the modern day, re-coded for playability on mobile devices.

Call of Duty (or COD) is one of the most successful videogames of all time, with over 1.6 billion hours of online gameplay logged through the *Modern Warfare 3*[4] release since 2011.[5] It is consistently at the top of the list in most-played games every year. *Call of Duty* is a game with few, if any, bright colours. And that has obviously not affected its many successes.

As noted in Misconception 1, what makes a game a game are four 'ingredients': goal(s), autonomy opportunities, rules and feedback. How you design these aspects, to include bright colours or not to include any colour at all, is dependent on the research requirements.

Misconception 4: games are about using fancy graphics

Games do not need advanced graphic content to be engaging. Similarly, to make an engaging and effective gamified survey or a research-game, you don't need to produce something that looks like *Call of Duty* where players can see wrinkles in a character's skin, or cinematic lighting and 3D effects.

Just like *Space Invaders* (first produced by Taito, 1978), and a host of other games, some of which are named in Misconception 3, engaging games can be made with a simple design, or low-fi or 8-bit graphics. Many of my own ResearchGame designs consist of 2D images of 3D backgrounds, 'flat' pictures, and have been successful research projects with high levels of participant engagement, and where the insight derived from the data has had positive real-world impact (case studies are noted in Chapter 11).

These 'low fi' games teach us that great gameplay doesn't need multimillion-dollar budgets, noise and fanfare. It shows us that fantastic game-design can be simplistic in its aesthetics, even beautiful, while still being intrinsically engaging.

With this in mind, rest assured *you* can produce an engaging and effective research-game or gamified survey even without *any* graphics at all. Text-adventure games, as mentioned earlier, are very successful. They are games because they include the game ingredients, and successful because they are well-designed. What do surveys consist of? Text on a screen. Learning from text-adventure games shows that as long as we understand the mechanisms of games, we can apply those mechanisms in our game-based surveys and open our eyes to the millions of ways there are to engage participants.

Misconception 5: game-based research is primarily about making research fun

The purpose of using GbRM is to intrinsically engage participants and encourage play because through that engagement and play we can achieve better data quality, provide solutions to the 13 adverse effects of low engagement (as described in Chapter 1) and improve the research experience. By using game-based research, we also take advantage of the capabilities inherent in digital games to gain untapped insights via emotive experiences and context-based simulations. That level of engagement isn't necessarily about fun.

Fun is a huge area of study, as is intrinsic motivation and engagement. Although there might be some overlaps, these terms mean very different things. For instance, we might think that being on a rollercoaster or taking part in extreme sports is fun. But being engaged in something might be less dramatic, like speaking to a friend on the phone, or writing an important email. Being *intrinsically* engaged can be where we experience flow – or 'being in the zone' (a concept we explore later on) while doing things like crafting a piece of art, writing a book, or spending extra time at work because we're really engrossed in a task. Fun can be an output of some – not all – types of engagement.

Being intrinsically engaged is first and foremost what we want research participants to be. If they have fun as an outcome of that process, that's great, but doesn't need to be the focus of our efforts as game-based research designers.

In the world of digital games, hundreds of thousands of players globally are hooked, and fun might not even be at the heart of their game-playing experience. As an example, let's look at award-winning app game *Monument Valley* (UsTwo, 2014). The game is stunning to behold. If ever there was an answer to the question 'Are videogames art?' a screengrab from this game would surely answer a resounding 'yes'. Playing the game is undoubtedly immersive, intriguing, mysterious and mesmerizing. But is it fun? Not necessarily. And that's not a bad thing. It hasn't stopped this game from being consistently voted as a top game app and earning US $14.4 million revenue in its first two years of release.[6] A game-based research designer must think 'engagement first' and 'fun' as a bonus.

Furthermore, 'fun' might not be tonally correct or appropriate for your research project if, for example, certain subjects in healthcare or social research are being discussed. However, engaging people in all research projects will always be necessary.

Misconception 6: games are primarily for male audiences

Games have always been played by both genders. So it's not only a misconception that games are played mostly by males but that game-based research is only for male participants. Women of all ages play videogames and in 2010, we saw an almost 50/50 gender split among US gamers. Since then, there has been a decline; in 2017, 41 per cent of US gamers were female.[7]

All human beings, male and female, have the psychological needs of mastery, autonomy, relatedness and purpose (as described in Chapter 4) that well-designed games can satisfy. That is why games, and therefore game-based research, appeals to *both* genders; because playing games makes all humans feel good.

Misconception 7: drag and drop functions make surveys gamified

While using drag and drop functions can increase ease of interaction within a survey, this has nothing to do with the goals, rules, feedback and autonomy opportunities inherent in games. The use of drag and drop has nothing to do with the definition of gamification. Just like the rewording of questions, adding fancy graphics and bright colours, these are superficial elements that you can certainly add to your research-game or gamified survey but do not constitute games or gamification.

Misconception 8: gamification is just a fad

The value of gamification has been questioned since people started talking about it. I have lost count of blogs or articles titled something like 'Is gamification just a fad?' or 'Is gamification here to stay?'.

The answer is simple – if you want people to engage with your brand, product, service, charitable cause and so on, then the answer is yes, gamification (and Serious Games) are here to stay because harnessing game techniques is about engagement. If engagement isn't important to your business, then gamification isn't important to your business.

We live in a world of supply and demand. Low engagement exists in a variety of areas; be it in education, in employee communications and training, be it in research surveys. Low engagement is an issue everywhere. This means tools to increase engagement are in demand. Games and gamification offer the supply. By tapping into what makes games so engaging and applying game mechanics to other activities, we see an increased number of gamification and Serious Game examples all around us, from loyalty cards with supermarket brands, to televised singing contests (like the *X Factor* and *The Voice*) and competitive job interviews (like *The Apprentice*).

And let's not forget that gamification was around long before the term gamification was coined. Have we not always used a carrot-and-stick approach with children to improve behaviour? McDonald's has been using gamification since the 1980s; using the *Monopoly* game to encourage more sales so customers can gain the stickers that come with purchases, that promise prizes.

According to research published in BusinessWire, the global gamification market (which covers the use of gamification in multiple industries) will be worth US $11.10 billion by 2020.[8] Gamification isn't a fad, it's lucrative.

Misconception 9: gamification is a quick fix for low engagement

While many gamification applications in multiple industries have been successful, simply adding goals, rules, feedback and giving opportunities for autonomy to an activity does not guarantee you an engagement hit. *Design is key.*

In 2012, a Gartner report forecasted that by 2014, 80 per cent of current gamified applications would have failed to meet business objectives primarily due to poor design.[9] While many articles have since argued whether that forecast bore any fruit or not, what is true is that *most things fail primarily due to poor design.*

Whether we're talking about the design of a website, a chair or a watch, if the design is poor, there will be a lack of buyers and/or participation. If that happens, businesses can't meet sales targets or objectives. The story isn't so much about gamification failing as a tool for engagement, but about the design of gamification applications in general. That's why slapping badges or points onto surveys for a quick miracle cure to low engagement is likely to leave stakeholders disappointed.

Working directly with clients, often my first job is to 're-lay' the foundations of the design or change aspects of accessibility before embarking on the game-based approach. The foundation elements might be things like ensuring questions are clear, even changing things like font style and size. In Chapter 13, which discusses ethics guidelines and in Part Two: World of Design, you will learn that building a solid design foundation is crucial before embarking on gamified surveys or research-game design.

Misconception 10: game-based research is just for research with gamers

The idea that only people who play games could be interested in game-based research is like saying that only people who believe in ghosts will like scary movies. Games are intrinsically engaging because they tap into four psychological needs: relatedness, autonomy, mastery and purpose (or RAMP) and every human has these psychological needs, whether they are gamers or not. This means that game-based research, when well-designed, really can engage anyone of any age, gender, culture and level of gaming experience. (More about our four psychological needs is discussed in Chapter 4).

Gamers and non-gamers have engaged in gamified programmes for more than 120 years. One of the first, if not *the* first, gamified loyalty programmes was introduced by a company called Sperry & Hutchinson in 1896. Even today, so much of what we interact with, such as aspects of advertising, customer loyalty and sales, is gamified. Developed by McCann Australia,[10] the app game *Dumb Ways to Die* (Metro Trains Melbourne Pty Ltd, 2013) promotes safety on Melbourne Metro trains. The game had reduced 'near-misses' by 30 per cent after the game and campaign were launched.[11] Gamers *and* non-gamers played *Dumb Ways to Die*. Or think of the stamps you collect whenever you buy coffee. These examples of games and gamification are used for non-entertainment purposes and have the participation of gamers and non-gamers alike.

Given that most people now play games and/or take part in at least one gamified activity every day, it seems we're all gamers; from being part of loyalty programmes, to offering incentives to our children for good behaviour, or being involved in some gamification activity in the workplace – we're all experiencing life as a gamification-player.

Misconception 11: participants will focus on the 'game' part and not the 'survey' part

If you have succeeded in developing a solid, coherent design for your game-based online survey, the 'game part' and a 'survey part' will be one and the same – the playfulness and 'gaminess' should be ingrained with the survey and work harmoniously with your research content. The game and the research are united as one, married to engage participants in the goal at hand, providing the researcher with quality data.

This is true especially if you are developing a research-game – a fully-fledged game for research. The 'survey' and the 'game' shouldn't be something you can even untangle and pull apart – they should end up being one and the same thing, working in complete harmony as the research objectives should be used to *drive* the game or gamification design. The game and the research must have a physiognomy to reflect the seamless blend of both.

Misconception 12: I'm not creative so I can't design research-games or gamified surveys

Wrong! Creativity doesn't always mean being good at drawing or painting. There are other types of creativity. Creativity can also mean problem-solving, and to be good at designing game-based surveys, you will need to be a good problem-solver.

I've trained people on GbRM for almost eight years. I almost always ask workshop participants to raise their hand if they think they're 'creative'. It's common to see only one or two hands raised. Yet by the end of the session, everyone has designed their own research-game or gamified survey, even those who were really adamant that they didn't have a creative bone in their body. Once researchers understand and learn the structure of effective game-based survey design, designing becomes a process like any other.

Researchers DO make excellent game-based research designers. They understand the rules of research, what to do and what not to do, and they have other useful skills like empathy, which is important in game-based survey design. Knowing about research is a crucial talent needed for game-based survey design. So basically, if you're a researcher, you're already halfway there.

Misconception 13: participants will find a way to cheat if the survey is a game

Researchers can only *wish* that participants would be engaged enough to want to cheat their survey! Cheating is an indicator of engagement; it requires time and research to figure out and apply loopholes.

People who take part in surveys, whether those surveys are game-based or not, already cheat. Straightlining answers in surveys is a form of cheating and is a real issue – where participants answer questions quickly, usually with the same answer and without thoughtful consideration, just to earn the incentive at the end (for example, money, vouchers or prize draws). Using game-based research actually deters this method of cheating because participants are intrinsically engaged in the process. As such, the data collected using a game-based survey is more reliable because participants *don't* feel the need to button-mash or straightline.

As the game-based survey designer, if you create a research-game or gamified survey where there is a lose state, and rules with loopholes, you may very well give participants the impulse to cheat. In the examples of ResearchGames in this book, you'll see there is no cheating, because the incentive for doing so is removed.

Misconception 14: the inclusion of a *single* game mechanic (like a goal or a rule) makes anything into a game, even a survey

As described by game designer and academic, Sebastian Deterding: 'No typical element (eg goals, rules) on its own constitutes a game, only assembled together do they constitute a game.'[12] This also applies to gamification, because gamification is the repurposing of games for non-game contexts. We must apply all four game ingredients (also known as 'elements') of goals, rules, feedback and autonomy opportunities to gain the kinds of engagement that games experience if we hope to create fruitful gamification platforms. This is why gamification platforms like *Codecademy*, *Foursquare* [13] and *SuperBetter* [14] have seen success, as they use the four game ingredients to engage players.

If all we need to do is add a rule or a goal to make something gamified, then this assumes that everything in life is gamified. For example, there are health and safety rules in working on a construction site, but this does not make building skyscrapers into a game or gamifies the working processes because there are rules.

Misconception 15: game-based research is really expensive

Your interpretation of this misconception is likely based on the answer to these questions: What do you deem expensive? What are you using as a point of comparison? For instance, if we compare the price of buying a licence from a DIY survey platform such as SurveyMonkey, versus buying a game-based study from a market research agency, the answer is yes, game-based research is likely to cost more.

The answer to these questions must be accompanied by several logistical, value-based and industry-based considerations.

Logistics considerations

- Price will differ depending on whether a gamified survey or a fully-fledged research-game is purchased.

- Price will vary depending on other factors such as survey length, complexity of the survey, complexity of the questions, inclusion of stimulus material (such as videos or photos) and quantity of questions.
- Price will vary depending on the quantity of required completed surveys.
- Price will vary based on the ease of access to targeted participants.

Value considerations

- **Prevention or cure?** As we explored in Chapter 1, the side effects of low participant engagement show that there are lots of time, human resources and money dedicated to *curing* low engagement issues. This can put a dent in the profitability of a research project. Ask yourself: is it better to spend money on a more engaging and valuable surveying method, or spend less money but endure the consequences of disengaged participants and questionable data quality? Prevention is better than cure.

- **Existing expectations and experience:** I've had clients note that the price of a ResearchGame is moderately more expensive than the traditional surveying methods they have previously bought, but they also say that they expected to pay more, and value the methodology better than traditional surveys. Other clients have been surprised (I assume pleasantly) that the price is the same as what they would usually pay for a traditional survey project. I'm making this point not to highlight the prices of my products; indeed, as I specialize in tailor-made ResearchGames, the prices all differ. Rather, the point is that the buyers' previous experiences and expectations mean that they alone can say if they think something is expensive or not.

Industry considerations

Game-based research is in its infancy: understanding of the methodology is limited and misinformation has spread. While there is growing industry confidence in the methodology, experiments with its features are few and far between in comparison to other methodologies, and the results of research based on games and gamification have varied. Pricing something people may not necessarily understand, or fully see the value of, is difficult. The list of factors below affect GbRM:

- **Supply and demand.** We have to think about the quantity of companies that are actually selling game-based research, and how many people want to *buy* game-based research. Supply and demand will always affect price.

- **Suppliers.** Has there already been an investment by companies to develop game-based research software and processes that can then make it easier for customers to buy into? (Hint, the answer is 'yes'.) This helps generate demand.

- **Competitor pricing.** While limited competition has its benefits, it also means a game-based research supplier has fewer companies to compare its own pricing with. In a new market, finding the sweet spot of pricing takes time. As such, as the seller, you can only price in a way that truly reflects your time and effort while making a profit. As a buyer, naturally, you can only purchase what you can afford.

- **What's really on offer?** Some companies may advertise that they offer gamified surveys or research-games, but in reality they are just producing more visual surveys. Visual surveys still have merit, but visual surveys alone are not game-based surveys. Then there are companies genuinely using gamification and games for research. With this in mind, there is often confusion and little room for like-for-like price comparison for the research buyer around what is actually being sold. In one example, a client mentioned they were speaking to three game-based research suppliers, of which Research Through Gaming was one. They said that, in every instance, the product they were shown was so different from the others, they were unable to carry out their usual price and capability comparisons.

- **Ready-made or tailor-made?** There are companies that offer gamified surveys and research-games which are pre-made, but other companies may offer tailor-made products. This also affects price from the seller and buyers' perspective. (More on this is explored in Part Two: World of Design.)

- **Platforms.** While we are not quite there yet, we also need to think about game-based research on different platforms and utilizing additional technology. For instance, a research-game using virtual reality may be more or less expensive then one using, say, augmented reality versus a text-adventure research-game.

With these factors in mind, we can see how it's less simple to answer the question: Is it more expensive? I reframe the question to help with an answer: 'Is it more valuable?' To that, my answer is a resounding yes, *if* the game-based approach is designed effectively.

Misconception 16: using game-based research requires a change in survey software

Many games, like text-adventure games, harness all the ingredients that make a game a game with nothing but text on a screen. Researchers can evoke intrinsic engagement and play without necessarily having to change survey software providers because like the text-adventure games that have engaged millions of players around the world, game-based survey designers can too use the capabilities available to them – even if that is just text on a screen – providing they understand the design fundamentals.

Essentially, how researchers approach their game-based survey design is up to them, and will depend on the types of interactions/behaviours they desire from participants, the nature and subject of the study, the age group of the participants and so on. If the researcher decides to make a highly visual, fully-fledged research game with avatars, virtual environments, music and sound effects, and other capabilities not normally found in traditional survey software tools, then yes, the researcher may want to invest in building his or her own game-based survey software, or buy into existing software that allows his or her designs to be realized.

With these myths explored, there is just one more common misconception to demystify: that games and gamification are the same thing. Often, researchers use these labels interchangeably to describe game-based surveys, with 'game' used to describe a gamified survey, and 'gamification' used to describe non-gamified research. It's important to explore the differences, understand them and work to define what it means to make a 'research-game' or 'gamified survey' because, once we know the rules, we can break them.

Notes

1 Barton, Matt (date unknown) [accessed 23 May 2018] The history of Zork, *Gamasutra* [Online] http://www.gamasutra.com/view/feature/1499/the_history_of_zork.php?print=1

2 The Entertainment Software Association (2017) [accessed 20 May 2018] Essential facts about the computer and games industry [Online] www.theesa.com/wp-content/uploads/2017/06/!EF2017_Design_FinalDigital.pdf

3   Ingram, Mathew (2010) [accessed 21 May 2018] Average social gamer is a 43-year-old woman, *Gigaom* [Online] https://gigaom.com/2010/02/17/average-social-gamer-is-a-43-year-old-woman

4   Activision Blizzard (2012) [accessed 21 May 2018] Activision blizzard announces better-than-expected first quarter 2012 financial results [Online] https://investor.activision.com/news-releases/news-release-details/activision-blizzard-announces-better-expected-first-quarter-2012?ReleaseID=672062

5   Dutton, Fred (2012) [accessed 21 May 2018] Call of Duty Elite has 10 million users, 2 million pay: Activision updates stats, announces revenue drop, *Eurogamer* [Online] www.eurogamer.net/articles/2012-05-09-call-of-duty-elite-has-10-million-users-2-million-pay

6   Sarkar, Samit (2016) [accessed 21 May 2018] Monument valley made $14.4m in two years, even with most downloads being free, *Polygon* [Online] www.polygon.com/2016/5/20/11724058/monument-valley-sales-revenue-download-numbers-ustwo-games

7   The Entertainment Software Association (2017) [accessed 20 May 2018] Essential facts about the computer and games industry [Online] www.theesa.com/wp-content/uploads/2017/06/!EF2017_Design_FinalDigital.pdf

8   Author unknown (2016) [accessed 21 May 2018] Global gamification market worth usd 11.10 billion by 2020 – analysis, technologies & forecast report 2016–2020 – key vendors: Faya Corp, Microsoft & Bunchball – research and markets, *BusinessWire* [Online] www.businesswire.com/news/home/20160218006350/en/Global-Gamification-Market-Worth-USD-11.10-Billion

9   Gartner (2012) [accessed 21 May 2018] Gartner says by 2014, 80 percent of current gamified applications will fail to meet business objectives primarily due to poor design, *Gartner* [Online] www.gartner.com/newsroom/id/2251015

10 McCann website (date of publication unknown) [accessed 21 May 2018] Dumb ways to die: The game [Online] http://mccann.com.au/project/dumb-ways-to-die-the-games/

11 Cauchi, Stephen (2013) [accessed 22 May 2018] No dumb luck: Metro claims safety success, *The Age* [Online] www.theage.com.au/victoria/no-dumb-luck-metro-claims-safety-success-20130214-2eelt.html

12 *Codecademy* website: www.codecademy.com

13 *Foursquare* website: https://foursquare.com

14 *SuperBetter* website: www.superbetter.com

Games and gamification

04

Exploring definitions and why games are so engaging

To develop an ontology of game-based research methods (GbRM) we must first explore the definitions and differences between games and gamification *outside* of market research to then use those definitions to construct definitions and frameworks of games and gamification *within* market research, to create definitions for research-games, gamified surveys and surveytainment.

With definitions and design constructs in place, researchers can understand the different processes and outcomes of creating and using these methodologies. As such, researchers can identify when to use research-games or gamify their surveys, or apply a fluidity between the two.

This chapter examines:

- the definitions of games, and what makes a game a game;
- game components and game elements;
- how the components and elements inherent in games drive desirable behaviours that are beneficial for market research.

There is another misconception within the market research community: that gamification and games are the same thing. Frequently, in articles, blogs, papers and conference presentations, the terms are used interchangeably and defined incorrectly – stating that merely using drag and drop functions or bright colours in a survey makes a survey gamified or a game. Using the terms interchangeably has led to mislabelling: where often a gamified survey is labelled as a game in the same paper, or even where a traditional survey is labelled as a gamified survey even though it does not possess the game mechanics and/or game elements to constitute gamification.

While there is, and can be, fluidity in game-based research approaches, it is important to understand how games and gamification are different so researchers can choose the methodology that best suits their needs. Not only are games and gamification different in many ways, but those differences impact:

- the best practices that the research community creates for both methodologies;
- the design processes;
- what researchers can achieve from participant interaction from a gamified survey versus a research-game – and the data results *will* be different.

So, it is important to define a gamified survey and a research-game, and also to discuss what some practitioners have named as 'gamified surveys' but are actually more 'surveytainment'. Surveytainment is a portmanteau of survey and entertainment, which refers to surveys that are not gamified or developed as games, but include more dynamic interfaces to be more engaging/entertaining for participants.

There is a large amount of information on the application of games and gamification outside of market research. This chapter considers broader arguments and discussions in these fields so that we can understand the differences between and definitions of games and gamification, in order to understand and define them as research methodologies.

Defining and understanding games, and exploring what makes games so engaging

If you are not a gamer or someone interested in studying games, the world of games can fall into one of two categories: 'that thing kids spend hours playing' or a nostalgic memory of your own gameplay as a child. But games have amassed as much academia and literature to rival any other subject. Much like Dorothy walking into Oz, learning about games makes this world go from grey to full Technicolor, where not only do we discover the breadth of games available, but also the breadth of *how games are defined*.

In this section, we are digging; we will dig to uncover the first layer – how games are defined, then dig to uncover *what* makes games so engaging, then finally dig through the final layer to uncover *why* games are so engaging.

Defining 'game' → GARF

The term 'game' is a contested term, with over 10 definitions to date, with some definitions more frequently used and accepted than others. In the book

Rules of Play: Game design fundamentals (2004) the authors Katie Salen and Eric Zimmerman create their own definition, through analysing and borrowing from previous descriptions: 'A game is a system in which players engage in an artificial conflict, defined by rules, that results in a quantifiable outcome.'[1] Meanwhile in the book *Reality Is Broken: Why games make us better and how they can change the world* by Jane McGonigal (2011),[2] games are described as having 'four defining traits': 'a goal, rules, a feedback system and voluntary participation'. Bernard Suits, author of *The Grasshopper: Games, life and utopia* (1978), offers his own definition: 'playing a game is a voluntary attempt to overcome unnecessary obstacles.'[3] By contrast, Espen Aarseth and Gordon Calleja, authors of the 2015 paper *The Word Game: The ontology of an indefinable object*, argue that games *can't* be defined. They say we can't define if something 'really is a game' or not 'any more than whether the feeling someone purports to have is "real love", "real guilt", etc'.[4]

Clearly, there is no one-size-fits-all definition of 'game'. The variety of games that exist and continue to evolve mean that separate definitions are needed to adequately describe the plethora of games available. For instance, how a sports game is described would be very different from how a board game is described.

There are also definitions of 'game' that are format and interaction dependent. Imagine trying to describe multiplayer or single player card games, real or virtual games of chess, or Scrabble, and a massively multiplayer online role-playing game (MMORPG) like *The World of Warcraft*; phew! It would be hard to find a single definition that justifies all occasions, formats and interactions.

The definition of games can also vary depending on who you are asking. If you ask a game designer to define 'game', she or he may have a definition different from that of a player or game academic. The definitions of games we looked at earlier, while useful, don't translate directly into useful definitions to help us define games as research instruments. For example, the definition offered by Bernard Suits would be redundant in game-based research because the obstacles to overcome in a research-game or gamified survey *would* be necessary as those obstacles have real-world impact. But there is one definition we can build on, and that is Jane McGonigal's 'four defining traits', with a few changes.

The four defining traits of games that McGonigal describes are: 'a goal, rules, a feedback system and voluntary participation'. In academia, these 'traits' are often described as game mechanics or game elements, and these terms are sometimes used interchangeably.

Game ingredients

To create a framework and a label that is more in line with research needs and less confusing, I propose to label the four defining traits as 'game ingredients' with a slightly evolved version of the four traits. These game ingredients are:

- Goal(s);
- Autonomy opportunities;
- Rules;
- Feedback.

As you can see from Figure 4.1 (see page 48), a goal is central to the other ingredients – every other ingredient links back to and works around the goal(s).

For memory's sake, we can try to recall these four game ingredients in the mnemonic 'GARF':

- **Goal(s)** is used instead of the singular 'a goal'; for example, smaller goals that work up to achieving an ultimate goal. When designing a game-based survey, note that while there can be more than one goal, don't overload the participant with too many goals as this can make the survey less focused and make the rewards for achieving goals feel less valuable.

- **Autonomy opportunities** has been used instead of 'voluntary participation' because voluntary participation accounts only for the users' will in playing a game in the first place. But autonomy – the freedom to do different things in games of our own choosing, like explore a virtual landscape rather than solely focus on the gameplay, is a fundamental part of what players enjoy. Autonomy opportunities also translates better in a market research context because while survey participation is voluntary, it's also often externally incentivized. By replacing 'voluntary approach' with 'autonomy opportunities', this makes it clear that researchers can still offer incentives, but it also prompts researchers to offer opportunities for autonomy *within* their game-based survey.

- **Rules** – this is kept the same from McGonigal's list of defining traits. Rules outline the limitations and opportunities that a player has in the game world; that is, what they can or can't do. For example, a game character can run only so fast before reaching a certain game level, or climb a wall but only with a special piece of equipment. Rules are already in place in online surveys; for example, to answer questions one at a time, or in sequence, or to choose only one answer from a list of responses. As a designer of game-based research, you already have the rules in place, so this game ingredient is largely supported by the rules inherent in the survey structure.

- **Feedback** is used instead of 'a feedback system'. 'Feedback system' implies a singular mode of feedback, and as such this terminology may make new game-based research designers feel restricted to designing just one type of feedback system. There are dozens of feedback mechanisms in games and there could be dozens of feedback mechanisms in game-based surveys. Feedback can be as simple as letting players (or participants) know how well they are doing or how their input is helping a wider cause. Feedback can be constant and multi-layered in games; from seeing how your avatar improves with every completed quest, to getting game stats on your speed and strength in fighting games like *Mortal Kombat*. By playing lots of different kinds of games, you can understand the multi-layered feedback mechanisms available and use this as inspiration for your game-based survey designs.

All game ingredients must be used to make a game

Another common misconception in the market research community is that using only *one* of the game ingredients, like a rule or a goal, constitutes a game or gamification. It does not. Imagine you need to pick up your child from school. Your goal is to get there on time but that does not make it a game. An employee receiving performance feedback is not a game.

In the paper *Gamification: Toward a definition* (Deterding *et al*, 2011) we can see that all the game ingredients must work together, and in harmony, to create a game. In this quote, the authors refer to our previously noted game ingredients as 'elements': 'No typical element (eg goals, rules) on its own constitutes a game ... only assembled together do they constitute a game.'[5]

It is important when designing a research-game or gamified survey to include *all* four game ingredients. Only when they work harmoniously together can they become a game or gamification.

Why are games so engaging? How games satisfy our psychological needs

Games (when well-designed[6]) are so engaging because they include those four game ingredients, and those four game ingredients directly satisfy the four human psychological needs. This is what makes games intrinsically engaging.

What are the human psychological needs? → *RAMP*

While some experts claim that humans have three psychological needs, I argue that there are four, by combining the works of three researchers.

Daniel H Pink, author of *Drive: The surprising truth about what motivates us* (2009)[7] argues that intrinsic motivation is born when our psychological needs are satisfied. He notes our psychological needs are:

1 **Mastery**: to continually improve at something.

2 **Autonomy**: the freedom to act of our own volition.

3 **Purpose**: to work towards a goal, with meaning.

This trifecta is aligned with the ingredients inherent in games. When we play games, we grow our skill and **mastery**. In a game, players have **autonomy** to move in different directions or undertake quests in whichever order they like. And players do all this with **purpose**, whether that purpose is a clear goal or to help the game narrative along.

However, researchers Edward L Deci and Richard M Ryan, developers of the Self-Determination Theory (SDT), say that our psychological needs are:[8]

1 **Competency**: to master one's environment.

2 **Relatedness**: to interact with other people and to feel connected. To have a sense of belonging.

3 **Purpose**: to work towards a goal, with meaning.

Both these lists are helpful but can be merged to provide a holistic view of all human psychological needs:

● mastery;

● autonomy;

● purpose;

● relatedness.

'Mastery' and 'competency' have similar meanings. I chose to keep 'mastery' because this term more accurately reflects the skill through which players are able to, with practice, 'master' a game and also describes how players can continually improve to master their environment. Onlookers watching a player in full flow don't think 'competent', they think 'master'.

'Autonomy' features on only one list, but it is key to human happiness. Having freedom to explore and make choices of our own volition is crucial to our wellbeing. Autonomy is also reported to (among other things) alleviate negative feelings, and boost productivity and engagement in the workplace and in education environments.[9]

'Purpose' is used in both lists, so it is included in the merged four-point list because a sense of purpose is also crucial to wellbeing.

'Relatedness' despite featuring on just one of the three-point lists, is indeed another human psychological need. Relatedness is about how we compare, communicate and relate to other people – this is core to human flourishing.

The mnemonic 'RAMP' (please see Figure 4.2) can help us remember these four human psychological needs. When we compare these psychological needs in Figure 4.2 with the game ingredients shown in Figure 4.1 we begin to see interesting alignments. Here we can see how games satisfy these needs:

- **R**elatedness: games give players a sense of belonging through collaboration with other players and non-player characters, and through a transcendent purpose of helping others towards a goal.

- **A**utonomy: games allow players to move how they wish albeit with a sometimes linear storyline and/or gameplay.

- **M**astery is to continually improve at something and master your environment. Games have levels in which continuous improvement is part of the gameplay process.

- **P**urpose: goals are met through the completion of levels and worlds, driving purpose.

These figures could overlap each other to create perfect parallels between what satisfies people psychologically and how those needs are satisfied through the game ingredients.

Figure 4.1 The four Game Ingredients should be used in game-based research to constitute a 'research-game' or 'gamified survey' (GARF)

Figure 4.2 The four human psychological needs as evolved from the work of other experts (RAMP)

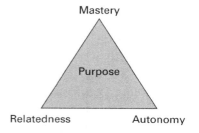

SOURCE © Betty Adamou, 2018

Goals help us towards a purpose. We understand our mastery through reaching our goals and getting feedback on reaching those goals.

Rules create challenges to overcome in which we elevate our mastery by overcoming those challenges. Rules are crucial at letting us understand the limitations within which we're operating to reach those goals. Rules provide a fair playing ground so we comprehend our mastery on a level playing field with others. Through a fair and equal system of rules, this lets us compare how we are mastering something to achieve goals compared with other people (which also provides relatedness).

Autonomy opportunities satisfy our need for autonomy. Autonomy isn't just an act of volition in *choosing* to play a game, but we can act voluntarily in *how* we play a game. Games provide players with a sense of autonomy in different doses and methods.

Feedback lets us compare how our mastery is evolving compared with others, and shared feedback (and goals) helps build stronger bonds with others – relatedness.

To illustrate the importance of all four of these elements, let's try a little exercise. Imagine your own life where just one of the four psychological needs is satisfied. Let's imagine you experience autonomy every day; you have the freedom to go wherever you wish and do whatever you please. Your life is limitless. But without a goal (purpose), or others to share your experiences (relatedness) and without the ability to evolve our inner selves and grow our knowledge (mastery), such an autonomous life would fast become boring.

Let's flip that around; imagine a life where *three* of the four psychological needs were satisfied. You live a life of autonomy, mastery and relatedness, but no purpose. Could such a life be fulfilling?

But a sense of purpose and mastery must be perpetuated, and this is why goals are so important. Once we reach our goals, we must evolve to achieve new ones – we must have not just one purpose but also multiple purposes. This is why games are so addictive: they feed into that constant cycle of satisfying our psychological needs for mastery through allowing players to achieve incremental goals towards an ultimate goal.

No single game ingredient can satisfy all psychological needs; only when all game ingredients are used can all psychological needs be satisfied so that a person becomes intrinsically engaged.

Now we understand why games are intrinsically engaging through understanding how the ingredients of a game satisfy our psychological needs, let's dig deeper. What happens when our psychological needs are satisfied? The answer lies in our biological make-up.

The science behind what happens when our psychological needs are satisfied and why this should matter to researchers

Human brains can release four, what are commonly known as, 'happiness chemicals'. Not only do the four game ingredients synchronize harmoniously with the four human psychological needs (which I'm calling HPN for short) – the four HPN also synchronize with these happiness chemicals. These are serotonin, dopamine, endorphin and oxytocin.[10] The release of these chemicals makes people feel good – hence 'happiness' chemicals.

Dopamine is released when game players achieve in a game, whether that's achieving smaller goals like collecting enough coins to make an in-game purchase, or larger goals like completing a level. In addition, working *towards* goals with positive expectations also releases dopamine. As such, game players are in an almost constant cycle of dopamine release between achieving goals and working towards them. It is here we see the linkage between:

- the game ingredient of **goal(s)** →
- the psychological need for **purpose** →
- the chemical that is released when goals are met: **dopamine**.

Why is this important to a researcher?

We have seen the importance of goals in engaging people through the satisfaction of their psychological need for purpose, but dopamine, the very chemical that is released when that happens, has an impact that is relevant to market research. The impact of dopamine is felt in many different areas, including but not limited to improved motivation,[11] memory,[12] cognitive abilities (like problem-solving or engaging in creative tasks),[13,14] focus[15] and attention.[16] So much so that doctors who play games before surgery have a 37 per cent reduction in errors.[17]

These outcomes align with what researchers want from participants. They want:

- participants to be motivated to participate in (and complete) research studies;
- participants to have better memory so they can retell their experiences with as much accuracy as possible;

- the full attention and focus of participants so they can respond to questions accurately and stay engaged for the entire period of the research;
- participants to harness their cognitive abilities to complete rudimentary and sometimes more advanced and creative research tasks.

Game components – 'CABIN'

It is now time to explore other aspects of games, and their advantages for market research. These other aspects of games are game components and game elements. It is important to note that while the game ingredients must be used together to constitute a game and encourage that all-important intrinsic engagement and play, any number of the game components and game elements are used in addition to the game ingredients to develop different types of games.

There are five key game components (although some ludologists would argue there are more, or fewer, or different ones):

- Collaboration;
- Aesthetic;
- Bonus features;
- Increases in difficulty;
- Narrative.

As an easy guide to remember these components, we can use another handy mnemonic: 'CABIN'. These components help to make games even more engaging and can be useful additions, where appropriate, to game-based research.

For each one of these five game components, there could be five further books. Indeed, there *are* entire books dedicated to exploring these components in games. In this book we will explore the function of each component and its usefulness in research as concisely as possible. To do that, we will look at digital games to understand how game components typically look and work in their 'natural habitat'.

In particular, we'll refer to the digital social game *FarmVille* by Zynga, as this game has examples of many of the game components. It is free to play and an easily accessible game for readers who would like to see the examples 'in the flesh'.

In *FarmVille*, players create a digital farm and earn experience points and coins by maintaining/growing their farm and maximizing its potential.

Players can plant a variety of vegetation and rear animals, which they can then harvest. While no goal is concretely defined, the goal is largely to develop the farm of your dreams. Some players develop farms mostly focused on growing vegetables, while others focus on rearing animals and so on. For a game like *FarmVille*, it seems much of the joy is in the playing of the game itself.

Collaboration

Working with other players in a game is commonplace. Some games focus on the collaboration component; these are called 'co-op games' (co-operation games) or multiplayer games. There are MMORPGs (massively multiplayer online role-playing games) with thousands of players, if not millions, many of whom will work together in large teams to overcome challenges. When the resources and skills of different players are combined, players can do things like defeat villains, conquer new worlds or gain even more resources.

Collaboration between players in games can reap many benefits including but not limited to:

- increased player engagement;
- increased rewards and/or resources (through working together to achieve goals);
- increased problem-solving skills (a problem shared is a problem halved);
- increased loyalty to the game, which encourages players to log in/play again and again.

In *FarmVille*, players can help each other on their farms, earning everybody more experience points and virtual money in the process. These collaborative components help players towards their goals, but also provide social interactions that satisfy our psychological need for relatedness.

How is collaboration useful in game-based surveys?

Encouraging collaboration (which includes a sense of community) in a market research context can, just as it does for games:

- increase engagement;
- increase problem-solving skills;
- encourage participants to want to take part in research in the future (the replay effect, spurred by engagement);
- encourage authentic behaviours and responses (accuracy and detail).

For years, qualitative researchers have encouraged participant collaboration in focus groups to increase engagement and boost insight. Collaboration can be asking participants to work together to solve problems, come up with creative ideas and critique ideas. Of course, market research online communities (MROCs) already have this game component. MROCs are, in many ways, the foundations of a MORPG (a multiplayer online role-playing game).

Think about harnessing a sense of collaboration with your participants in your game-based survey to gain these benefits. For example, can you let participants know how many *other* people have taken part in the study so far to give a community/collaborative feel? Can you let them know how their collaboration is going to help a wider cause?

Evoking a sense of collaboration and community works in games and works in research (as we see in MROCs) and should be harnessed in game-based surveys too.

Aesthetic

Aesthetic includes quality and type of graphics – for instance, if the graphics are highly detailed or fairly low-fi 8-bit style. If I were to say 'Super Mario', 'Sonic the Hedgehog' or 'Pong', you will probably be able to conjure the graphics in your mind's eye. How games look is key to how we think of and remember them.

While the brightness of colours or the sophistication of graphics are not core to evoking play or even core to creating intrinsic engagement, the aesthetic of a game can play a role in engagement. For instance, the app game *Monument Valley* (UsTwo Games) has such a unique aesthetic that its labyrinthine MC Escher-style look is the main talking point among fans and journalists.

If you visit the site www.pottermore.com/patronus you can explore how a polished and relevant aesthetic can be engaging. On the 'To discover your Patronus' first screen, the cursor is followed by sparkles, the buttons change colour when the cursor hovers over them, and the background slightly moves with our movements. This aesthetic, like so many other fantastic digital experiences, shows that thinking about your design is core to providing engaging experiences.

As we will explore later in Part Two: World of Design, the aesthetic of your game-based survey must harmonize with the research content.

How is aesthetic useful in game-based surveys?

Many traditional online surveys don't look like anything else on the internet today. Being more focused on the aesthetic can not only bring surveys up to speed, but also help research suppliers differentiate from one another. Finally, and most importantly, the aesthetic that researchers use can include visuals, which can aid a participant in understanding the research process and content through the meanings derived from visuals – and this is semiotics.

Just like the 'Patronus' site from Pottermore, or indeed some of the most popular websites around today like Facebook, Google and Amazon, a good aesthetic is consistent with great user experience and design. This should always be at the forefront of a research designer's mind as good user experience and design equals engagement.

Bonus features (and novelty)

Novelty should not be underestimated as a tool for engagement, and bonus features in games are just one of many ways they provide novelty. The delight of novelty – 'the new' – releases dopamine in the brain, which is, as we have already explored, one of our four happiness chemicals.

Bonus features and novelty are also important not just in games, but life in general. Whether serendipitous or planned, novelty or 'bonuses' help to keep things interesting; finding a £10 note in an old jacket, going on holiday to new places, even having a novel digital experience. Novelty breaks up the monotony of everyday life, and games, like life, would be pretty boring without any surprises or new experiences.

In *FarmVille*, the availability of bonus features encourages players to log in as often as possible because they want to see what is new to buy, or what 'gifts' they might have been given by a fellow farmer. Such bonus features give players something different to look forward to, which is different from the standard farm equipment, animals and plants on offer. And *FarmVille* is truly the master of bonus features: for every special event in the real world, *FarmVille* offers related items for sale in the digital world. At Christmas and Thanksgiving, players can log in and see new items to buy such as festive trees, reindeer, snow blankets and turkeys. At Halloween, you can buy green cows and pumpkins. Some bonus features, however, cannot be bought, as they are awarded only when players conduct special tasks.

Bonus features in games need not be confined to in-game purchases though, or necessarily have positive outcomes. In *Super Mario 3*, uncovering a hidden whistle can transport players to much later levels, but it may be that they find those later levels too difficult to complete. In *Monopoly*, the 'Chance' and 'Community Chest' cards are inbuilt bonus systems but don't always lead to happy results. Bonus features can also be things like limited edition armour or costumes for your avatar, new/special virtual experiences within a game, or even items of 'urban myth'. These are often referred to as Easter Eggs. The term is another way to describe what is basically a 'hidden gem', or secret thing within a game (often, the more limited the item, the more sought after it is). Hunting Easter Eggs can spur many hours of game-play and research for a player.

A testament to how bonus features and novelty increase player engagement lies within the willingness to pay for such items. A report in a 2012 Forbes article showed that about 2 per cent of Facebook users spent collectively over US $1 billion on virtual goods, including items for games.[18] Players use *real money* to get virtual money to purchase things like in-game cows and sheep, energy packs and other novelty items.[19] Just for pixels on a screen. But why? What are the true benefits of bonus features and novelty in games? Bonus features and novelty in games can:

- allow players to achieve their goal(s) faster;
- be used as tools to keep players feeling valued;
- increase loyalty through curiosity: the anticipation of such surprises, or 'the new', is part of what encourages players to come back to play the same game again and again.

How are bonus features and novelty useful in game-based surveys?

Researchers can harness bonus features and novelty in all types of research *without* using the game ingredients, although using this component alone certainly isn't a long-term solution to low participant engagement problems. There are three key ways researchers can encourage participant engagement through novelty and bonus features.

1 Design the survey (or face-to-face research experience) to look/feel different from anything else participants are likely to have experienced before   From the first ResearchGame that Research Through Gaming ever released to the most recent, participants comment that the platform is 'novel'. The newness of the methodology appears to contribute to their engagement. This should prompt researchers to think that whether or not they use game-based techniques, how can they make their survey look different from other traditional surveys?

2   Avoid repetition and introduce different interactions, and often

Introducing novelty and bonus features can break up the monotony and repetition we often see in online surveys. A survey that has a grid on every screen, or a scale slider, would quickly become boring. Introducing a mix of ways that participants can answer questions or respond to scenarios will help to keep their attention and engagement.

3   Provide unexpected, useful and interesting bonuses   In Research-Games released by Research Through Gaming, bonus features have included bonus online diaries, bonus rewards such as a downloadable certificate bearing the participant's name, QR codes that participants can scan to receive secret messages on their phones to help them in later levels, extra points or completing challenges in a certain time frame and VIP access codes to unlock new levels. These bonuses and novelty experiences help participants feel valued, keep their engagement, and help turn something viewed as 'cumbersome' into 'exciting'. In a ResearchGame called *Dubious*, rather than introduce a digital diary activity as an extra task, it was re-framed as a bonus. Nineteen per cent of participants voluntarily completed this non-mandatory digital diary, and with rich detail.[20]

The kinds of bonuses a researcher can offer in game-based and even non-game-based research are only limited by imagination. Bonus features and novelty items should relate to the research content and/or the narrative in the research-game or gamified survey.

The feedback gained by some participants after playing *TESSA Undercover Agents* (a ResearchGame produced by RTG) shows that novelty, bonuses and a mix of questions keep participants alert, engaged, enjoying the experience and wanting to come back for more. Here is some of the feedback written by the participants:

> thank you very much, this survey was new and different and kept me on my toes!! It didn't feel like a survey which is often boring, very good way to keep me alert!! thanks!

> A novel and interesting way of conducting a survey that also focuses the mind on specific answers. Would definitely do again.

> I love this way of conducting surveys and I would have absolutely no hesitation in completing one again. Fantastic!

> prob on of the best and inventive surveys I done, if only more were like this. Interesting and enjoyable to participate. would participate in these again.

Increases in difficulty

Games get harder as we play them. In *FarmVille*, a player begins with just a few patches of land. The increased difficulty over time is because as the farm becomes larger, it becomes more of a challenge to maintain. In other games, increases in difficulty might be embodied by a higher quantity of villains, or more skilled villains, or the level is longer in duration thus testing our stamina and patience, or environments are harder to navigate. Game designers have no shortage of ways in which they can make games challenging.

Overcoming obstacles and facing challenges is part of what makes games intrinsically engaging, as overcoming obstacles to achieve goals is linked to our psychological needs for mastery and purpose. This is why games begin as easy and then become more difficult, as this technique of incrementally increasing difficulty taps more effectively into our needs for mastery. This means that as players overcome smaller obstacles to gain confidence and skill, they can then defeat bigger, badder obstacles later in the game.

But there is also another reason why games (largely) begin as easy. For players experiencing a new game, there is a wealth of new things to learn: pressing 'B' means my character 'jumps'; pressing B and A means my character runs. Bumping into this mushroom will weaken or kill me, but that mushroom will make me bigger and stronger. The initial, easy levels of a game act as a learning-by-doing tour of the game world and its rules. Game designers have become experts at the easy/difficulty ratio of games – it is a science. The perfect balance between challenge and success and the balance between hard work and reward are two of the reasons games are so addictive. By contrast, games that are too easy or too difficult can quickly disengage players.

Overcoming obstacles and facing challenges in games all sounds pretty stressful, and you would be right. But it's a different kind of stress – a stress called 'eustress'. While this is described much more adequately by Jane McGonigal in her book *Reality Is Broken* (2011),[21] the layperson's definition is that eustress is 'good stress'. This 'good stress' makes people more focused – another desirable behaviour researchers want from participants.

How can increases in difficulty be useful in game-based surveys?

Increases in difficulty can help researchers structure their surveys by:

1 **Engaging participants**. Researchers shouldn't be afraid to challenge the participant – as we've seen, challenges engage people but be sure to offer rewards that are reflective of efforts.

2 **Building a sense of mastery**. Think about how to place simple/easy questions at the beginning of a survey and ease into more complex questions or challenges later in the survey. This will help build a sense of mastery, which is one of our psychological needs.

3 **Building trust**. For research content of a sensitive or taboo nature, researchers can use the initial questions in a survey to develop trust with the participant before asking what might be tougher questions, thus building a sense of trust and rapport with the participant.

Narrative

In the book *Storytelling Animal: How stories make us human*,[22] the author writes that humans spend most of every day and night engrossed in narrative through daydreaming, dreaming, reading stories, watching stories, telling stories, imagining future scenarios; story is part and parcel of being human.

Humans tell stories and engage in stories. This is another reason why games are so engaging; they allow us to consume a narrative while actively contributing to it. Games like those produced by the Telltale Games studio ensure that the player is actively involved in progressing the narrative through making conscious choices about what to do when a different facet of the narrative presents itself. In the market research industry, there's already a fascination with 'storytelling' as a technique to engage research buyers in research results and insight, but such an emphasis on using narratives to immerse the participant is not as prominent.

Games can tell great stories and don't necessarily need words to convey a narrative; music, virtual environments and visual metaphors can help tell a story. Some games, like text-adventure games, are more literal with text on a screen and where the narrative unfolds as the player inputs his or her own ideas to evolve the storyline.

Some game narratives aren't clear, but it is in their conceptuality and mystery that the narrative becomes a source of engagement and intrigue. App games like *Monument Valley* (UsTwo) may not have a clear narrative, but are able to convey to players a certain mix of emotions to empathize with Ida, the central character, even though the narrative is abstract.

How can narrative be useful in game-based surveys?

In every story, there is trouble to overcome. This can help your participant feel valued; what is the trouble that the research buyer or supplier has, that the participant can help overcome? Essentially, how can the participant solve a problem and become the hero or heroine?

In RTG ResearchGames, realistic, fantasy-based (and somewhere in the middle) types of narratives have been used to help engage participants in the research content. In cases where our clients have allowed us to articulate the problem to the participants, we have done so, with some elements of role-play. For example, saying things like: 'We have no idea what to name this product, what flavour it should be, or what the packaging should be. Can you help us?' In other studies, where we've not been able to say what the problem is, we've created a fantasy-based narrative, but that in itself can help engage participants in the research content. By using relevant storylines, we have encouraged participants to imagine the future (to the benefit of allowing our client to understand the impact of specific future-scenarios), become fashion designers, and create their ideal lunch product.

The use of metaphorical or realistic narratives in game-based surveys must uphold the research objectives at hand, and it really doesn't matter if the narrative is realistic or entirely fantastical, as long as the narrative serves to immerse the participant in the research content and appropriate emotional contexts. As described by Rigby and Ryan (2011) 'despite the fictional nature of the content (in games), a good story can be just as meaningful as "real" experiences and used as a vehicle for genuine growth'.[23] However, the suspension of disbelief is crucial, which is why a narrative, if used in a game-based survey, must harmonize fully with the research content, otherwise confusion and frustration can arise and actually serve to disengage the participant. It is the suspension of disbelief that can help immerse participants in another world completely and emotionally.

Game elements – 'ATARE'

We have explored game ingredients and game components, but there are other aspects of games that create further engagement. Below is a list of game elements. Again, some opinion leaders argue there are more or fewer or different game elements. Note: this list may expand as games evolve over time and capabilities/game features change:

- Avatars;
- Timers (giving players specific time periods to achieve a goal and can also regulate the speed and rhythm of the game);
- Audio (such as background music, sound effects and spoken dialogue);

- Role-play;
- Environments (virtual or otherwise).

Such elements can and have been used in game-based research.

Avatars

Many digital games require players to take on a character. A character may be seen in a game as visual representation (ie through an avatar) or the player embodies a character but sees no visual representation of that character (for example, in a first-person game).

The term 'avatar' is loose in its meaning, as avatars come in all shapes and forms; from simple pseudonyms to role-play and visual avatars in human-like or non-human forms. People have grown up with avatars in their lives in some form or another, even if they don't play videogames. Toys are types of avatar – Action Man and Barbie dolls allow children to play out their stories as they take on certain characters or extend their sense of 'self'. Online chatbots and virtual assistants are other examples of avatars – digital characters that help users with anything from online banking to sales calls.

To understand how avatars are used in digital games, and indeed how they can be used in game-based surveys, it is important to understand the different types of avatar. 'Visual' avatars (which can appear in human and non-human forms) can come in three broad types:

1 **Non-customizable pre-existing characters**: these are pre-made avatars that players can select from a menu, but can't customize anything about the character or its avatar. For instance, in videogames like *Super Mario* or *Street Fighter*, the characters have different and unique characteristics, which (most times) cannot be changed by players unless they gain in-game achievements or 'suits' that can alter the abilities of their chosen characters. For instance, if Super Mario earns a 'feather' in *Super Mario 3*, it allows him to run and fly for a limited time, which he cannot do usually.

2 **Pre-existing 'base characters' with customization options**: this is a 'base' character that the player can then evolve. For example, in the game *World of Warcraft*, players can choose to be one of many races, like a Troll or a Dranei, and from there choose their 'class', such as a Hunter or a Priest. While these avatars are preconceived and come with a set of unique abilities, a player can do things like change the hair colour, clothing, face-shape and other elements to make the avatar unique.

3 **Fully customizable avatars made from scratch**: players can build these avatars from 'the ground up', customizing anything and everything about their avatar. For example, the Nintendo Wii allows players to make an avatar from a myriad of choices of hair, eyebrow shape, lip fullness and so on, but there is no 'character' which the avatar embodies.

Why are avatars useful in games?

- **Avatars can be a key onboarding engager** – something that initially engages a player in a game. Usually, creating an avatar is the first thing players do in a game and this engrosses them in the overall gameplay process.

- **The inclusion of avatars can perpetuate engagement.** The evolution/ growth of an avatar can in itself be a feedback mechanism – where the avatar constantly evolves as the player achieves goals. Seeing your avatar evolve is also a source of aesthetic and bonuses/novelty, as sometimes improvements to an avatar can be sought because a player wants a beautifully crafted weapon or clothing for their avatar. Sometimes these improvements are a bonus, perhaps where a player unexpectedly finds a piece of armour while exploring terrain. Avatars also tie in with narratives, as the way an avatar changes over time in a game can be reflective of changes in the storyline.

- **Avatars are a source of emotional connection** with a game and can help players behave as their true selves and explore the different roles we play in life. This is also applicable to the relationships and emotional connections developed with other avatars, even those that don't have a human controlling them. These are known as NPCs – non-player characters.

How can avatars be useful in game-based surveys (and online market research in general)?

In research, avatars can be useful as they can:

- help to onboard participants in the research process (if creating an avatar is one of the first things participants can do when starting the survey);

- help participants engage right through to the end of the study because they want to see their avatar evolve if avatars change over time during the game-based survey process;

- help encourage people to come back for more research (especially true if participants can build an avatar one time, and then as they participate in more surveys, gain bonus content – like unlocking hair colours and styles – for their avatar. The *Harry Potter Hogwarts Mystery* app game does exactly this – check it out for inspiration at www.harrypotterhog wartsmystery.com);

- help participants behave as their true selves and express more freely the different roles we play in life: wife, daughter, sister, dog-mum, entrepreneur, artist, home owner etc. – Even though avatars can be a source of anonymity, it is this anonymity that enables players (and can enable participants) to act authentically. As Oscar Wilde put it, 'give a man a mask and he will show you his true face';

- give researchers an understanding of a participant's preferences without necessarily asking questions when avatars are made in the participant's image.

Avatar Creator Tools can be customized to include content that is relevant to the research objectives. For example, if you want to understand what car a participant drives, or what brands he or she wears, you can show visual images of these things in the tool itself and observe the choices people make.

If other avatars are seen in the game-based survey (as other participants controlling those avatars, or as NPCs) then this can encourage collaboration, emotional connection and thus researchers can observe the content of more natural conversations as players talk to each other, rather than answering research questions. These kinds of 'conversations' that take place by answering questions is a feature already inherent in games – this is called interactive storytelling, where the player's decisions have narrative weight and can shape the direction of the game. This is seen in games like *The Wolf Among Us* (Telltale Games), *Mass Effect 2* (Electronic Arts), and in app games like *Episode* (Episode Interactive LLC) and *Choices* (Pixelberry Studios) where players can converse with others and change the direction of the narrative depending on how they react to certain situations and respond to other characters. **Games are already tasking players to answer questions. Games are already evolved versions of surveys.**

When including participant-made avatars in your game-based survey you should consider three things:

- the need for using avatars (is it crucial/appropriate/relevant to the research objectives?);

- your time;

- your budget.

Developing an Avatar Creator Tool (as my team and I did at Research Through Gaming) can take several months and involve people with different sets of skills; researchers need to be involved in the process, as do concept artists, graphic designers and programmers. You will also need to think about how detailed or sparse your Avatar Creator Tool will be. Do you want to give participants deep levels of detail in the thickness of lips and shapes of eyebrows? Or do you want only a few options available per facial feature, clothing, accessories and so on? No matter what your initial design, an Avatar Creator Tool for game-based surveys is never a finished product – but one that is constantly updated for years to come.

Timers

Timers (invisible or visible countdown clocks in a digital game) give players specific durations in which they can achieve goals. Countdown timers can also regulate the pace and rhythm of a game. They are also used to count down the start of specific in-game events, which helps to create anticipation, engagement and focus. Often, timers in games go hand-in-hand with music, as the music will speed up as time runs out to encourage players to speed up their movements. Little has been written about the use of timers in games compared to other components and elements, like avatars and audio, which is surprising as timers are key in engaging players because they help to build emotion (such as anticipation, relief and urgency) and can be key in nudging desirable behaviours (such as completing a level within a certain time to gain further points).

How can timers be useful in game-based surveys (and online market research in general)?

- Time limits can help boost focus and productivity, as participants would feel less inclined to procrastinate or waiver their attention if they only have a certain window in which to complete a task.

- Time limits, especially time limits per question or per scenario, can discourage deliberation and encourage more top-of-mind responses. Arguably (and where relevant), these types of responses are said to be more truthful, as they can reveal hidden biases that people might not even be aware of, let alone be able to articulate. This thinking has already been harnessed in the Harvard Implicit Association Tests[24] (or IATs).

- Countdown timers to begin specific tasks within a survey can create a sense of anticipation, and that can create engagement and encourage focus.

Audio

You don't think of videogames without thinking of the music and sound effects. Videogames are audiovisual in their nature. Audio plays such an important role in games that there is a relatively new genre of games: audio-only[25] (or where the audio becomes part of the gameplay itself). For example, in the *Zombies, Run!*[26] app game (designed to help those who like to run or jog) the sound of zombies gets louder to make the player run faster, thus the sound is integral to the gameplay, player behaviour and the game's emotional impact on the player. Music can boost emotional impact and steer the player's interpretation of the visuals by providing context.[27]

As well as sound effects and background music, audio also encompasses dialogue between characters, like the language Simlish, spoken in *The Sims* game, which helps to convey the emotional state of the characters. How a non-player character (NPC) delivers speech in a game can also make the difference between trusting the character or not. In the game *L.A. Noire* (Rockstar Games) players are asked if they can trust an NPC by the sound of its voice (as well as its body language).

In this sense, audio for a game-based survey can be broken down into these groups:

- information audio (like narration, or dialogue between game characters);
- environment audio (for example, the sound of splashing in a game when in water, or the light 'tink tink' sound if walking on a tiled floor);
- music audio (background music that changes when the game environment evolves, or helps to set the pace or emotive contexts);
- audio that does all of the above.

Audio forms part of feedback systems, a form of information sharing. For instance, if a player does x, then the sound effect, dialogue or music can inform a player if they've won an award in a game, defeated a villain, levelled up and so on. Background music can also do things like set the emotional tone of a game, communicate a change in the narrative, or warn the player if danger is on the horizon – thus audio conveys information about the environment.

Audio can also trigger different player behaviours; if a player is running out of time, the music might speed up to encourage the player to move faster. If a player needs to tread carefully within enemy territory, the music may slow down and become quieter.

Audio in games can be such a key element to the gameplay experience that some people attend concerts by orchestras that specifically play music from games,[28] and some games even have their own soundtrack albums. When we hear a piece of music we like, dopamine, one of the four happiness chemicals (of which the benefits, like increased motivation, have been discussed earlier) is released.[29]

The increased understanding of how music can change human behaviour has had many commercial benefits, from playing classical music on trains to deter antisocial behaviour[30] through to how music in marketing affects purchase intent and shapes brand perception.[31] Some companies running call centres have researched to find the perfect accent because the accent heard on the phone can make or break a sale.[32]

Deane Alban, health information researcher, author and co-founder of Be Brain Fit, writes a comprehensive and evidence-based list of the positive effects of music in the article *How Music Affects the Brain*.[33] (Note: the citations below are taken from the citations referenced in Deane Alban's article.) The benefits include:

- enhancing performance on cognitive tasks, which improves accuracy, and enables the completion of repetitive tasks more efficiently;[34]
- improved quality of work;[35]
- improved productivity;[36]
- increased creativity and quantity of ideas;[37]
- increased inclination to spend time and energy helping others.[38]

Other benefits include:

- increased emotional engagement;[39]
- increased ability to recall, spurring improved memory in different ways;[40]
- places listeners in a relevant mindset and can increase motivation.[41]

How can audio be useful in game-based surveys (and online market research in general)?

Researchers want all these behaviours and outcomes from participants!

Audio in game-based research can also:

- work with behavioural economics to induce a sense of urgency or limited time for the participant to react to certain scenarios with faster paced audio. This can discourage deliberation and encourage top-of-mind responses (the opposite also works, as slower music can encourage more time and thus deeper thinking);

- immerse the participant in the narrative (if a narrative is being used);

- encourage a relevant emotional state (for example, high-pitched noise might induce feelings of stress or softer tones can induce relaxation).

For participants who have visual challenges, audio is a *crucial* component. It can let them know how they are progressing through the survey, if they have pressed something incorrectly, if they have selected the correct quantity of answers and so on. By including audio, be it narration, sound effects or music, we can help people who are visually impaired take part in research and feel valued.

If we look again at the www.pottermore.com/patronus website and find out what our Patronus looks like, we see that the website marries a polished aesthetic (one of the previous game components) along with audio to engage us. The sound of twinkly bells ring out as we move the cursor and hover over buttons and this makes us want to press and move things – it makes us want to participate. The multi-sensory nature of videogames (and now more commonly, other digital media like the Pottermore Patronus site), create the 'Triple E Effect' of engagement, emotion and experience.

Role-play

In games, role-play is a prominent feature. Players can be placed in the shoes of almost any character, real or metaphorical or a parody of the real. Some game genres focus on role-playing, such as MMORPGs (massively multiplayer online role-playing games) or simply RPGs (role-playing games) which can, and have, existed digitally in games such as *Final Fantasy*, and in non-digital games, like *Dungeons and Dragons* (first published in 1974, but so popular that people still play different versions of this game today).

But what is the role of role-play in games, and what are the benefits? Role-play helps to build empathy,[42] places people in situations they would otherwise never experience, and even helps players learn about different subjects that they may never have experienced before.

Many readers may associate role-play with constantly being the hero of a story, or the villain: some kind of 'extreme'. But actually role-playing games have evolved to become a bit more 'low key' than that, and are still incredibly engaging. In games like *FarmVille*, players take on the role of a farmer, and can actually build empathy regarding the amount of time, labour and maintenance involved in the farming process, despite the fact that it is a completely digital simulation of an unreal event. In other games like *That Dragon, Cancer* (2016) the player experiences the heart-wrenching highs and lows of being a parent of a young boy with cancer.

In the book *How Games Move Us: Emotion by design* (Isbister, 2017)[43] the author describes how games not only create empathy, but also emotion. When you can place yourselves in someone else's shoes, you can begin to replicate the kinds of emotions that person goes through. The author, like others, reminds us that the emotions felt in games *are real*, and in fact some emotions that are felt during gameplay, such as guilt, complicity and grief, are not felt (at least not in the same way) through any other medium.

In short, role-play equates to empathy and emotion and is part and parcel of being able to simulate and replicate experiences, which will help researchers understand those experiences through observation.

How can role-play be useful in game-based surveys (and online market research in general)?

The connection between role-play and the benefits to market research are obvious; in fact, so much so that many market research techniques already use forms of role-play such as projective techniques and personification techniques. These are used in both qualitative and quantitative research to allow participants to think about things that they might not otherwise think about in day-to-day life, giving researchers insight that they might not have if they asked direct questions about a participant's own specific experiences. For example, let's say we wanted to know how a participant thinks that a brand's marketing disaster should have been better handled; what would they have done instead? Or – let's look to the future – what would the participant do if he or she were in charge of marketing for an upcoming campaign? But this kind of role-play can only become believable and immersive if participants begin to empathize with the other person's position, and games are great at getting players to do that.

The success of role-play is already being used in market research to help with future forecasting[44] and to understand buying intentions. This ability to hypothesize about situations (past, present or future) has been labelled

System 3 thinking[45] and combined with role-play can be useful in the following ways:

- Building empathy and emotion through role-play can help participants better understand the research content/situation being discussed.
- Building empathy and emotion through role-play can help participants give more thought-out responses to hypothetical past, present or future situations.
- If the participants are putting more thought into responding to scenarios, then this can help produce more reliable data.

But, how accurate is this information? There are arguments to say that simply asking participants to imagine 'what they would do/buy/feel/want/ say if ...' is as unreliable as asking someone what he or she will want to eat for breakfast tomorrow. The answer is, we simply just don't know until we are placed in that time, and in that context, with the limitations and opportunities available to us in which we can make the final choice. This is why role-play *in* a simulation, with the relevant contexts in place, can lead to more accurate insight, and games are great at creating multi-sensory and contextual experiences.

Even if the role-play is far removed from the participant's reality, if designed well, there can still be an emotional connection that allows the participant to be immersed in someone else's position. As Meg Jayanth, multi-award winning writer, and writer of Time Game of the Year 2014 '80 days' (Inkle, 2014), writes in an article for *Polygon*: 'As I play through the lives of the characters ... these highly specific experiences are at times strange, but they are not estranging.'[46]

Environments (virtual or otherwise)

Game environments can be extremely diverse, from sprawling cities or forests to tunnels and castles. Game environments also deal with scene geometry, for example a spacious hallway or a narrow corridor,[47] and such spatial geometry can contribute to player emotion, like relaxation or stress. Indeed, designing game environments is a specialist job and skill in the games industry.

Games environments, like the one pictured in Figure 4.3 from *Monument Valley* 2,[48] can become a source of the gameplay themselves, where the game environment becomes the problem that players need to solve. Other game environments can be realistic and detailed in their graphical content, like in the *America's Army* game.[49] Game environments can also act as feedback mechanisms where the game world evolves as you level up, letting players know that they are achieving.

Figure 4.3   A screengrab from the multiple-award-winning app game
Monument Valley 2. The game environment itself becomes the
source of the game challenges – the user must navigate around MC
Escher-style labyrinthine buildings to complete levels

SOURCE © Ustwo Games 2018

How can environments, conceptual or realistic, be useful in game-based surveys (and online market research in general)?

Virtual environments are not just a key element in games but should be in future market research if researchers want to collect information on subconscious biases and the impact of environment on consumer behaviour.

While 'virtual supermarket environments' have been created for online research, researchers can take much more advantage of virtual environments to observe behaviours and choices in relevant contexts. In one example, a virtual reality environment was used to place participants in a digital store to test in-store communication effectiveness. The results were high participant engagement, self-reported enjoyment and spontaneous recall, which was spurred by the use of the virtual environment.[50] In my own ResearchGame designs, digital kitchens, design studios, undercover agent hideouts and

Table 4.1   The building blocks of games and game-based research: Human Psychological Needs, Game Ingredients, Game Components and Game Elements

Human Psychological Needs (*RAMP*)			
Relatedness	Autonomy	Mastery	Purpose

Game Ingredients	Game Components	Game Elements
(*GARF*)	(*CABIN*)	(*ATARE*)
Goal(s)	Collaboration	Avatars
Autonomy opportunities	Aesthetic	Timing
Rules	Bonus features	Audio
Feedback	Increases in difficulty	Role-play
	Narrative	Environments

doctor waiting rooms have been used as environments in which to stimulate the participants' memory, immerse them in the research content using conceptual narratives, and house stimulus material to collect information on how participants change their choices and behaviour depending on different contexts.

Table 4.1 shows the building blocks of games so researchers can reflect these game ingredients, game components and game elements in game-based surveys.

Now that games have been explored, it's time to look at gamification.

Defining and understanding gamification

The definition of 'gamification', like the word 'game', is also contested. However, there are two widely accepted definitions:

1 'the process of using game-thinking and game mechanics to engage users and solve problems';[51]

2 'the use of game elements in a non-game contexts'.[52]

While these definitions are useful, they can be problematic:

- If you don't know what a game mechanic is, or a game element, then it's difficult to understand these definitions.

- Even for those literate in game phraseology, the terms 'game mechanic' and 'game element' are *also* contested. In my interview with Professor James Newman,[53] author of *Playing with Videogames* (2008), he notes that game mechanics describe the way a game operates – as in, the more literal mechanics of a game; pressing 'B' is jump, pressing 'A' with the down arrow makes your game character squat, and so on. However, other academics have said that game mechanics are things like rules and challenges.[54]

- The terms 'game mechanics' and 'game elements' are often used interchangeably. For instance, one publication may describe things like goals and rules as game elements,[55] while elsewhere goals and rules will be labelled as game mechanics.[56]

To lessen the confusion of the widely accepted definitions, my suggested definition is:

Gamification repurposes superficial aspects of games (such as points and badges) to gain the engagement that games can create for activities that are not games.

This definition identifies that gamification borrows *from* games, and is not a game in itself. Gamification mostly harnesses:

- social media style interactions (such as likes and shares);
- social status (which can be reflected in the form of badges);
- feedback mechanisms in the form of measuring things like behaviour and productivity, where there are often many ways to level up, and a user's level/badge/measurements and so on are often displayed in leaderboards.

Gamification is also synonymous with data collection, as every user interaction with digital gamification platforms is often recorded.

While gamification can use the four game ingredients, it is the way they are used that will determine whether a research-game or gamified survey is produced, and how the finished designs impact participant interaction. For example, whether participants feel they were playing a game or not will give an indication on the type of platform created. In many ways, the product is not defined by the maker, but by the users; did they feel like they were *taking part* in a gamified survey, or *playing* a game?

ACTIVITY

Gamify your life

- As a way to dip your toes into applying game ingredients in the real world, think about how you can apply the four game ingredients to 'gamify' an aspect of your life or create a fully-fledged Serious Game to help you reach an objective. For example, can you use the game ingredients to help you achieve a life goal like learning a language or writing a book, or even build a gamification strategy to do things like spend more time with a loved one, or explore new experiences?

- After thinking about or designing your gamification strategy or Serious Game, check if there is a business that has *already* used gamification to reach the same or similar goals. Take inspiration from it and see how it has applied the game ingredients, game components or game elements to gain user engagement.

Notes

1   Salen, K and Zimmerman, E (2004) *Rules of Play: Game design fundamentals*, MIT Press, Cambridge, MA

2   McGonigal, J (2011) *Reality is Broken: Why games make us better and how they can change the world*, Penguin Press, New York

3   Suits, B (1978) *The Grasshopper: Games, life and utopia*, University of Toronto Press

4   Aarseth, E and Calleja, G (2015) [accessed 27 May 2018] The Word Game: The ontology of an indefinable object, *FDG* [Online] https://tinyurl.com/yb5zceep

5   Deterding, S, Khaled, R, Nacke, LE and Dixon, D (2011) [accessed 21 May 2018] *Gamification: Toward a Definition*, Proceedings of CHI 2011, Vancouver [Online] http://hci.usask.ca/uploads/219-02-Deterding,-Khaled,-Nacke,-Dixon.pdf

6   I say 'well-designed' because like any platform we interact with, poor design leads to lost attention. Therefore, it is important to note that 'slapping on' game ingredients to a survey is not going to fix low engagement issues as there are design guidelines to adhere to. These guidelines are explored in Part Two: World of Design.

7   Pink, DH (2009) *Drive: The surprising truth about what motivates us*, Riverhead Books, New York

8 Ryan, RM and Deci, EL (2000) Self-determination theory and the facilitation of intrinsic motivation, social development, and well-being, *American Psychologist*, 55 (1), pp 68–78 [Online] http://dx.doi.org/10.1037/0003-066X.55.1.68

9 Belle Cooper, Beth (2016) [accessed 21 May 2018] The key to happiness at work isn't money–it's autonomy, *Quartz* [Online] https://qz.com/676144/why-its-your-call-is-the-best-thing-you-can-say-to-keep-employees-happy/

10 Breuning, Loretta (2014) [accessed 21 May 2018] Meet your Happy Chemicals, *SlideShare* [Online] **www.slideshare.net/LorettaBreuning/happy-chemicals-33377349**

11 Patel, Sujan (2015) [accessed 21 May 2018] The Science Behind Motivation, *Forbes* [Online] www.forbes.com/sites/sujanpatel/2015/01/09/the-science-behind-motivation/#14f7ebec49d9

12 Sample, Ian (2014) [accessed 21 May 2018] Curiosity improves memory by tapping into the brain's reward system, *The Guardian* [Online] www.theguardian.com/science/2014/oct/02/curiosity-memory-brain-reward-system-dopamine

13 Ashby, FG, Valentin, VV and Turken, AU [accessed 21 May 2018] *The effects of positive affect and arousal on working memory and executive attention: Neurobiology and computational models* Chapter 11 [Online] https://pdfs.semanticscholar.org/b807/257f90dd433a7ef1b073195b6acd87ed2627.pdf?_ga=2.259998474.1464839100.1533553513-856830954.1526937094

14 Boot, N, Baas, M, van Gaal, S *et al* (2017) [accessed 21 May 2018] Creative Cognition and Dopaminergic Modulation of Fronto-striatal Networks: Integrative Review and Research Agenda, *Neuroscience & Biobehavioral Reviews*, 78, 10.1016/j.neubiorev.2017.04.007 [Online] www.researchgate.net/publication/316155666_Creative_Cognition_and_Dopaminergic_Modulation_of_Fronto-striatal_Networks_Integrative_Review_and_Research_Agenda

15 Mandal, Dr Ananya MD (2017) [accessed 21 May 2018] *Dopamine Functions*, *News Medical* [Online] www.news-medical.net/health/Dopamine-Functions.aspx

16 Palladino, LJ (2008) *Find Your Focus Zone*, Simon & Schuster, London

17 Garret, Ural (2013) [accessed 21 May 2018] Florida Surgeons Play Video Games Before Surgery, *Tech Times* [Online] www.techtimes.com/articles/104/20131014/florida-surgeons-play-video-games-before-surgery.htm

18 Yung-Hui, Lim (2012) [accessed 21 May 2018] 1.6% of Facebook Users Spent Over $1 Billion on Virtual Goods, *Forbes* [Online] www.forbes.com/sites/limyunghui/2012/08/02/1-6-of-facebook-users-spent-over-1-billion-on-virtual-goods

19 Chahal, Gurbaksh (2010) [accessed 21 May 2018] There's Real Money in Virtual Goods, *TechCrunch* [Online] https://techcrunch.com/2010/06/23/real-money-virtual-goods/

20 Adamou, B and Birks, Dr D (2013) [accessed 22 May 2018] ResearchGames as a Methodology: The impact of online ResearchGames and game components upon participant engagement and future ResearchGame, Proceedings of 'Critical Reflections on Methodology and Technology: Gamification, Text Analysis and Data Visualisation' conference, the Association of Survey Computing (ASC), University of Winchester, UK, 6–7 September 2013 [Online] www.academia. edu/9487108/ResearchGames_as_a_Methodology_The_Impact_of_Online_ ResearchGames_Upon_Participant_Engagement_and_Future_ResearchGame_ Participation

21 McGonigal, J (2011) *Reality is Broken: Why games make us better and how they can change the world*, Penguin Press, New York

22 Gottschall, J (2013) *Storytelling Animal: How stories make us human*, Mariner Books, New York

23 Rigby, S and Ryan, MR (2011) *Glued to Games: How video games draw us in and hold us spellbound*, p 81, New Directions in Media, California

24 Readers can participate in Implicit Association Tests here: https://implicit. harvard.edu/implicit/

25 Röber, Niklas and Masuch, Maic (2005) [accessed 21 May 2018] Playing Audio-only Games: A compendium of interacting with virtual, auditory worlds, *Digital Games Research Association* [Online] www.digra.org/dl/db/06276.30120.pdf

26 *Zombies, Run!* (2016). Published and developed by Six to Start and Naomi Alderman

27 Tammen, Hendrik and Loviscach, Jorn (2008) [accessed 21 May 2018] Emotion in Video Games: Quantitative Studies? Proceedings of the Emotion in HCI – Designing for People International Workshop (2008) pp 25–29 [Online] https://tinyurl.com/y8bm2vm3

28 Collins, K (2008) *Game Sound: An introduction to the history, theory, and practice of video game music and sound design*, MIT Press, Cambridge, MA

29 Bergland, Christopher (2012) [accessed 27 May 2018] The Neuroscience of Music, Mindset, and Motivation [Blog] *Psychology Today* [Online] www.psychologytoday.com/us/blog/the-athletes-way/201212/ the-neuroscience-music-mindset-and-motivation

30 Shilling, Jane (2017) [accessed 27 May 2018] A musical approach to anti-social behaviour might just hit the right note, *The Telegraph* [Online] www.telegraph.co.uk/news/2017/08/06/musical-approach-anti-social-behaviour-might-just-hit-right/

31 Morris, JD and Boone, MA (1998) The effects of music on emotional response, brand attitude, and purchase intent in an emotional advertising condition, *Advances in Consumer Research*, 25, pp 518–526 [Online] www.acrwebsite. org/search/view-conference-proceedings.aspx?Id=8207

32 Reuters (2009) [accessed 21 May 2018] Revealed: The perfect telephone call center accent, *Reuters* [Online] https://uk.reuters.com/article/us-britain-branding-accents/revealed-the-perfect-telephone-call-center-accent-idUKTRE5AN37C20091124

33 Alban, Deanne (date of publication unknown) [accessed 27 May 2018] How Music Affects the Brain, *Be Brain Fit* [Online] https://bebrainfit.com/music-brain/

34 Angel, LA, Poizella, DJ and Elvers, GC (2010) [accessed 27 May 2018] Background Music and Cognitive Performance, *NCBI* [Online] https://www.ncbi.nlm.nih.gov/pubmed/20865993

35 Lesiuk, Teresa (2005) [accessed 27 May 2018] The Effect of Music Listening on Work Performance, *Sage* [Online] https://graphics8.nytimes.com/packages/pdf/business/LESIUKarticle2005.pdf

36 Fox, JG and Embrey, ED (1972) [accessed 27 May 2018] Music – an Aid to Productivity, *Applied Ergonomics*, 3 (4) pp 202–205 [Online] www.sciencedirect.com/science/article/pii/0003687072901019

37 Ritter, Simone M and Ferguson, Sam (2017) [accessed 27 May 2018] Happy Creativity: Listening to happy music facilitates divergent thinking, *PLOS* [Online] http://journals.plos.org/plosone/article?id=10.1371/journal.pone.0182210

38 North, Adrian C, Tarrant, Mark and Hargreaves, David J (2004) [accessed 27 May 2018] The Effects of Music on Helping Behavior: A field study, *Sage* [Online] http://journals.sagepub.com/doi/abs/10.1177/0013916503256263

39 Saarikallio, Suvi, Nieminen, Sirke and Brattico, Elvira (2012) [accessed 27 May 2018] Affective Reactions to Musical Stimuli Reflect Emotional Use of Music in Everyday Life, *Sage* [Online] http://journals.sagepub.com/doi/abs/10.1177/1029864912462381?journalCode=msxa

40 Proverbio, CA Alice Mado, Lozano Nasi, Valentina *et al* (2015) [accessed 27 May 2018] The Effect of Background Music on Episodic Memory and Autonomic Responses: Listening to emotionally touching music enhances facial memory capacity, *NCBI* [Online] www.ncbi.nlm.nih.gov/pmc/articles/PMC4606564

41 Bergland, Christopher (2012) [accessed 21 May 2018] The Neuroscience of Music, Mindset, and Motivation, *Psychology Today* [Online] www.psychologytoday.com/us/blog/the-athletes-way/201212/the-neuroscience-music-mindset-and-motivation

42 Parkin, Simon (2015) [accessed 21 May 2018] Role Play in Gaming is an Empathy Machine, *Wired* [Online] www.wired.co.uk/article/gaming-role-play-empathy

43 Isbister, K (2017) *How Games Move Us: Emotion by design*, MIT Press, Cambridge, MA

44 Knowledge at Wharton (1999) [accessed 21 May 2018] Role Playing as Forecasting Tool, *Knowledge at Wharton*, University of Pennsylvania [Online] http://knowledge.wharton.upenn.edu/article/role-playing-as-a-forecasting-tool/

45 Caldwell, Leigh (2018) [accessed 21 May 2018] Introducing System 3: How we use our imagination to make choices [Blog] *GreenBook* [Online] http://greenbookblog.org/2018/04/24/introducing-system-3-how-we-use-our-imagination-to-make-choices/

46 Jayanth, Meg (2017) [accessed 21 May 2018] What Big Publishers Can Learn About Representation From Small Games, *Polygon* [Online] https://www.polygon.com/2018/1/12/16878196/butterfly-soup-best-games-2017-year-in-review

47 Tammen, Hendrik and Loviscach, Jorn (2008) [accessed 21 May 2018] Emotion in Video Games: Quantitative studies? Proceedings of the Emotion in HCI – Designing for People International Workshop (2008) pp 25–29 [Online] https://tinyurl.com/y8bm2vm3

48 *Monument Valley* game: www.monumentvalleygame.com

49 *America's Army* game: www.americasarmy.com

50 Bramley, I and Salmon, J (2018) 'Researching in-store, at home', Paper presented to the IMPACT MRS Annual Conference, London, 13–14 March

51 Definition provided in Zichermann, G (2011) *Gamification by Design*, O'Reilly Media, Sebastopol, CA

52 Deterding, S, Khaled, R, Nacke, L, and Dixon, D (2011) *Gamification: Toward a definition*, In CHI 2011 Gamification Workshop Proceedings, Vancouver, BC

53 Adamou, B and Newman, J (2014) Expert interview with author James Newman on understanding intrinsic engagement with videogames, Web interview, 19 November

54 Sicart, Miguel (2008) [accessed 27 May 2018] Defining Game Mechanics, *Game Studies* [Online] http://gamestudies.org/0802/articles/sicart

55 Bartholomeus, Ellis (2011) [accessed 27 May 2018] What are Game Elements? Pacman as a reference, *Ellis in Wonderland* [Blog] [Online] www.ellisinwonderland.nl/what-are-game-elements

56 Lee, JJ and Hammer, J (2011) Gamification in Education: What, how, why bother? *Academic Exchange Quarterly*, **15** (2)

The differences   05
and similarities
between games
and gamification

There are six key differences between games and gamification outside of the context of market research that impact how we apply games and gamification *within* market research. The first difference between games and gamification is their definitions, as we have already explored in the previous chapter.

The other differences are:

- win/lose states;
- intrinsic engagement versus extrinsic engagement;
- play versus taking part;
- the design processes;
- the outcomes in terms of user data and behaviour.

Win/lose states

Games have a win/lose state. Player actions have consequences and there are elements of jeopardy.[1] By contrast, many gamification platforms have a win state; there doesn't tend to be a lose state. As such, participation in a gamified activity has less risk and consequence to the user. If you know there is no consequence to your action (or inaction), there is less engagement and emotional investment. For example, imagine you have forgotten your loyalty card (loyalty cards are gamification examples) while buying a coffee. While this is frustrating, the customer does not experience a 'lose' state as a player does in games. Without that important sense of challenge, one could argue that even the initial inspiration to take part is lessened.

We know how it feels to be genuinely challenged; how many times have players shouted 'YES!' when winning at a game, or 'no, no, no...!' when they think they are about to lose? Gamification doesn't give us the same intensity of emotion. When that perception of risk is removed, the sense of challenge is also removed and can negate user engagement.

Intrinsic engagement versus extrinsic engagement

Jay L Wenger in the book *Psychology of Motivation* (2007)[2] quotes from Deci and Ryan (1985)[3] to offer a helpful understanding of extrinsic motivation and engagement: 'Extrinsic motivation refers to our tendency to perform activities for known external rewards, whether they be tangible (eg money) or psychological (eg praise) in nature.'

Intrinsic engagement is said to be when people find joy in the doing of itself, even without reward. As we explored in Chapter 4, games are intrinsically engaging because they satisfy four human psychological needs. This helps us enjoy the process of playing games and, in general, players play games for that sense of enjoyment as well as the in-game 'wins'. By contrast, gamification adopts the 'do x, get y' (often called the 'carrot and stick') approach relying on extrinsic motivators. It's argued that gamification is similar to the operant conditioning explored by psychologist and behaviourist BF Skinner, where experiments showed that rewards can be used to change and reinforce behaviours.[4] As such, it is contended that gamification isn't anything new[5] and cannot promise the intrinsic motivation and engagement that is produced by the medium gamification tries to imitate: the game.[6] As such, gamification as a tool to increase engagement in online research is limited owing to its very nature. Research tells us that extrinsic motivators (like financial incentives) aren't always infallible. If they worked, then online market research wouldn't have any issues with engagement. Gamification still harnesses the very problem we are trying to solve: the problem of ineffective extrinsic motivators, while games create intrinsic engagement and play.

We see this with loyalty cards, which are helpful examples of gamification. Let's take on a little challenge – take out any loyalty cards from your wallet or purse and see how many are from competing brands. I have a points card for Caffe Nero and Starbucks. I have loyalty cards for two competing beauty and pharmacy stores. Because of the extrinsic rewards inherent in loyalty programmes, it means lots of consumers are not intrinsically engaged with a single brand or store, and the irony is that they become disloyal because they are extrinsically motivated by competing brands.

Play versus taking part

We *play* games, we *take part* in gamified activities. This is one of the fundamental differences between games and gamification.

Do we feel like we're playing a game when the coffee store barista stamps or swipes our loyalty cards? Do we feel we're winning at a game when we get triple points for buying products? No. Do we feel like we're playing when we're engaged in *Candy Crush*, *Call of Duty*, *Monopoly* and *Chess*? Yes. Play is key to increasing problem-solving abilities, improved creativity, helps to induce a flow state, and many other behaviours. While simple participation has its benefits, from a sense of collaboration to feelings of inclusion, play creates specific behaviours that are commercially advantageous to market researchers, as we explore later in Chapter 7.

The design processes

There are huge differences between the design processes of creating a digital game compared to creating a gamified platform, in and outside of market research. Traditionally, the process for a game designer (who will make games for entertainment) is as follows (Figure 5.1):

1 The designer will have a game idea and create the game.

2 When players engage with it, they will behave in specific ways: trash talking their competitors; sitting on the edge of their seat; planning a strategy for a dungeon raid and so on.

3 Those behaviours will generate:

 – in-game outcomes, such as how many quests are completed, how many lives are saved and so on);

 – real-world outcomes, such as the players' emotional state and their psychophysiological response like increased heart rate or sweaty palms.

If we take the augmented reality mobile game *Pokémon Go* as an example, we can see the behaviours and outcomes clearly:

Figure 5.1   The process of making entertainment games: a diagram. A designer usually executes a game idea, and the players display certain behaviours during their game play, of which those behaviours have different outcomes

SOURCE © Betty Adamou 2018

1   The game: collect digital Pokémon in the real world.

2   Behaviours: players work in teams or alone. They leave the house. They walk or they run. They move around. They work collaboratively.

3   Outcomes: players are exercising, experiencing new places; this helps them feel good and engaged.

By contrast, gamification designers tend to work backwards. They will plan the desired outcomes of user interaction first, then think about the behaviours that will drive those outcomes, and finally that understanding drives the design that will nudge the desired behaviours and outcomes.

In market research however, gamification is often seen as an 'add-on' to traditional surveys. Gamification is not something you can sprinkle on a survey and hope everything will be better by adding a leaderboard here and a points system there. This won't gain researchers the participant behaviours and outcomes they desire. Instead, the inclusion of the four game ingredients, game components and/or game elements should be designed and developed as part of the survey from the start. Indeed, there is a pushback in the gamification industry to re-educate and rethink gamification to stop it from being thought of as a bolt-on solution to low engagement, but an ingrained *part* of the design process from the start.[7]

Serious Game designers 'work backwards' too; even though they are creating fully-fledged games, they are doing so with a purpose, be it to help students learn or allow players to empathize with different groups of people. Research-games *are* a type of Serious Game, and as such, game-based research designers (whether you are using gamification or reimagining your survey as a fully-fledged game) should also use the 'working backwards' approach, and start their design with the end goal in mind (Figure 5.2).

Figure 5.2   The differences in design process for Serious Games and gamification versus games

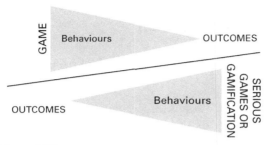

SOURCE © Betty Adamou 2018

The outcomes in terms of user data and behaviour

If researchers choose to develop fully-fledged research-games, they will evoke play and intrinsic engagement. If researchers choose to gamify a survey (especially if they 'add on' the superficial elements like points and badges to traditional online surveys) they will still rely on extrinsic motivators and may not necessarily evoke a sense of play or develop intrinsic participant engagement. As such, the participants' behaviours will be different as will the way they respond to questions/scenarios, and the data derived from their interactions will be different.

Researchers are encouraged to test the differences in participant behaviours and data outcomes by comparing research-games and gamified surveys for their own studies, within their own business contexts. While we could compare the outcomes of a number of research-games and gamified surveys, the results won't be comparable to your own tests and results. For example, if a case study from company *x* shows that a research-game gained more or less participant engagement than a gamified survey, those results won't necessarily occur in your tests because your study will have different research and business objectives, different types of participants and the design is likely to be entirely different. How I approach the design of a game-based survey could be completely different from you; it's a creative methodology so every approach will be different. As such, experimenting with design and execution within your company or department is encouraged.

The similarities between serious games and gamification: from engagement to applying the four 'game values'

Why do people choose to use gamification or Serious Games, and what are the similarities?

- **Engagement**: Serious Games (like research-games, exergames and advergames) and gamification (like loyalty cards, or where gamification is used to improve learning in education) are used to engage people, but crucially, to gain more user engagement than an organization would have without the use of game techniques.

- **Commercial gain**: increasing user engagement is for (mostly) commercial gain. Whether gamification and/or Serious Games are used for training, learning or some other endeavour, the end goal is either saving money, making money or raising money.

- **Behaviour change**: Serious Games and gamification also spur changes in behaviour. For example, Serious Games and gamification can be used to do things like raise awareness of an issue, increase productivity, increase collaboration, increase creative ideas and so on.

- **Include the four game ingredients**: both Serious Games and gamification include the four game ingredients and can include game components and game elements.

It is how Serious Games (like research-games) and gamification (like gamified surveys) are designed and applied that places them in one category type or another.

Learning from four game values: inspiring participants for higher response rates and perpetuating engagement for higher completion rates

Another element that Serious Games and gamification have in common is the *value* they provide to users. I have identified four, what I call, 'game values' – the value that games give players. Researchers can apply these values in both gamified surveys and research-games:

- self-discovery value;

- transcendent value;

- narrative value;

- knowledge value.

If these values are articulated at the beginning of the game-based survey, it can help participants understand straight away what they are going to get out of the experience and why they should give their time. These values can spur user inspiration to take part, curiosity, engagement, and evoke emotional investment for higher probability of onboarding and activity completion. Nowadays, offering value to users when involved in any digital content is crucial, and the same principles apply to market research participants. Brands will increasingly view their research outputs as additional communication tools, so how they treat consumers during the research process will matter more than ever before.

Applying any or all of these values to your own game-based survey would be considered 'quick wins' because the feedback system of learning something about yourself (as in the self-discovery value), or learning about how you are contributing to a wider cause (as in the transcendent value) *becomes* the goal of the game-based survey. These values can be implemented whether you are making a highly experiential and dynamic game-based survey, or just using text-on-a-screen. A breakdown of these values, and how they have been used in entertainment games as well as Research Through Gaming's ResearchGames, follows.

Self-discovery value

What is it?

Providing self-discovery experiences, or self-discovery value, allows participants to find out something about themselves. The uncovered information is usually something the participant didn't know before. Self-discovery experiences can increase feelings of mastery, purpose and relatedness, especially as self-discovery results can be compared with results from other people.

Examples from games and elsewhere

In games, self-discovery can come in a variety of forms. Self-discovery in games can be as simple as a player seeing his or her experience points (XP) grow or getting an award for his or her efforts. Serious Game *SuperBetter* (SuperBetter, LLC) also offers self-discovery value, as the game encourages players to overcome mental and physical obstacles to improve wellbeing.

As players complete quests, they can view their progress over time, learning more about themselves. Fitbit, which records the physical endeavours of players in a gamified way, also provides self-discovery value. These are just two examples of many in the 'quantified self' movement.

Online quizzes are also apt examples of self-discovery value. Quizzes that ask 'what kind of Disney princess are you?' gain huge engagement on social media. In many ways, horoscopes are a kind of self-discovery value, and there is engagement there as well.

The *BBC Class Calculator*[8] launched in 2011 is essentially an online survey, styled as a quiz. The information asked is quite personal; for example, what kind of property you own, your annual income and so on. These are questions that participants notoriously dislike responding to in surveys and can cause drop-outs. However, 160,000-plus participants have taken part to date because they are engaged to discover something about themselves.

How a ResearchGame used self-discovery value

> Having to answer such questions that I have been avoiding in my head has cleared to me what exactly I want. I feel more confident. Adding a few more questions could improve it some more.
>
> Participant feedback from the *What Kind of Student Are You?* ResearchGame
> by Research Through Gaming Ltd. Launched in July 2017 to
> prospective students of the University of Surrey, UK.

In a ResearchGame I designed on behalf of the University of Surrey in the United Kingdom, we harnessed self-discovery value so the participating prospective students could learn which one of six student types they were, and gave the option to share their results on social media. This segmentation study was played by thousands of prospective students, and achieved a 97 per cent completion rate from those who started the segmentation questions to achieving their profile result, showing that self-discovery value in a game-based research context can have benefits in driving engagement (especially with hard-to-engage audiences like students) but also driving more honest responses.[9] If you know you are about to learn something about yourself, you will be inclined to offer accurate information.

Thinking points

- Can your research-game or gamified survey offer the participants information in which they can learn something about themselves, from the data already collected as part of the survey?

- Could participants share the information they gain about themselves with others, for example on social media, as a form of social currency? (And even spread the word about your survey, if that's appropriate to your study.)

There are times when, as a designer, finding enough information to offer engaging self-discovery value is difficult. Perhaps I'm not able to share certain types of data with the participants, or perhaps my audience research indicates that the data I have for developing self-discovery value wouldn't necessarily engage them say, as much as another value type. If this is the case, I look to the other values.

Transcendent value

What is it?

Games are great at offering transcendent value – they tell players how their contributions are part of something bigger than themselves and that creates transcendent purpose. In your research-game or gamified survey, there are super simple ways to offer transcendent value – research is, after all, an instrument by which to change the world around us somehow; we just need to better articulate that to participants.

Examples from games and elsewhere

In games like *World of Warcraft*, transcendent value is offered in almost every challenge a player undertakes. In one example, even something so mundane as 'pounding the contents of rice baskets' keeps players engaged, because the player knows it will help others. Look at how the quest is described by a non-player character:

> 'There are certain things that everyone needs, from the basic household cook to the master chef. One of the city's most important staples is rice flour. Most families keep at least one basket of rice in their houses and the residents of the Craftsmen's Terrace and Tradesmen's Terrace are no different. I often ask my students to help with the task of pounding rice into flour since it's good practice and an endless task. Why don't you give it a try?'

This quest lets players know who they are going to help and why it's important. We can apply this approach in game-based research easily.

Figure 5.3   Screengrabs from a ResearchGame where participants were given a sense of transcendent purpose by seeing that their efforts could affect the real world, by knowing the name they chose for a product could be made and be available in stores

SOURCE © Research Through Gaming Ltd

How a ResearchGame used transcendent value

In a ResearchGame for an FMCG company, I articulated transcendent value simply by letting the participant know what the problem is to solve and what will happen if the participant chooses to help (Figure 5.3).

A simple note like this can help participants realize their impact on others around them and create engagement. In my experience, many participants self-report to enjoy helping in their voluntary feedback, for example:

> I liked that it's interactive. Was a topic I love and was glad to help.
>
> Participant from the *Designer for a Day* ResearchGame,
> developed on behalf of a Fortune 500 company,
> by Research Through Gaming Ltd

Thinking points

- Can you communicate how the participants' contribution will help a cause bigger than themselves?
- Can you let participants know why you need their help specifically?
- Can you let participants know how many other people have taken part so far, thus creating a feeling of community spirit and collaboration?
- Can you let participants know if/when you will give them the results of the study after they have been analysed and where they can find the information?

Again, if for whatever reason, these kinds of information can't be shared with participants, then we can create 'artificial value' through a storyline as we see next in narrative value.

Narrative value

What is it?

Games harness storytelling to immerse us in characters, missions, quests and more. Narratives help to show an evolution of your strengths as a player, and can even shape the virtual game world.

In the case where self-discovery value and transcendent value can't be offered, perhaps due to confidential research content (ie sharing information about the study back to the participant) then rewards, goals and feedback systems can be constructed through a narrative that relates to the research content. If you choose narrative value as your driver, remember to offer what I call narratologically relevant rewards. Rewards (be it in-game promotions, badges, points and so on) need to be tied in harmoniously to the storyline and make sense in the 'world' you have created.

Examples from games and elsewhere

Overarching storylines and character backstories are another big feature in games. As we have previously explored, narrative is an important game component.

While some games like *World of Warcraft* have complex weaves of story, other games can be more linear in their approach, while others allow players to shape the narrative through the way they answer questions like in the app games *Episode* (Episode Interactive LLC) and *Choices* (Pixelberry Studios) and in other games like *The Wolf Among Us* (Telltale Games), *The Stanley Parable* (Galactic Cafe) and *Life Is Strange* (Square Enix). Being able to change narrative through conscious choices makes the player complicit in the outcomes. Stories help immerse us in the personality of characters, the missions and quests, and can even show an evolution of your strengths as a player.

How a ResearchGame used narrative value

In the case where self-discovery value and transcendent value can't be offered to the participant because of client confidentiality then the game ingredients can be constructed through a narrative that relates to the research content. For example, if participants are tasked to review a holiday experience, why not place them in a role-play of being a travel blogger for the day, and allow them to level up with the more information and detail they contribute? If participants need to imagine a new food product, why not place them in a narrative where they are an inventor with a budget, who needs to create the world's best dish?

Thinking points

- Can you identify the problem that you need the participant to overcome, and 'storify' this?
- Can the narrative be accompanied with role-play and projective techniques to engage and immerse participants?

Knowledge value

What is it?

If you are unable to provide self-discovery value, transcendent value or narrative value, you may find yourself bereft of options as I did creating a ResearchGame design for a global consultancy brand. Without being able to share information about the study, share data with participants about their responses, and no room for a storyline, the only 'currency' I had was the value of knowledge.

Games impart knowledge in a variety of ways: through feedback mechanisms about our gameplay performance, to knowledge about secret missions, quests and rewards. Games are synonymous with gaining knowledge; not just through the gameplay but even the way players explore information about a game afterwards, seek out knowledge through video guides on how to combat a baddie, and read up about upcoming games.

Examples from games and elsewhere

Lots of games for entertainment, Serious Games and gamified platforms share knowledge and players can gain knowledge as they take part. *Mathletics*, the game to help children with maths, allows them to gain knowledge as they play (see http://us.mathletics.com).

How a ResearchGame used knowledge value

In designing a ResearchGame for a C-level executive audience, it was apparent through my research that the thing they would find most valuable, and what they trade on, is knowledge. The study, which was about data warehousing, had three levels. At the beginning of the study, I introduced a quiz:

three questions about the subject at hand, but unrelated to the questions for the survey itself. Participants would guess the answers to these quiz questions, but only one answer was revealed after completion of each level. As well as letting the participants know if they were correct, close to the right answer or wrong, the design also included the capability to compare their answers with those of other participants and the experts working within the research buyers' brand. This type of 'knowledge value' was a great way to intrigue the audience to test their knowledge, give them interesting information as a trade for their time, and a handy workaround given that the client wasn't able to let me share any actual survey data back to the participants.

In another ResearchGame, I tasked participants to imagine specific aspects about the future. Depending on how they responded to questions and scenarios, this told us if they predicted a dystopian or utopian future. Using an algorithm, we gave participants 'future summaries' at the end of every level – a summary of the future as they saw it, based on what they answered. This summary feedback didn't actually give participants any survey data, thus 'knowledge value' was offered while still keeping client confidentiality.

Participants have reported to have learned something and enjoyed the experience of learning:

> This was really fun and a cute way to stay informed about what it costs for our clothes thanks again and i will start looking for (the brand's) products next time I go shopping
>
> Was a refreshing approach to gain shopper insights and desires in their apparel line.
>
> Participants from *Designer for a Day* ResearchGame
>
> I enjoyed playing this game very much. I am not a gamer and neither do I use smart phone or phone apps but I also learned from this gaming experience
>
> Male participant of *TESSA Undercover Agents* ResearchGame, aged 72

Thinking points

- Can you provide knowledge value? Perhaps offer information about the wider issues relating to the research content, interesting facts or wider industry knowledge?

- If you are not able to share research results, can you send a 'summary' of information, based on what participants shared with you?

- Can you let participants know if/when you will give them the results of the study after they have been analysed, and where they can find the information?

Is it better to offer just one game value or all four values?

There are so many ways a game-based survey designer can approach each of the values to encourage initial onboarding and drive engagement through to survey completion – it's just about experimenting during the design stage to find the perfect balance of what will spark the interest of your audience while immersing the participant in the research context.

And guess what? You can offer any and ALL of these types of value to participants to engage them just by using text on a screen! Remember, as the game-based survey designer, you can offer these values as part of simulations if you wish, or with just text on a screen, in quant or qual research and even using technologies like augmented reality and virtual reality.

ACTIVITY

- What platforms can you think of that provide one or more of the four game values? How do they offer those values, and how can this inspire your surveys?

- How do your existing surveys offer any of these values already? Or is your survey offering the value of extrinsic motivators like cash incentives? If so, what kind of value can you offer for a 'quick win' in increasing participant engagement?

Notes

1 Adamou, B and Newman, J (2014) Expert interview with author James Newman on understanding intrinsic engagement with videogames, Web interview, 19 November

2 Wenger, JL (2007) The implicit nature of goal-directed motivational pursuits, in *Psychology of Motivation*, ed LV Brown, p 143, Nova Science Publishers, New York

3 Deci, EL and Ryan, RM (1985) *Intrinsic Motivation and Self-Determination in Human Behavior*, Springer Science & Business Media

4 Skinner, BF (1938) *The Behavior of Organisms: An experimental analysis*, Appleton-Century, New York

5 Fleming, Nic (2014) [accessed 27 May 2018] Gamification: Is it game over? *BBC* [Online] http://www.bbc.com/future/story/20121204-can-gaming-transform-your-life

6 Bogost, Ian (2011) [accessed 27 May 2018] Gamification is bullshit, *The Atlantic* [Online] https://www.theatlantic.com/technology/archive/2011/08/gamification-is-bullshit/243338/

7 Jacobs, Melinda (2013) [accessed 27 May 2018] Gamification: Moving from 'addition' to 'creation', Proceedings of CHI'13, 27 April–2 May 2013 [Online] http://gamification-research.org/wp-content/uploads/2013/03/Jacobs.pdf

8 BBC, *Class Calculator* [Online] www.bbc.co.uk/news/magazine-22000973

9 Gray, Michelle and Adamou, Betty (2018) Game design: Engaging students to evolve university marketing [Conference presentation] Proceedings of the IIeX (Insight Innovation Exchange) conference, Amsterdam, 20 February 2018. Presentation synopsis [Online] https://iiex-eu.insightinnovation.org/agenda/session/218271

An ontology of game-based research methods

06

Defining research-games, gamified research and surveytainment

In this chapter, we:

- explore the existing definitions of research-games and gamification used in market research;
- create new definitions of game-based research methods, research-games, gamified research and surveytainment;
- understand how to know if we have created a research-game or gamified survey;
- learn when to use games or gamification in market research.

In previous chapters we have explored the definitions, components and elements of games and gamification, and their parallels/benefits for market research. Using this knowledge, we can now define the umbrella term 'game-based research methods' and the definitions this term encapsulates: 'research-games' and 'gamified research', and also discuss 'surveytainment'.

In defining these terms, do not be alarmed by the lengthy descriptions! As game designer Chris Crawford describes in his book *Chris Crawford on Game Design*,[1] his own dictionary used 6.5 column inches to define the word 'game', and 12 column inches to describe 'play'. In addition, there are (at the time of writing) more than 10 definitions of the word 'game', with each expert creating his or her own description to fit their understanding. And as games evolve with technology, so does the way we define them.

Over time, it is likely that these definitions will evolve as we discover sub-branches of research-games and gamified research, but should suffice for researchers to use today as a means to explore the meaning of different game-based approaches.

Definitions of game-based research methods in the market research industry so far

I coined the term 'game-based research methods' (GbRM) to encompass any market research methodology using games, gamification or game-like techniques, but what has the market research community thought of 'gamification' and 'game' as applied in market research so far?

There are no widely accepted definitions of gamification research (or gamified surveys) or research-games. There is also little to no expertly peer-reviewed literature in these fields (peers who are perhaps expert in game and gamification design processes), partly because the methodology is very young with no set of established best practices.[2] But crucially, the mislabelling of gamification in research, and what some practitioners are labelling as 'gamification', is incorrect.

A definition of 'gamification' (in the context of market research) appears in the book *Answers to Contemporary Market Research Questions*, in which gamification is described as 'the process of using elements of gaming to improve respondent engagement with the survey process. In some cases the gamification process can be as slight as improving a layout. In other cases gamification is used to turn a survey into a game.'[3] This definition is quite correct, the one caveat being that slightly improving a layout would fall under 'surveytainment' – a definition we will explore later.

It is easy to understand why market researchers would think that improving survey layout is what gamification is, because that's what we've been told in countless blog posts, articles, papers and conference talks. Market researchers during conference talks within the last five years have mentioned that gamification for research is all about using bright colours, using drag and drop functions, adding more images and changing the wording of questions. Market researchers have also used the terms 'gamification' and 'games' interchangeably.

Owing to the mislabelling, and somewhat confusing definitions, it is necessary to use the definitions of games and gamification that we have already explored in Chapter 5 to create new and more accurate working definitions, and create a useful taxonomy of game-based research.

Defining game-based research methods (GbRM)

GbRM is an umbrella term to describe any research approach that uses the four game ingredients with the addition of any mix of game components and/or game elements (such as narrative, role-play, audio etc) to increase participant engagement and data quality, whether the research is created as 'gamification' or a fully-fledged game. Game-based research covers the use of games and gamification in both online, non-digital (analog) and mixed-reality research methods. For researchers who wish to describe their approach more specifically, more exact terms can be used such as 'game-based online research' or 'game-based focus group'.

While 'surveytainment' is not a branch of GbRM, it is often confused as 'gamification' and as such, Figure 6.1 describes the differences and succession of more game-like research experiences.

Another way to define research-games and gamified surveys is to look through a lens of understanding their differences.

Figure 6.1   Game-based research methods (GbRM) describes any research methodology using the game ingredients (GARF), the game components (CABIN) and the game elements (ATARE). While 'surveytainment' is not a branch of GbRM, it requires clarification as it is often confused with gamification in the market research community

Research-Game	Gamified Survey	Surveytainment
A fully-fledged game created for research purposes.	A survey that has been gamified.	Many surveys of this type are labelled as gamified surveys but do not use all four game ingredients. Commonly, there is a focus on rewording the questions and/or adding graphics to an existing survey to make them more enjoyable for participants.

⬅   ⬅   ⬅

The more the survey is realized as a fully-fledged game the more intrinsic engagement and play can be evoked in the participant.

SOURCE © Betty Adamou

Figure 6.2   Research-games versus Gamified Surveys: Game-based research
methods (GbRM) describe any research methodology using the
game ingredients. This chart shows the key differences between
research-games and gamified surveys

Game-based Research Methods (GbRM)	
Research-Game	**Gamified Survey**
A fully-fledged game created for research purposes.	A survey that has been gamified.
The game ingredients, components and elements are designed as part of the research experience from the start.	The game ingredients, components and elements are added on to the survey and not designed as part of the experience from the start.
◄ Both methods aim to increase participant engagement. ►	
Creates intrinsic engagement & play.	Relies on extrinsic motivators; a 'do x, get y' approach.

SOURCE © Betty Adamou

Figure 6.2 shows that while research-games aim to elevate what research
can do in terms of offering experiential platforms, through intrinsic engagement and play (with the ability to observe behaviours in context), gamified
research is limited in terms of its potential to engage on an intrinsic level.

Research-games can harness the instinctive, the implicit and the subconscious. They are fluid. If there's anything I've learned from reading about
games, interviewing game practitioners and academics, and of course playing
games, it is that games are a hugely versatile medium, just as research-games
are, and should continue to be versatile, because gamified surveys and
research games can *blend.*

Think of them separately and structurally at first, and as your design
confidence grows, bend the rules, mix-and-match game components, and
experiment with design to suit your research needs.

Definition of research-game

A research-game is a game designed for research purposes where data is
collected from the actions participants take while playing the research-
game, and the *way* they play the game itself.

The use of the four game ingredients (goals, autonomy opportunities,
rules and feedback) constitutes a research-game, with the addition of any

mix of game components (such as bonus features and narratives) and game elements (such as avatars and audio) that the designer deems fit-for-purpose in order to intrinsically engage participants in the research and encourage play. However, the interaction of 'play' with a research-game is subjective; it can only be the participants who can describe if they feel they were playing instead of taking part.

A research-game can be executed as digital, analog or mixed reality where the designer can decide the approach that he or she deems suitable for the study. For instance, a designer can choose if 3D graphics, or low-fi 8-bit visuals, or an entirely text-based approach (like a CRPG – computer role-playing game) or a face-to-face approach is the most effective.

Research-games provide participants with an experience that aids their understanding of the research content and ability to respond/react honestly to in-game questions or scenarios. Research-games seamlessly integrate research material into a game world that can be created in a way that engages the participant in accordance with, and in relevance to, the research objectives. Research-games can include the use of virtual environments, audio, avatars, and other game components and game elements to compliment the game ingredients in such a way that the designer deems fit-for-purpose. Research-games should be developed with the mindset of 'designing with function' in which the designers can consider how they use narrative, linguistics, semiotics, rewards and so on to appropriately engage their participants and gather the necessary insights to satisfy the requirements of stakeholders.

From the outset, a research-game will be designed with the various aspects of the research study in mind, to engage the audience while encouraging truthful participant responses. The ages, culture, lifestyle and other aspects of the participant audience are considered for the research-game design, where the design is driven by the research objectives.

A taxonomy of research-games

For researchers who wish to describe their approach more specifically, they can use more exact terms such as 'digital research-game', 'augmented reality research-game', 'virtual reality research-game' and others. Indeed, we can develop a taxonomy of research-games to be even more specific.

The paper *The Future of Research Through Gaming*[4] (Adamou, 2011) outlined a taxonomy of ResearchGames. The taxonomy in this book is an evolution of that noted in the paper to account for more varied ways one can approach a research-game design. The different types of research-games can be blended to create entirely different genres; for example, an avatar-based, role-playing simulation research-game. Don't feel restricted by this taxonomy, but let it inspire you so you can see the different ways you can approach your own design, and mix/match these genres together to suit your research requirements. Below are some base-types of research-games to consider:

- **Avatar-based research-games** – research-games that encourage participants to create an avatar of themselves, and where data are collected through the choices and behaviours of the participants via their avatars and how the participants choose to build their avatars. The avatar doesn't necessarily have to embody a character or role, as the participants can play as themselves through their avatars.

- **Role-playing research-games** – research-games that harness role-play where the participants are in the mindset of a 'character', such as the CEO of a company or someone in charge of town planning, with or without the use of visual avatars.

- **Narrative-based research-games** – research-games that use a storyline that is relevant to the research content and appropriate to the type of participants required. A narrative-based research-game will also offer participants narratologically relevant rewards; that is, rewards that relate and harmonize with the selected narrative.

- **Text-based research-games** – research-games that use only text to convey the game ingredients and can include additional game components and game elements such as narrative and bonus features. Text-based research-games borrow from the principles of text-adventure games or CRPGs (computer role-playing games) where few to no images are used, and only text on a screen is used to convey the game and allow players to respond as required.

- **Simulation-based research-games** – research-games that use simulations to observe participant behaviours in context. Such simulations can be conceptual (for example, simulating how participants might build their ideal home if they won the lottery), to past-focused (that is, a simulation replicating a real-life experience that may have already happened so that researchers can understand past behaviours and choices based on observation and context), to future-focused (that is, creating a simulation for an experience that has not yet occurred for the participant).

- **Questions as mini-games** – any type of online survey, even one that is not game-based, can create questions as mini-games (Figure 6.3). Imagine there was a long piece of text that you needed participants to read. Imagine also, that this piece of text is fairly boring, like an end-user agreement or a piece of insurance documentation. Now imagine you have added in a couple of fake clauses in there such as 'and on the first Friday of every month, you will be sent a free chocolate donut' or something equally daft. Challenge the participants to spot what they think is the lie. Not only will this keep them reading attentively, but it will also be useful in letting the research buyer know what else might be deemed to be far-fetched, even if it was not a lie. This is just one example of many of how a single question can be stylalized as a mini-game in itself.

Figure 6.3 An example of a question as a mini-game within a ResearchGame environment. Here, participants are tasked to name the celebrity behind the tiles – if they name the celebrity correctly, they can move on to the next secret celebrity image. If the participants guess incorrectly, they lose a 'life' (one of the hearts) but this still provides useful data on the other celebrities who may be top-of-mind

SOURCE © Research Through Gaming Ltd

Researchers can, and are encouraged to, select and blend the types of research-games listed here. Truly in this case, game-based research designers are only limited by their imaginations, and the requirements of the study.

Definition of gamified research

Gamified research is where gamification is applied to any research method or approach and, as such, 'gamifying' it. Where research-games encourage intrinsic engagement and play, gamified research relies on the extrinsic motivators inherent in gamification (such as points, badges and collecting items) and, as such, it is argued that while participant engagement can be increased, gamified research is unlikely to encourage intrinsic engagement.

Gamified research can still use the four game ingredients, with any mix of the game components and game elements in addition; however, the execution of the design is what will or will not transform the study into a research-game or gamified research. It can be argued that if participants felt they were playing a game, then the platform can be described as a 'research-game'.

Often the gamification is 'applied to' research as opposed to being created as a gamified research experience from the outset. The taxonomy below lists some examples.

A taxonomy of gamified research

- Gamified focus groups
- Gamified online surveys
- Gamified hall tests
- Gamified depth-interviews
- Gamified market research online communities (MROCs)
- Gamified door-to-door surveys

Definition of surveytainment

Surveytainment is a portmanteau of the words 'survey' and 'entertainment' to describe any survey (or any research approach) that has been designed as a more engaging and/or entertaining experience for participants. While I've known of this term for a good many years, I'm afraid I don't know who first coined it.

Modes of surveytainment include but are not limited to the use of more dynamic answer options (such as drag and drop features), more graphical content used (if online) and where the wording of questions has been altered by the designer to seem more challenging and/or fun. Easily confused with gamified research, surveytainment does not include the use of the four game ingredients working harmoniously together, but may include fewer than four (such as the inclusion of a goal) to try to make the research more enjoyable. The application of surveytainment has historically been confused with gamified research, but has yielded positive, negative and mixed results in terms of participant engagement and feedback.

How do I know if I've created a research-game, gamified my research or created surveytainment?

Three things will help you to understand the content you have produced:

- your own understanding and intuition;
- the participant feedback;
- the data.

Your own understanding and intuition

We all know what it feels like to play a game, or take part in a gamified activity. We also know what it's like to play a game that feels more like click-bait (where a game includes a variety of paywalls, and the game encourages players to buy rewards like gems and coins and so on) and we also know what it feels like to participate in a playful experience. As mentioned previously, the game-based design approach can be fluid – there is no right or wrong, as it is all about the effectiveness of your design. However, trying to understand and categorize our work as researchers, in any methodology, is important. Your instinct will help to inform you of what you have designed.

The participant feedback

Did participants report they felt they were playing a game? Did they use words like 'play', 'experience', 'game', or did they use other terms that can help you determine how participants perceived the platform? The feedback will either contradict or confirm your initial intuition. Participant feedback is always encouraged through constructed questions and open verbatim responses.

The data

As we explored in Chapter 5, the approach and design you choose will have an impact on participant interactions, behaviour and engagement and that will impact data. To determine whether or not participants were intrinsically engaged versus extrinsically engaged, researchers can ask themselves things like:

- Did participants do more than was expected of them?
- Did they give richer detail in open verbatim responses than in other traditional surveys of a similar length or subject?
- Did the study finish earlier because participants were more engaged, and thus response and completion rates increased?
- How often, or little, did participants straightline?
- How often, or little, did participants button-mash (write gobbledegook in the open-responses)?

These factors will help determine the levels of engagement and play that participants may or may not have experienced.

When to use research-games, gamified surveys and surveytainment

The needs of the study and where you are in the process of the study will determine which methodology to use.

The needs of the study

Do you require participants to be ultra-creative, come up with innovative ideas, be engaged for a long time in the study, and answer lots of open-ended questions? Do you need to replicate the emotions and contexts found in the real world to understand how emotion and context drive behaviour and choice? If so, then intrinsically engaging participants and encouraging play using a game will help boost problem-solving and creativity. It will also increase the chance of participants experiencing flow, which can help if a researcher requires participation for some time or at high frequencies throughout a longer process. By using the capabilities inherent in games, you can also create relevant emotional 'states' and contexts – using elements and components like music, virtual environments and timers.

However, if the research requirements are to simply elevate participant engagement, and there isn't a need to conduct a full review of the design, then a gamification or even a surveytainment approach may be the most effective.

Where you are in the process of the study

If you are at the very early stages of a research study, and have some time, you can begin to think about how to apply your research as a fully-fledged game. However, if the survey or online community has already been created, then at this point it is worth considering what game ingredients and/or game values you can apply to amplify engagement and data quality. The design processes are further explored in Part Two: World of Design.

Notes

1 Crawford, C (2003) *Chris Crawford on Game Design*, New Riders Publishing, Indiana

2 Wiszniowski, David (2014) [accessed 27 May 2018] Gamification in market research: Interest, curiosity and misconception, MRIA *VUE* magazine, July/August 2014, pp 14–16 [Online] https://issuu.com/mria-arim/docs/vue-julaug-2014

3 ESOMAR (2014) *10 Answers to Contemporary Research Questions*, 3rd edn, p 167

4 Adamou, B (2011) [accessed 27 May 2018] The future of research through gaming, Proceedings of the CASRO conference, Las Vegas, 3–4 March [Online] www.academia.edu/9487174/The_Future_of_Research_Through_Gaming

The scientific foundation for using game-based research methods

07

The six vital states and their benefit to market research

> Games can inspire the loftiest form of cerebral cognition and engage the most primal psychical response, often simultaneously.
>
> Frank Lantz, Rules of Play (2004)

This chapter explores:

- the six vital states of game-based research:
  - inspiration;
  - motivation;
  - intrinsic engagement;
  - play;
  - flow;
  - enjoyment;
- that these states, induced in game players, have parallels with and are beneficial for market research;
- behavioural economics and personalization as sciences inherent in games, and their parallels and benefits for market research.

It is impossible to talk about games, or game-based research, without exploring the plethora of disciplines, frameworks, systems and sciences inherent in games. Indeed, over time ludologists have attempted to identify and define all the elements inherent in games, and it is a difficult job, given that games are so wide-ranging with new designs pushing the boundaries of what games are and what they can do.

One thing is clear though: that the frameworks, features, disciplines and sciences that exist separately *from* games, also work together *in* games and what's more, work harmoniously to create the kind of intrinsically engaging, emotive and experiential videogames we see today. From Self-Determination Theory to positive psychology, flow, immersion, linguistics, fun, semiotics, emotion, psychophysiology, user experience (UX), happiness, gestalt principles, inspiration, paideia, cognitive neuroscience and play – games harness *all* of these principles and many more. Simply search online: "*(insert word)*_____ in games" (insert any term from neuroscience to flow to gestalt principles and so on) and you will see volumes of papers, books and articles on each of these areas in games. And there are further publications on the effects of specific game features: the impact of avatars in games, narratology, virtual environments, personalization, sound and more.

Why is this relevant to a market researcher? Because all of those disciplines matter in market research and indeed many market research methodologies already harness some of these principles. However, games harness them more effectively with better intrinsic user engagement and better user relationships than market researchers do (as illustrated in Chapter 8). The way games use these principles can help researchers amplify their data quality and participant engagement.

Six of these disciplines, sciences and frameworks make up what I call the 'six vital states' – emotional states that should be induced in research participants to get the kinds of intrinsic engagement, creativity and collaboration we see in game players in order to increase response rates, completion rates and engagement, which will lead to improved data quality and increase the likelihood of participants returning to participate in more research in the future.

Introducing the six vital states for increasing response rates, completion rates and data quality

We have explored the benefits of implementing the four game ingredients, game components, game elements and game values in market research. Their implementation evokes the 'six vital states'; a flow of emotion that I have

Figure 7.1 This diagram shows the contribution and benefits of the six vital states in online GbRM

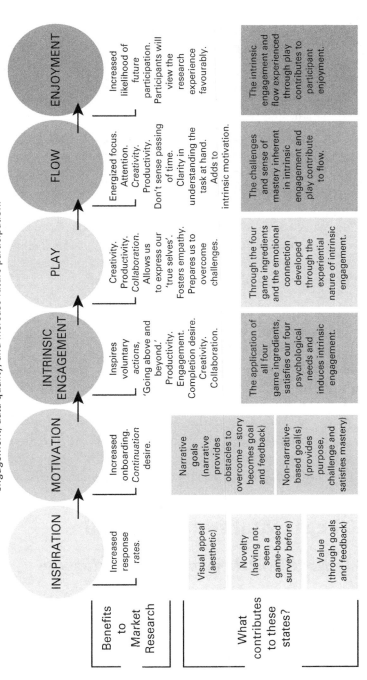

SIX VITAL STATES FOR PARTICIPANTS IN GAME-BASED RESEARCH

Desirable behaviours to increase response rates, completion rates, engagement, data quality, and increase future participation.

INSPIRATION	MOTIVATION	INTRINSIC ENGAGEMENT	PLAY	FLOW	ENJOYMENT

Benefits to Market Research

Increased response rates.

Increased onboarding. *Continuation desire.*

Inspires voluntary *actions,* 'Going above and beyond.' Productivity. Engagement. Completion desire. Creativity. Collaboration.

Creativity. Productivity. *Collaboration.* Allows us to express our 'true selves'. Fosters empathy. Prepares us to overcome challenges.

Energized focus. Attention. *Creativity.* Productivity. Don't sense passing of time. Clarity in understanding the task at hand. Adds to intrinsic motivation.

Increased likelihood of future participation. Participants will view the research experience favourably.

What contributes to these states?

Visual appeal (aesthetic)

Novelty (having not seen a game-based survey before)

Value (through goals and feedback)

Narrative goals (narrative provides obstacles to overcome – story becomes goal and feedback)

Non-narrative-based goal(s) (provides purpose, challenge and satisfies mastery)

The application of all four game ingredients, satisfies our four psychological needs and induces intrinsic engagement.

Through the four game ingredients and the emotional connection developed through the experiential nature of intrinsic engagement.

The challenges and sense of mastery inherent in intrinsic engagement and play contribute to flow.

The intrinsic engagement and flow experienced through play contributes to participant enjoyment.

Source: © Betty Adamou

identified to be the flow of emotion in game players. These are: **inspiration, motivation, intrinsic engagement, play, flow** and **enjoyment**.

We need participants to be **inspired** to take part in market research. Inspiration inspires action and will help to increase response rates. That inspiration needs to quickly turn into **motivation** to make participants go from being inspired to participate (clicking on the link to the survey) to actually begin participating (begin answering the first few questions). That motivation must develop into **intrinsic engagement** and **play** so that researchers can gain the benefits of these elements, such as increased creativity and collaboration and to complete the survey to the end. During the process of being intrinsically engaged and involved in play, participants should experience **flow**, so participants feel immersed in the research experience, and don't feel the passing of time to be a taxing experience (as is often the case with traditional online surveys). Finally, participants must experience **enjoyment** so they want to come back and take part in more research in the future, to the commercial benefit of everyone involved.

Figure 7.1 shows an overview of the six vital states, how they are induced and their benefits to market research.

This process should not be undervalued for its commercial benefit in the relationships between research buyers and suppliers. If participants are engaged, focused, attentive, with increased completion rates meaning less time in field, then research buyers will gain the quality data they desire with the speeds they need. This increases the chances of research buyers doing business with the research suppliers who have the engaged, attentive, motivated, focused, collaborative and creative participants who are happy to go over and above their call of duty because they enjoy these new valuable research experiences.

The six vital states in detail

1 INSPIRATION = a desire to participate

Many organisms engage in exploratory, playful and curiosity-driven behaviours, even in the absence of reinforcement or reward[1] because they are inspired to do so.

What causes inspiration?

Inspiration needs periods of gestation 'spending time in your own head' through neuroplasticity, which can lead to better problem-solving and creative ideas.

Inspiration is synonymous with change. It is an active, positive disruption to the norm; a shift in one's mental state. Being inspired is often said to be a 'eureka' moment, or that 'something has clicked'. Being inspired is a joy in itself, often with the urgent need to create or contribute – to materialize an idea or share thoughts with others. Inspiration changes behaviour.

Inspiration is powerful, and as such, should not be underestimated as the first of the vital states in how participants experience research-games or gamified research. The initial inspiration is the hook; it is how researchers can ensure response rates are higher because, either through novelty, through an intriguing aesthetic or the values and goals articulated at the very start, the desire to participate is ignited.

As such, inspiration is the first step in the building block to creating participant engagement. And how can researchers provide inspiration? By giving them a motive through the four game values and game ingredients. The process of inspiration is STIMULUS -> CHOICE -> RESPONSE. The participant must be stimulated (inspired), then make a choice for action, then take action (response).

That's why in the *very first* interaction with the participant, such as the email invitation to the survey and/or the first screen of your game-based survey, a researcher must illustrate how the participants' four psychological needs will be met by articulating:

- clear **goal(s)** (to satisfy desires for **purpose** and **mastery**);
- what the **feedback** and **values** will be (such as **self-discovery value** and **transcendent value** to satisfy our needs for **mastery, purpose** and **relatedness**);
- the **collaborative** opportunity there will be to help in a situation (to satisfy our needs for **relatedness**);
- what the participant should or shouldn't do (to make sure the **rules** are clear from the start, introduce the sense of **challenge** and articulate the **autonomy opportunities**).

Once the participant chooses to respond, their initial inspiration must quickly turn into motivation.

2 MOTIVATION = better onboarding

It's not enough to inspire participants to click the link to your survey. Even if they are inspired to open your online survey, you need to keep their attention in the first few seconds to ensure they are properly onboarded and likely to continue taking part. This means the initial inspiration must quickly transcend to motivation. As researchers Richard Ryan and Edward Deci note: 'To be motivated means to be moved to do something. A person who feels no impetus or inspiration to act is thus characterized as unmotivated, whereas someone who is energized or activated toward an end is considered motivated.'[2]

What creates motivation?

Motivation is created by goal-setting, gaining feedback, having a sense of challenge that we can adequately overcome, with varying degrees of autonomy. As we've already explored, these components are the mechanisms of what makes a game a game: our four game ingredients.

Motivation comes in two types: extrinsic and intrinsic. Intrinsic motivation arises from a person's will to carry out a task simply 'because it is inherently interesting or enjoyable' whereas extrinsic motivation 'refers to doing something because it leads to a separable outcome'.[3]

In games, intrinsic motivations are described as the 'psychological needs that drive behaviour without extrinsic motivation, such as a game score'.[4] It is not enough for game-based surveys to inspire participants to click or begin, but they must also be motivated to *continue*. That motivation must therefore become intrinsic engagement to go from the initial onboarding to completion, and continue the research experience with focus, care, creativity and attention.

3 INTRINSIC ENGAGEMENT = a desire to complete, create and collaborate

What creates intrinsic engagement?

As we explored in Chapter 4, the satisfaction of our four psychological needs generates intrinsic engagement. While the four game ingredients can help generate motivation, perpetuating participation can only be achieved through the *constant* and *consistent* use of the game ingredients – that is, *further* goal setting, *further* challenges, feedback and autonomy. This is why games include levels and incremental goals, because it's this that feeds into player motivations to continue playing a game. As participants continue, their motivation will evolve to intrinsic engagement if the platform is well-designed and perpetually satisfies the four psychological needs.

Why is intrinsic engagement beneficial for market research?

Intrinsic engagement inspires:

- voluntary actions (going over and above the call of duty);
- a desire for continuation and completion;
- focus and attention;
- creativity;
- collaboration.

These are desirable behaviours and outcomes to induce in research participants and benefit market research. Researchers require participants to be focused and attentive to read instructions and answer questions appropriately. Researchers want to harness their creativity and collaboration for ideation, co-creation and other innovation-led tasks. Participants enjoy the opportunity to be creative, as some participants have shown:

> I thought this survey was extremely creative, loved making my own workout pants. Thank you.
>> Participant feedback quote from the 'Designer for a Day' ResearchGame
>> by Research Through Gaming Ltd

Researchers want participants to continue and complete surveys. This has been proven not just by continuation rates that have been measured with Research Through Gaming studies using ResearchGames, but in the responses we've had from participants. Here are a few feedback statements of the hundreds we receive:

> Super fun survey! Extremely unique, never have taken one like this. Enjoyed customizing my ideal pants. Would love to take again.
>
> I thought it was fun! and different! it made doing a survey a lot more enjoyable and I would like it if more surveys like this one, followed their model!
>
> Loved it!!! If I can be part of this again ... Sign me up!!!
>
> Amazing way of conducting a survey. Very interesting and fun to do. I wish all the survey's are like this. Feels like I am playing a game. Hats off to whoever has come up with this unique idea.
>
> This was pretty cool and interesting also very exciting and I would love to fill out another survey like this one. Also just imagine if all surveys were

> like this or even most of them? I'd be doing surveys a lot more often than I do them now.
>
> It was so much fun I wish I could do it again! Thank you.
>
> I loved it! I would definitely do this again if given the chance!

Researchers would also like participants to go 'over and above', as evidenced by participants taking part in ResearchGames without incentive and participants doing extra activities (even though the incentive didn't increase if more work was done). We also see a desire for participants to 'do more' in feedback:

> It was super fun! I Really Enjoyed making the leggings, i just wish there was more to choose from! :) I had a lot of fun, thanks!

The enthusiasm shows enjoyment, which occurs through intrinsic engagement. It's only when we're intrinsically engaged that a sense of play can be induced, and play also has useful outcomes, as we explore next.

4 PLAY = creativity, collaboration and allowing participants to express their true selves

> An hour of play reveals more than a year of conversation.
>
> Anonymous

Play is a hot commercial commodity. Play consultants work globally to induce playful work and education environments to boost problem-solving, creativity and engagement (among other benefits) which have commercial value in increasing profit, saving money, increasing sustainability and beating the competition. Play, a seemingly purposeless pastime, has become lucrative and highly regarded for what it can, and has, achieved. As Dr David Whitebread writes in *The Importance of Play*: 'Play in all its rich variety is one of the highest achievements of the human species, alongside language, culture and technology. Indeed, without play, none of these other achievements would be possible.'[5]

What factors induce play?

Play is mostly internally generated and spontaneous, but constructs like activities and games can be created to encourage play and playful behaviours.

Therefore, if researchers want to get the benefits of play with participants, then they're going to have to make a game or create more playful research experiences by gami*fying* surveys.

Stuart Brown, author and founder of the National Institute of Play, shares the work of historian Scott Eberle in his book *Play: How it shapes the brain, opens the imagination and invigorates the soul* (2010)[6] to tell us how play is supported. The six-step process of play is aligned with the game ingredients, game components, game elements and the four game values (explored in Chapter 4).

Play involves anticipation, surprise, pleasure, understanding, strength and poise. It's easy to see the parallels between these six steps and the features of games. **Bonus features** in games and **novelty** contribute to **anticipation** and **surprise**. The **experiential nature of games** can lead to **discovery** and **surprise**. Acquiring new knowledge, inherent in understanding, is born from the four game values of **self-discovery, transcendent value, narrative value** and **knowledge value**. **Strength** is born from **mastery**, one of our four psychological needs that is satisfied through the **game ingredients**. The contentment that comes with **poise** is satisfied through the **enjoyment** of **playing games**.

Benefits of play in market research

Play induces many desirable outcomes for market research. Stuart Brown notes that play:

- energizes us;
- enlivens us;
- eases our burdens;
- opens us up to new possibilities;
- increases creativity, productivity and innovation;
- is the truest expression of our individuality;
- allows us to find and express our own core truths;
- fosters empathy;
- induces a continuation desire;
- harnesses the imagination and allows us to explore a different self and our selves in future scenarios;
- prepares us for, and to overcome, challenges;
- 'one of the hallmarks of play is that *anyone* can do it';
- lets us try out things (new concepts, role-play) without threat to our physical or emotional wellbeing.

In an edition focused on play from *New Philosopher* magazine, the editor notes that 'play *reveals us* – to ourselves and to others'.[7] And don't we want participants to reveal themselves, to their true opinions and beliefs? Researchers need to encourage these feelings. We also want participants, who feel that surveys are cumbersome, to have that burden eased. We want participants to be open to new possibilities when we are testing new ideas and products. We want them to be creative, productive and innovative during the research process, and we want them to be able to express themselves in their true nature.

As play also includes the ability for pretence, play can aid immersion in role-play, which is important for times when researchers want participants to answer questions like 'what would you do if...?' while being able to empathize with the context in which the role-play exists, and in a fashion that feels safe and non-threatening to participants. Play also harnesses the imagination. Research buyers are very interested in how consumers will or won't engage in brands, products, services and environmental facilities in the future, and often task participants to imagine future scenarios. A sense of play can harness the consumers' imaginations so they can articulate imagined experiences. As Stuart Brown notes: 'in play we can imagine and experience situations we have never encountered before and learn from them.[8]

If we present participants with challenges – with a problem to solve, a sense of play can help the participants feel that they can overcome it. And because we know that all humans, no matter their age, benefit from play, then that's useful because researchers need to speak to, and benefit from, the desirable behaviours of play with *every* participant.

Play also 'provides freedom from time. When we're fully engaged in play, we lose a sense of the passage of time'.[9] This is beneficial if we want participants to be engaged in research that takes a long time to complete, or has multiple touchpoints through several days, or weeks. A sense of time passing is one of the properties of flow – thus play induces flow.

While play is undoubtedly useful in market research, **play is also a data generator,** where information can be collected by observing *how* people play games. Therefore, play is useful in two ways for market researchers: 1) play induces desirable behaviours in participants that benefit researchers; 2) play is a data generator, therefore *how* participants play a game-based survey can lead to insight.

Participants, of all ages, have shown their engagement and creativity through playing RTG ResearchGames:

> That was the best survey I've ever done. Really imaginative and engaging.
>
> I thought this survey was extremely creative, loved making my own workout pants. Thank you.

> This was the best research I've participated in, it was very entertaining and creatively fun!
>
> This was fun and original. Instead of asking endless questions, you make a game out of it and make it lots more fun and we can show you what we want or don't want much easier this way.

5 FLOW = full immersion and not noticing the passing of time

Flow is created through being engrossed in an intrinsically engaging activity. To be in flow is to be in the zone, where distractions are ignored and the task at hand has our full focus. With so many distractions competing with researchers for participant attention, it's therefore wise to induce a flow state. But researchers cannot gain the benefits of inducing flow without inducing intrinsic engagement and play.

Mihaly Csikszentmihalyi, author of *Finding Flow*,[10] describes accurately how it feels to be 'in flow' in his TED talk *Flow, the secret to happiness* (2004).[11] In his talks he lists seven feelings involved when experiencing flow. These feelings are what researchers should want their participants to feel:

1 Completely involved in what we are doing – focused, concentrated.

2 A sense of ecstasy – of being outside of everyday reality.

3 Great inner clarity – knowing what needs to be done and how well we are doing.

4 Knowing that the activity is doable – that our skills are adequate to the task.

5 A sense of serenity – no worries about oneself and a feeling of growing beyond the boundaries of the ego.

6 Timelessness – thoroughly focused on the present, hours seem to pass by in minutes.

7 Intrinsic motivation – whatever produces flow becomes its own reward.

These feelings are aligned with games. While traditional surveys are unlikely to induce flow, games are well known for doing so. Indeed, the digital games *Flow*[12] and *Journey*[13] were born from the study of flow in games. Designer Jenova Chen (founder of *That Game Company*[14]) developed these games from his study of Mihaly Csikszentmihalyi's flow theory and used his academic findings and research (which can be found in Chen's PhD thesis)[15] to develop these award-winning games.

It is common for Research Through Gaming participants to comment on the passing of time after playing a ResearchGame. As one participant put it: 'That was such a great way to complete a survey. I thoroughly enjoyed it and the time went so quickly. Totally engaging.' If some surveys are long and/or with multiple touchpoints, then the passing of time while enjoying and engaged in the experience is beneficial to both the researcher *and* the participant.

So where are the parallels between games and the feelings that Csikszentmihalyi describes? The four game ingredients: goals, autonomy opportunities, feedback and rules, directly contribute to these feelings. Through **feedback** we understand **how well we're doing** which taps into our needs for **mastery**. Through being intrinsically engaged we are focused and so **understand what needs to be done**. Through our **four psychological needs** being satisfied we are **completely involved** and experience intrinsic engagement. The features inherent in games, like **virtual environments, avatars** and **role-play** allow us to be outside of our **everyday reality. Knowing that the activity is doable** is helped through the incremental **goals** inherent in the **game ingredients.**

Games, as we have already explored, **intrinsically motivate** us by satisfying our psychological needs, and therefore the experience becomes **the reward in itself,** which is enjoyable. As we explore next, participant enjoyment is also commercially valuable in market research.

6 ENJOYMENT = increased participant loyalty; participants will come back for more research in the future

Intrinsic engagement, play and flow can create enjoyable research experiences. A participant who enjoyed the research experience is a happy participant. Happy participants will tell their friends about your survey company, and come back to do more research with you in the future – just as people do with anything else. A happy customer who has enjoyed a dining experience will likely recommend it to a friend and return in the future. Therefore, participant happiness is not something to be undervalued; without happy participants, market research will continue to face the challenges it does today.

When we play games, and are intrinsically engaged and enjoying something, our brain releases dopamine. This is another important chemical in happiness and is 'triggered' when the 'reward/achievement' part of our brain lights up. This happens when we play games. It is therefore not much of a coincidence that dopamine is one of four what are known as 'happiness chemicals'[16,17] where dopamine's impact on the body is felt in various areas, including but not limited to improved motivation, memory, attention, and learning.[18] Again, this has parallels and benefits for market research as we want participants to give the survey their attention, we want them to be motivated to take part, to quickly learn what the study is about and what is expected of them and to have improved memory when recalling experiences.

Therefore, enjoyment, and how it can spur these benefits as well as providing an increased chance that participants will return for more in the future and even make recommendations about a good survey company to their friends, is commercially beneficial for all involved.

Non-vital but useful other sciences, disciplines and frameworks inherent in games that are beneficial for market research

Throughout inducing the six vital states, researchers can use other sciences, disciplines and frameworks for further benefit, from harnessing gestalt principles to semiotics and more. This section focuses on behavioural economics and personalization. These disciplines are already used in traditional market research surveys, but have strong parallels with games and could be used in game-based research to amplify their positive outcomes.

Behavioural economics

Behavioural economics (or BE) is harnessed in some form or another in almost all games. On the *Pottermore* website, the online portal for all things Harry Potter-related, players can play *Discover your Patronus* (a Patronus is an animal-shaped form of magic that can protect the witch or wizard, or those around them, after producing the Patronus Charm). The Patronus is said to reflect the witch or wizard's personality. Immediately, the user understands the self-discovery value of the experience.

To find out what your Patronus animal is, the website puts you through a time-limited questionnaire, with ambient and atmospheric audio and visuals, which encourages System 1 thinking to try to gauge the players' top-of-mind responses. The time limit also adds to the engagement and urgency of what is, essentially, a questionnaire. Players can select choices based on pretty conceptual questions, or without questions at all. In one example, a player may simply see the words 'Leaf', 'Blade' and 'Thorn' on the screen. The participant is encouraged to gravitate to one answer before thinking too much. In fact, if a player has not made a selection quickly enough, the process begins again. Like *Pottermore*, countless videogames encourage 'System 1' thinking. Music and time (or lack thereof) both contribute to the ways in which the participant is encouraged to use more System 1 thinking to discourage deliberation.

In the *Pottermore* example, we can see that by encouraging System 1 thinking, *Pottermore* is trying to get to the 'true you' to uncover your Patronus. Market research uses BE for the same reason. BE has been one of the main research methodologies in the limelight since I became a market researcher; its application in other industries and the evidence in which its use helps to determine anything, from how we price products to how participants answer questions, has been key to how research buyers rethink their marketing, product design and more.

But BE in market research, harnessed in a game, can be even more powerful. Through the use of BE in game-based surveys, we can create context-based simulations, use timers and other nudges to see what participants would do in various situations. The passive data collected can allow us to understand subconscious preferences and biases, which is what the implementation of BE in research sets out to understand.

Personalization

What is personalization? Personalization helps increase engagement and revenue. In its most basic and non-digital form, personalization can be the simplicity of going into your favourite restaurant and the waiting staff remembering your name and what you ordered before, while giving you recommendations about other food and drink you might enjoy, based on what they know about your likes and dislikes. By knowing your likes and making recommendations, the staff ensure that the customer is likely to have another satisfying dining experience and will come back again in the future. Thus, they become engaged with the restaurant, the staff, and more revenue is generated from their next visit.

Personalization is used in games but also in many other forms of media. Anything from Santa Claus video messages to books and websites can be personalized in simple ways, such as using the participant's name, to more advanced forms of personalization such as a digital program understanding your age, lifestyle, budget and brand preferences by giving you suggestions on what to buy, much like many websites do, and Amazon does.

How is personalization used in games? Some games are not personalized at all, while others are personalized to the nth degree. Players can make avatars, while their real names or pseudonyms are used frequently to create/perpetuate engagement.

How can personalization be used in game-based research to amplify participant engagement and data quality?

Personalized experiences are engaging, and personalization happens in varying degrees. From things like our names being used in email marketing through to children's books using the readers' names and even their friends' names as part of the story. In RTG ResearchGames, personalization has been used in many ways, from personalizing rewards (such as downloadable certificates) and including the names of people the participant knows (or can give pseudonyms to) so they feel connected to NPCs – non-participant characters, to make them feel like they are talking to someone they know (Figures 7.2 and 7.3).

Figure 7.2 A screengrab from the *Dubious* ResearchGame produced by Research Through Gaming on behalf of the IMPRINTS Futures academic study. In the story, the participant must convince three people that they are really from the future by answering questions about what the year 2030 is like. The participant puts in the names of a best friend, doctor and teacher or colleague. The names of these people pop up again throughout the game, such as 'Will asks if ...' or 'Sarah asks what ...' and so on

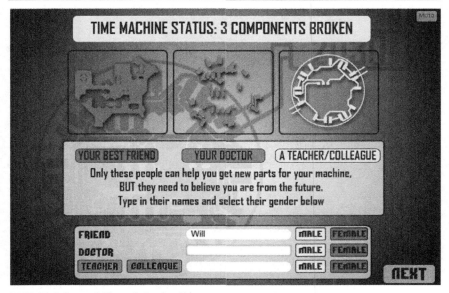

SOURCE © Research Through Gaming Ltd

Figure 7.3 As the ultimate reward, the participant levels up to Super Designer status to mark the completion of the study, and the extra reward is a personalized certificate. Once participants input their name, they can download the certificate.

SOURCE © Research Through Gaming Ltd

Notes

1 White, R (1959) Motivation reconsidered: The concept of competence, *Psychological Review*, **66**, pp 297–333, 10.1037/h0040934

2 Ryan, RM and Deci, EL (2000) Intrinsic and extrinsic motivations: Classic definitions and new directions, *Contemporary Educational Psychology*, **25** (1), pp 54–67

3 Ryan, RM and Deci, EL (2000) Intrinsic and extrinsic motivations: Classic definitions and new directions, *Contemporary Educational Psychology*, **25** (1), pp 54–67

4 Roohi, Shaghayegh, Takatalo, Jari, Guckelsberger, Christian and Hamalainen, Pertty (2018) [accessed 25 May 2018] Review of Intrinsic Motivation in Simulation-based Game Testing, Proceedings of the CHI [Online] https://tinyurl.com/yd6gm3x7

5 Whitebread, Dr David (2012) [accessed 25 May 2018] The importance of play [Online] www.importanceofplay.eu/IMG/pdf/dr_david_whitebread_-_the_importance_of_play.pdf

6 Brown, S and Vaughan, C (Collaborator) (2010) *Play: How it shapes the brain, opens the imagination, and invigorates the soul*, Avery/Penguin Group, New York

7 Baag, Zan (2018) Play, Editor's note from *New Philosopher* magazine, 20 (May–July)

8 Brown, S and Vaughan, C (Collaborator) (2010) *Play: How it shapes the brain, opens the imagination, and invigorates the soul*, p 34, Avery/Penguin Group, New York

9 Brown, S and Vaughan, C (Collaborator) (2010) *Play: How it shapes the brain, opens the imagination, and invigorates the soul*, p 17, Avery/Penguin Group, New York

10 Csikszentmihalyi, M (1997) *Finding Flow: The psychology of engagement with everyday life*, Basic Books, New York

11 Csikszentmihalyi, Mihaly (2004) [accessed 25 May 2018] *Flow, the secret to happiness* [Video] Proceedings of TED2004, Monterey, California [Online] www.ted.com/talks/mihaly_csikszentmihalyi_on_flow/transcript

12 *Flow* game: http://thatgamecompany.com/flow/

13 *Journey* game: http://thatgamecompany.com/journey/

14 That Game Company website: http://thatgamecompany.com/

15 *Flow in Games*: a Jenova Chen Thesis [Online] https://www.jenovachen.com/flowingames/Flow_in_games_final.pdf

16 Nguyen, Thai (2014) [accessed 25 May 2018] Hacking into your happy chemicals: Dopamine, serotonin, endorphins and oxytocin, *Huffington Post* [Blog] [Online] www.huffingtonpost.com/thai-nguyen/hacking-into-your-happy-c_b_6007660.html

17 Breuning, Loretta (2014) [accessed 25 May 2018] Meet your happy chemicals, *Slideshare* [Presentation] [Online] www.slideshare.net/LorettaBreuning/happy-chemicals-33377349

18 Lee, Kevan (2017) [accessed 25 May 2018] Your brain on dopamine: The science of motivation [Blog] [Online] http://blog.idonethis.com/the-science-of-motivation-your-brain-on-dopamine/

Game culture   08

A showcase of intrinsic engagement to help market researchers

This chapter explores:

- the 12 signs of intrinsic engagement among game players;
- desirable participant behaviours; how intrinsic engagement, like the type we see between player and game, can be useful in market research;
- case study examples: how game-based research has already harnessed intrinsic engagement to nudge desirable participant behaviours.

I have spent years researching and understanding 'engagement'; what do people do when they are intrinsically engaged? Why is intrinsic engagement useful? And what displays of intrinsic engagement do players show with games, and how would harnessing such behaviours be useful for market research?

A series of interviews with expert game designers, game professors and other professionals in and outside of the games industry formed part of this research, and the insight was eye-opening. The breadth of how intrinsic engagement is displayed among game-players is wide. A thematic analysis of those interviews helped to create the 12 signs of intrinsic engagement among game players noted in this chapter.

One of the expert interviews was with Rommel Romero,[1] the then community manager for independent games studio Minority Media, shortly after the release of their debut videogame *Papo and Yo* (released in 2012). I wanted to understand if intrinsic engagement among gamers evolved over time as a player continued to play the same game time and again, or could intrinsic engagement occur with a new game, and from a new games studio that gamers previously did not have a relationship with? This information would help me understand if it was feasible for game-based surveys to generate intrinsic engagement in participants, whether it was their first time playing or not, and whether or not the participants had an established relationship with a research supplier.

The answer was a resounding 'yes'. In my interview with Romero, it was clear players were already displaying the kinds of intrinsic engagement normally associated with more established games and game studios. Players had sent in drawings of new characters and ideas for new stories that they thought would complement the *Papo and Yo* game. Players even offered to work for their company and fix bugs in the game, for free. Some players have even got tattoos of game characters.

In another interview[2] with James Newman, author of *Playing with Videogames*,[3] he confirmed that these displays of intrinsic engagement are commonplace, no matter how new or established a game or game company might be 'providing that the format (of the game) is compelling'.

These experts assured me that intrinsic engagement can be generated even if it's the first time a person plays a game. As such, I was encouraged that game-based surveys, especially fully-fledged research-games, could be intrinsically engaging, even if participants had never taken part in this style of research before.

Displays of intrinsic engagement exist in other areas outside of games. Kevin Kruse,[4] employee engagement expert, says that intrinsic engagement in the workplace can lead to a plethora of benefits:

> the engaged computer programmer works overtime when needed, without being asked... the engaged retail clerk picks up the trash..., even if the boss isn't watching.

Across various organizations and industries, such intrinsic employee engagement has led to increased profits, productivity, and even product and service innovations,[5] showing that intrinsic engagement has tangible and quantifiable value.

In another example, Philip Schlechty, student engagement expert, shows that intrinsic engagement benefits students too. They are reported to 'persist despite challenges and obstacles, and take visible delight in accomplishing their work'.[6]

This evidence on the effects of intrinsic engagement may seem obvious; we all know what it feels like to be 'in the zone' when the task is something we care about or will help us better ourselves. Which begs the question: what is the *real* incentive for a research participant? Why should they take part in surveys? Unlike the engaged employee, game player or student, participants aren't necessarily invested in the 'greater good' and there is (largely) no immediate impact on their lives and no instant gratification, reward or self-progression. While the researcher and research buyer certainly benefit, the participant, by and large, does not.

This is why market research needs an intrinsic engagement culture and the best place to learn about such culture is by putting player interaction with games under the microscope. Games have those four ingredients of goal(s), rules, feedback, and autonomy opportunities that can motivate *and* perpetuate intrinsic participant engagement, especially when it doesn't come naturally. Games are an artificial construct of intrinsic engagement; rather than rely on life circumstances to serendipitously bring us joy, people play games instead that genuinely satisfy their four psychological needs.

Game culture

Games are so intrinsically engaging that they have their own thriving and diverse cultures that exist *outside* of direct game play. Players collaborate and dedicate thousands of hours to make things like the entire *Games of Thrones* world Westeros, using the environment from the game *Minecraft*,[7] or use games like *The Sims* to re-enact weekly episodes in the style of a TV show.[8] The internet is full of player-produced fan art and fan fiction inspired by favourite games. These examples, and millions more, are instances of people creating beautiful things and working together for the sheer joy of it. And the majority of this textual production is voluntarily made, for free.

Intrinsically engaged players have started their own game conventions, will know the names of programmers who developed a game they love (despite having never met them), be able to recite game-character scripts, and draw virtual or imagined environments from their favourite games. This is a world where game designers and game developers are rock stars, and people share moving stories of how games have affected them emotionally or even changed their lives in some way.[9]

Such examples of engagement say clearly that when people are truly inspired, there is no end to their motivation. If we, as researchers, could generate just a fraction of that inspiration and engagement in our participants, we would have a completely different industry.

Intrinsic engagement in games and what it can do for market research

Here we explore the typical outcomes and behaviours of intrinsically engaged players, and explore what researchers can learn from such behaviours. The following list has been compiled using a thematic analysis from several expert interviews.

Twelve signs of intrinsic engagement among game players[10]

1 Show curiosity in aspects of the game, like the narrative or the aesthetic. Curiosity can be displayed in-game (such as exploring an environment or different directions of a game narrative) or outside of a game (that is, asking questions about a game in online forums or seeking 'background' knowledge about a game via reviews, blogs and so on).

2 Seek direct contact with the development team (for example, making contact with game developers and game designers via social forums, email, handwritten letters and so on).

3 Provide voluntary feedback (either as positive feedback or constructive criticism).

4 Provide voluntary textual production. Many examples are highlighted in this chapter, such as fan art, fan fiction, cosplay, creating Let's Plays (or LPs – which are videos of people playing games), fan sites and so on.

5 Watch others play games (learning from other players' techniques, or simply watching for enjoyment).

6 Replay games.

7 Display emotional and psychophysiological connections and reactions (increased heart rate, sweating, happiness, frustration).

8 Play *with* a game (for example, players can create their own rules to change the game dynamic – like seeing how fast they can finish a game, or if they can complete a level without collecting any points).

9 Create game modifications (through hacking or for cheating).

10 Experience flow – players can lose track of time when playing games.

11 Share content: players may share content with other players and non-players, from sharing videos to conversations, fan art, fan fiction and so on, either online or face-to-face.

12 Able to recall in-game events, characters and other game items with high levels of accuracy.

This aligns with existing definitions of engagement, for example: 'Follow-up behaviour including seeking out more information, disseminating information, talking to others, and attitude are all indications that engagement did in fact occur.'[11]

This analysis can be grouped into two broader categories – that intrinsically engaged people voluntarily:

CREATE (through writing, making, drawing, painting, etc);

COLLABORATE (share ideas, make things together, solve problems together, etc).

Researchers and research buyers *need* creative and collaborative participants.

Researchers regularly ask participants to perform creative tasks, like sharing ideas or solving problems (ie 'what name would you give this product?'), and collaborate through an array of market research platforms such as online communities and through long-term diary studies. If we break down the contributing actions that lead to creativity and collaboration, we can see there are five key actions:

- reading;
- writing;
- watching;
- listening;
- designing/making.

(and, in some cases, all of those things combined) with passion and attention. Researchers would benefit from such actions because *all* these actions are required from participants, yet, we are told that participants will never read, write, watch, listen or make as much as we would like them to. Clearly, the disconnect is not in how people interact with digital media; it's how the digital media engage people that matters, in order to encourage desirable behaviours.

Next are examples of games that ask players to perform those five actions, with a specific look at why and when researchers would find such actions desirable. ResearchGame examples from Research Through Gaming will be used to evidence how a 'player-style engagement' has been captured when a survey has been restyled as a game, with information on the research outcomes.

Actions of the intrinsically engaged: towards participant creativity and collaboration using games

Reading

We all read now more than we have ever done in history: blogs, online newspapers, social media updates, and more. Yet, many survey participants struggle to read all research questions and instructions, or with the same attentiveness they give to other digital content. By contrast text-adventure games like *Zork*, which are entirely text-based, are as popular now as they've ever been, and the genre has seen a revival with modern text-adventure app games like *Blackbar*[12] and *Grayout*.[13]

Even games that are *not* text-adventures may still include lots of text; text is often used to transcribe conversations between characters, and characters may send or receive virtual letters. In many multi-player games, quest instructions (of which a player could read hundreds over the course of their gameplay) can be the equivalent of two to three paragraphs each.

Figure 8.1 shows a screengrab from award-winning game *That Dragon, Cancer* (2016, Numinous Games). In this section of the game, the player reads letters from the parents, friends and family of a young boy who has cancer. This letter is one of many that players can read. A player could spend around 15 minutes reading these letters in this level alone. In this example, we see how intrinsically engaged people are happy to read lots of text thus debunking myths that research participants are only capable of reading very little. It also contradicts research that tells us attention spans are in decline.[14]

While writing surveys in a concise manner is important, examples from many digital games show that it's not the quantity of text on screen that is the issue; it's the inspiration to read it. Players don't just read during gameplay; they read a lot of content outside of direct gameplay too. Game players, or those simply engaged with the games industry at large, will also read *about* games. Magazines like *Edge* and *PC Gamer* provide commentary on the

Figure 8.1 A screengrab from *That Dragon, Cancer* game showing one of many letters players could read in this level

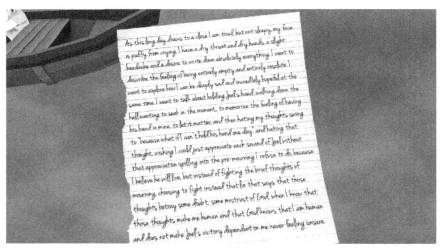

SOURCE Image used with kind permission of Numinous Games, 2016 © copyright Numinous Games

games industry, news about new releases, game reviews and more, while other magazines might be console or genre specific such as *Xbox Magazine* and *PlayStation Magazine*. Such magazines see circulations and subscriptions in the hundreds of thousands annually.

As interest in games has increased, even highbrow publications include regular content about games. There is also an endless array of game blogs, such as *Game Skinny*, *Kotaku*, and *IGN.com* and even more reading takes place via the social media networks and newsletters of game studios. While most of this content is free, some of it requires payment. This means gamers, who already spend money on consoles, the games themselves and other paraphernalia/equipment, (and are likely to be time poor and financially squeezed by this point), are still engaged enough to invest their limited resources to do *more* reading.

Why is it useful to research suppliers and buyers that participants are engaged in what they are reading, or are able to read more content?

Market researchers are often told to ensure participants need to read as little as possible in online surveys. But there are cases where not only will researchers need participants to read lengthier text, but also be engaged enough to read with high levels of attentiveness. This is because:

- being engaged enough to read survey questions, answer options or instructions in detail can help participants answer questions with more accuracy as they understand the question and/or context better;

- if participants understand the empathic value of the project/situation through reading, they will care more and are more likely to put more effort into their responses, and sustain such efforts because they are engaged;

- researchers can include more context to a question, and/or more answer options where needed to gain the data that research buyers need.

When would researchers want participants to read?

- In surveys, for questions and instructions.

- In online focus groups – participants are often encouraged to read comments from a moderator and read comments from other participants.

- Testing on financial agreement documentation, end-user licence agreements, etc.

- Testing instruction manual content, or similar.

- In some cases, text-based marketing communications may be tested.

How ResearchGames have encouraged participants to read more

My team and I created two ResearchGames: *TESSA Undercover Agents* (referred to as *TESSA* for short) and *Dubious*, on behalf of an academic study named IMPRINTS Futures. The list below illustrates how much content the participants were tasked to read.

The *TESSA* ResearchGame included:

- seven statements about things that may have happened to the participants' bank cards in the past (such as 'I've lost my card' or 'my card was damaged');

- testing 14 card types that the participant may own (eg credit cards, bank cards, loyalty cards, etc);

- testing 10 present-day forms of identification and authentication in conjunction with context and purpose (eg 'I have used 3D body scanning at an airport');

- 26 agree/disagree statements based on the Hofstede's Cultural Values scale[15] (phrases like 'Group welfare is more important than individual rewards');

Figure 8.2   Screengrab from *TESSA Undercover Agents* (2014) in which participants would take the top three items from a safe out of five items that were chosen in a previous level

SOURCE © Research Through Gaming Ltd

- testing four futuristic forms of identification and authentication (eg smart tattoos, smart jewellery etc) using a Likert scale, with text-based descriptions about the forms of ID;

- 15 statements on desires for future modes of identification and authentication (statements like 'I wish my card would beep when criminals are nearby').

In total, *TESSA* included 48 statements and 28 futuristic and current forms of identification and authentication to test. This excludes further text that helped to establish the ResearchGame narrative and progress the story (as pictured in Figure 8.2).

The *Dubious* ResearchGame included:

- three futuristic garment types to test (these were included in the Research Through Gaming 'Avatar Creator Tool' within the ResearchGame itself). Each of the three garment types had been used twice where the participants were asked to create/dress an avatar of themselves and then create/dress a friend, colleague or teacher, choosing one of the three garment types again. Each of the three garments came with a tooltip, explaining the function of each garment, as seen in Figure 8.3.

- 12 futuristic accessories (again, used twice when the participant created an avatar of themselves and then another avatar of a friend, colleague or teacher). These futuristic accessories also came with tooltip-style explanations.

- 15 current and futuristic forms of identification and authentication (again, each one with text tooltips to explain their function).

- Testing another 14 current and futuristic forms of identification and authentication (again, each one with text tooltips to explain their function).

- 20 statements based around a theoretical framework that the client was using as part of the analysis (statements like 'Is it true that in the future, all systems I use will utilize my data to "act" without me? For instance, my TV will turn on to my favourite channel so I don't have to do it myself?'). An example statement can be seen in Figure 8.4).

- And finally, a *Day in 2030* digital diary (included in the ResearchGame itself) broken down into two areas: morning/afternoon and evening.

Figure 8.3   A customized version of the Research Through Gaming 'Avatar Creator Tool', featuring futuristic clothing and gadgets, and tooltips to explain the function of the items. Screengrab taken from *Dubious ResearchGame*, published in 2013

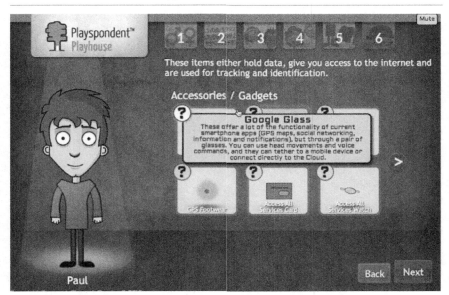

SOURCE © Research Through Gaming Ltd

Figure 8.4 One of the statements from the 'doctor' character in the *Dubious* ResearchGame

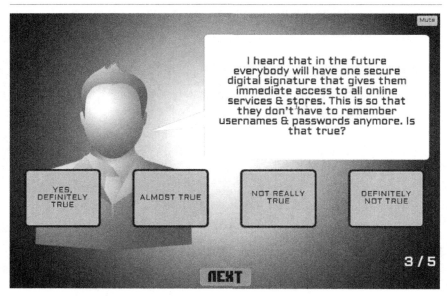

SOURCE © Research Through Gaming Ltd

Figure 8.5 A screengrab from *Dubious* ResearchGame, published in 2013. After each level, participants received three rewards, among them was a summary of the future, based on the way participants responded to the earlier questions

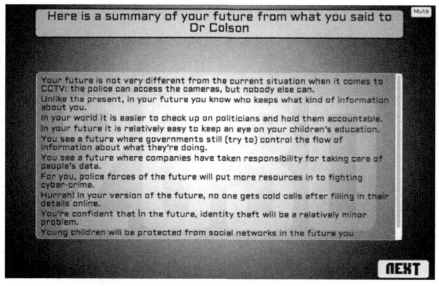

SOURCE © Research Through Gaming Ltd

In total, *Dubious* included 20 statements and 59 forms of identification and authentication to test/choose. As with TESSA, this list doesn't include the ResearchGame narrative text, or other components such as the Avatar Creator Tool choices like hair colour and hair style. The participant was given text-based feedback, to read, which summarized their version of the future based on the responses they had previously chosen (Figure 8.5).

It is clear these were text-heavy ResearchGames with a large number of statements for participants to consider. The client was clear that things like the wording of the statements couldn't be changed (a common client request) so unfortunately, the quantity of words or quantities of statements couldn't be decreased. In addition, text-based tooltip definitions were provided for clarity as some terminologies had a duel meaning and others may not have been easily understood.

Results

Earlier, we looked at the 12 signs of intrinsic engagement among game players. From the results (including statistical results and participant feedback) from both the *TESSA* and *Dubious* ResearchGames, we were able to recognize 7 of the 12 signs of engagement, such as 'voluntary background research' and 'seeking direct contact with the games studio'.

Despite heavy reading requirements, 91 per cent of *TESSA* participants left feedback categorized as positive, with many participants commenting that they had 'enjoyed the experience'. There were also feedback comments of gratitude:

- 'Thank you very much. This survey/game was very exciting!'
- 'Amazing! Loved this "ResearchGame" – best survey I have ever taken. Thank you for allowing me to participate.'
- 'thank you, weirdest yet most interesting survey I've ever done.'
- 'Great experience – thank you!!'
- 'far more fun than ANY survey I have participated in before – THANK YOU!'

Seventeen participants voluntarily asked for opportunities to play more ResearchGames in the future. The continuation desire was expressed in many cases enthusiastically from people of all ages. These feedback statements are from people aged 40 to 55:

More of these please please please

Man this type of survey is totally awesome and ground breaking in its method. Please please please sign me up for any future projects. xxxx@hotmail.com or xxxx@yahoo.co.uk.*

(*Note: the participant was not asked to provide email addresses)

While looking at participant enjoyment is useful, other aspects of the survey experience are also important. One aspect we wanted to keep a close check on was the continuation rate to see if we could gain the kinds of replay effects normally seen in games. Of participants who completed *TESSA*, 81 per cent played *Dubious* four months later. This continuation rate was 11 percentage points higher than predicted by the panel company we hired, as they had predicted a maximum 70 per cent continuation rate[16] based on the past rates of traditional online surveys of a similar length.[17] While 11 percentage points doesn't sound like much, this can make a significant difference if many thousands of participants are required for surveys.

When we look at the earlier 12 signs of intrinsic engagement, the following results correspond to 4 of those 12 signs:

- **Voluntary feedback**: 27 per cent of the participants who took part in *TESSA* gave voluntary feedback (N=376).

- **Voluntary positive feedback**: Across all feedback gathered from *TESSA* participants, the most frequent adjectives and adverbs used when leaving feedback (in order of most to least frequent) were fun, interesting, different, enjoyed, great, good, enjoyable, unusual and novel.

- **Voluntary constructive criticism.**

- **Seeking direct contact with development team.**

After playing *TESSA*, one participant found my email address (I assume somewhere online as it wasn't provided as part of the ResearchGame) and sent a positive email about her ResearchGame experience with some constructive criticism. Participants were not required to do this. What was surprising, and what is an indicator of this participant's intrinsic engagement, is not that she gave constructive criticism or even that she had spent time to find my email address, but that she tried to refresh twice, and spent over an hour taking part, showing a strong continuation desire. (The name is changed to protect the participant's identity. The writing style is kept as originally written.)

Dear Betty,

just completed a panel survey & thought you should know that your survery was amazing, one of the best i've ever done & i've done a lot of panel rearch/ feedback face to face & over the internet since i was a young child. thought you should know that many of the pages failed to load fully - we have pretty typical noncable broadband here - the sort most people complain over. so i was unable to fill in the questionnaire page of your survey. as a last resort the next page i refreshed twice before finally being able to click yes. it may be worth considering that many users do not have amazing broadband speeds available in their area?

anyhow, thanks for the most not boring survey ever!

Many thanks, Julie

p.s took over an hour to complete....

The heaviness of the content and the quality of the data as well as the participant feedback has proven that using games as a research tool can ensure participants can become intrinsically engaged, read more and read with high levels of attention. And even when their internet fails them, they are determined to read the full content.

Notes:

- The *TESSA* and *Dubious* gameplay video can be viewed here, using the access code DUBTES2 when prompted:
  www.koganpage.com/gamesandgamification
- This case study is discussed further in Chapter 11.

Writing

There are seemingly no limits to how much intrinsically engaged players will read, and the same applies to how much they will write. Computer role-playing games (CRPGs – often called text-adventure games) require players to progress in the game by writing, which can continue for many hours. But what about writing outside of direct game play?

The *World of Warcraft* wiki[18,19] is one of the most heavily cited examples of voluntary textual production. At the time of writing, it has 297,240 pages of voluntary input from *World of Warcraft* players around the world. They made this wiki to help other people play the game and document the games' changes.

Engaged players will also voluntarily produce fan fiction.[20] Examples of fan fiction fill in the missing backstories of game characters, imagine how the game narrative evolves in the future, or simply reimagines the characters in other ways. One such example is a parody based on the *Angry Birds* game

(Rovio Entertainment Corporation) where a player published a series of letters titled 'Angry Birds – Letters from the Front Lines':[21]

My Dear Amanda,

I hope this letter finds you in good health. We have sustained significant casualties in levels 3-17 and 3-18. Those loathsome green pigs are starting to build their fortresses with stones now. Sergeant has ordered backup from those black birds that explode. I pray they arrive in time. I've seen too many of my brother red birds thrown against stone walls to no avail. I'm having trouble making sense of all this, Amanda. They tell me I can come home after we get three stars on 3-18. I would like to believe it's possible, but my heart is heavy with doubt.

Yours always,

Red Bird

© Chris Riebschlager, reproduced with his kind permission.

This example, and many more, show that not only can intrinsically engaged people write lots of text and with high attentiveness but do so with imagination, creativity, intellect and clarity (and even a little humour) – all things researchers would want from market research participants.

Why is it useful for researchers and research buyers for participants to be engaged in what they are writing, or be able to write more content?

Researchers often forego the inclusion of open-end responses (that is, survey questions where the participant has an input field where they can write 'free' text) because we are told that participants are deterred by these opportunities to write. Perhaps it is deemed too cognitively taxing, takes too much time for the participant, or both.

But if we can create surveys as games, we can harness the types of creative, thought-out and detailed writing like the kind we see within games and in fan fiction. This could be beneficial for researchers in terms of richness of insight.

When would research suppliers and buyers want participants to write?

- in online or offline diary studies;
- as part of online focus groups and in market research online communities (MROCs);

- to write their feedback when discussing customer service experience, or other kinds of feedback;
- to write about their ideas and opinions in open-end responses.

When a ResearchGame got participants writing

In the ResearchGame *Dubious*, we included a digital diary entry for participants to imagine a day in their lives in the year 2030. The diary was split as two sections: morning/afternoon and evening.

Of participants who took part in *Dubious*, 19 per cent chose to complete the Bonus Level 'Diary Study' filling out both the 'morning/afternoon' and 'evening' sections. This activity was entirely optional. The buttons 'WRITE' and 'SKIP' were clearly visible on the screen (Figure 8.6). Just the 'morning /afternoon' section was filled out by 21 per cent of participants. This result was higher than both our client and I had expected, particularly as this was the final activity in the *Dubious* ResearchGame, after approximately 25–30 minutes of gameplay, and after completing the *TESSA* ResearchGame four months prior to completing *Dubious*.

While the length of what was written voluntarily by participants was impressive (long diary entries were common throughout the dataset) the

Figure 8.6 Bonus Level diary study in *Dubious* ResearchGame

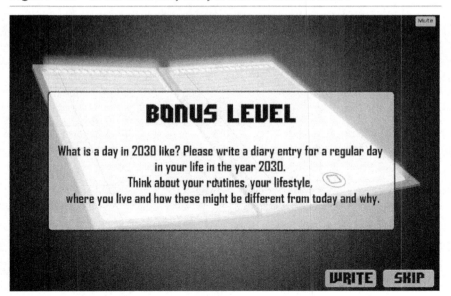

SOURCE © Research Through Gaming Ltd

content was said to be one of the most insightful parts of the data for our client, especially as they were detailed and emotive. The data illustrated the fears and hopes people had about the year 2030, indicative of things people thought would largely stay the same, as well as what would be new, including lots of ideas for innovations. For example, smart fridges were mentioned, 4D TVs, 'integrated keep-fit machines which read bio-data and feed to the doctor for recording and early warnings', through to self-prepared breakfasts served by androids, virtual bars and food-as-pills. We also got to see how people envisioned the world of work: 'travel to work via beam of light.10 hour shift of manual labor for gov, 1 break of 10 mins' to 'The office is clean with automatic cleaning machines. Almost all work is computer based with video conferencing instead of meetings.'

The following extract (which keeps in the participant's exact response including typos) is illustrative of the length and detail of the majority of entries for the same activity:

MORNING/AFTERNOON

07.00 Wake Early, take three capsules for breakfast. 09.00 connect the children to the education channel and download today's study programme - must check back in one hour to verify their results and communicate with their professor09.15 I teleport myself to the office , complete my duties for the day and am teleported back home for 10.0010.00 Childrens professor is happy with their study results and awards them a PHd12.00 I take the children out for lunch, they love the Hamburger pills - they really taste just the same as the burger I had when I was their age.13.00 We have a marathon games session at the games palace. The children meet their friends online and play all afternoon. They take a shower and we set off for home - individual teleports- the children prefer to travel with their friends.

EVENING

7.30 Meet up wit friends, we have evening pills, much bigger choice in the evening. catch up with the day in the office.we move to the electronic communications and book a teleporter around the world. We stop in Kuala Lumpur for a stroll around Petronas tower and move to Singapore for a few minutes. Next we go to Manila for some live music. Tokyo was very quiet, we decided to leave Tokyo until the week-endNew York is always special for me but just a few minutes before the teleporter whisks us back home10.15 back home take uv shower and tiredness pill, relax and watch a video from the 1980's. I have to ask the children to show me how to make the video player work

Some participants wrote about their future lives with storytelling techniques in their delivery:

> Went to work as usual. Got a message over the CCTV / Voice system as I made a mistake and was asked to explain to the boss. (Jesus, can't even breathe without the boss knowing about it) Never mind it wasn't a major issue just gotta watch your back. Finished work and went for a beer, found some cash in the street and was immediately informed that it had been noticed by camera operators and to hand it in or be charged with theft. Better luck next time eh? Still, enjoyed the pint. Expensive as it was. Made way home and switched the TV on en route along with closing curtains and switching on the lamp. At least I won't get burgled this way. Stayed in watched TV had a couple of beers and then early night as up early for work and don't want to go through what I did today. Night Night. At least the dreams are mine !!!

Voluntary feedback was provided about the ResearchGame itself, where participants wrote more; 83 per cent of the feedback received was categorized as positive towards the *Dubious* ResearchGame format. These results, like so many other examples from ResearchGames, show that games encourage creative writing, thoughtful responses and even ideation.

When looking at the feedback and the kinds of behaviours displayed by participants, this links to more of the 12 signs of intrinsic engagement: voluntary textual production and voluntary feedback.

Designing/making

Fan art is where players pay homage to their favourite game, or reimagine their favourite game characters, using all sorts of artistic expression. Super Mario has been reimagined as abstract art to stained glass and Renaissance style paintings.

Just search the web for "fan art for…" and insert the name of any game, and you'll likely see hundreds if not tens of thousands of hits of fan art. Some of it is digital fan art, some of it hand drawn, but whatever the medium, it is always born from intrinsic engagement.

One of my favourite examples of player-made fan art is that of popular and award-winning app game *Monument Valley*[22] by Ustwo Games. Take a look at their fanart website[23] and see how children aged under 10 and people aged over 50 are producing such impassioned works. These examples show that when intrinsically engaged, research participants *can* produce equally passionate and intricate depictions of what they like, don't like, or what they want, for market research purposes.

Engaged players (again, of all ages) also make costumes to look like their favourite game characters, and wear such costumes at events and other conventions. This is called 'cosplay' – costume play.

People can spend hours, if not days, sewing in all the intricate details of footwear, clothing and other accessories. In one story shared on social media, Leo Simons, under the name 'Elmins Cosplay', had spent 1,000+ hours creating his own *League of Legends* (Riot Games, Inc.) costume and spent US $1,000 doing so. For a week, the world was fascinated by this man's dedication, with the story reported in British newspaper *The Mirror*.[24]

His efforts making mechanical wings (Figure 8.7) complete with blue LED lights wowed readers. While developing game content like costumes and accessories is impressive, what is equally if not more awe-inspiring is the high level of problem-solving and engineering required to recreate in reality the digital content seen in games. For many cosplayers, they don't necessarily have the skills to make such things, but through their intrinsic engagement, they even learn new skills to make these products. Again, if researchers could harness this dedicated design and/or build power, it could equate to lots more creative ideas and problem-solving from participants.

Figure 8.7   Giant motorized wings, made by artist Elmins Cosplay, who spent over 1,000 hours building the piece. Image used with kind permission from Leo Simon 'Elmins Cosplay'

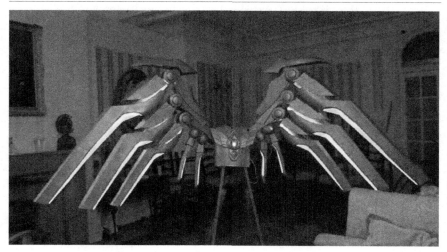

SOURCE © Elmins Cosplay

Why is it useful to researchers and research buyers for participants to be engaged in what they are designing or making?

Participants may be required to get involved in designing or making to:

- idealize prototypes of products including furniture, homewares, apparel and so on;

- idealize prototypes of apps and other software products;

- idealize their versions of neighbourhoods, schools or other buildings or environments.

In creating such products, in reality or even as digital designs, researchers would require that participants show high levels of detail so it is easy to understand the ideas.

When a ResearchGame tasked participants with designing

In 2015, I designed the *Designer for a Day* ResearchGame on behalf of an apparel portfolio Fortune 500 brand. The participants were placed in the role of being a leisurewear designer and through three levels, could visually build their ideal activewear bottoms (such as leggings or jogging bottoms) for an activity of their choice (yoga, pilates, boxing and so on).

The participants had a lot of choices in designing their ideal activewear. Specifically, participants could choose:

- 1 of 8 different styles of bottom (such as leggings, boyfriend style, harem style etc);

- 1 of 3 styles of rise (high rise, mid and low rise which means that a high rise was over the belly-button, and the low rise was under the belly-button);

- 1 of 4 lengths (full length, ankle length, capri and short);

- 1 of 2 types of logo (which would feature on the pant);

- 1 of 12 colours (including 2 prints and 9 block colours);

- 1 of 2 types of fabric texture;

- 1 of 5 locations for a first pocket;

- 1 of 5 locations for a second pocket;

- up to 5 pocket types (eg with zipper, with flap, small or large etc);

- up to 4 fabric performance types;

- up to 5 fabric features;

- up to 5 choices on sustainability;

- 1 of 2 seam styles.

Figure 8.8 A screengrab from the *Designer for a Day* ResearchGame, published by Research Through Gaming in 2015 on behalf of an apparel portfolio Fortune 500 brand

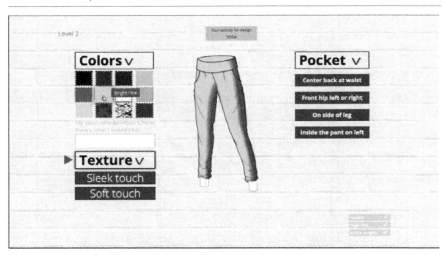

SOURCE © Research Through Gaming Ltd

In all, participants had 62 choices relating to their design where a minimum of 13 design decisions were required to create the ideal activewear bottoms, in addition to answering questions to explain design choices (Figure 8.8). There were more than 8 trillion possible design combinations.

Again, even with the quantity of choices and combinations available, which may be viewed as taxing in a traditional survey environment, 99 per cent of the voluntary feedback was categorized as positive; the most popular words to describe the ResearchGame were 'fun', 'awesome' and 'cool'. In addition, 82 per cent said they would like to play a ResearchGame again in the future.[25] The client deemed the insight as actionable, and had put much of their learnings into action within weeks.

This case study illustrates that reframing so many choices as a creative endeavour within a game (rather than grids, drop-down menus and other usual question interactions used in a traditional survey) can be instrumental in participant enjoyment, but also shows how important visual aids are in quantitative research. We can take advantage of the capabilities inherent in games so participants can see their creations 'come to life'. Such visuals, with permission, can be directly used in the insight reporting processes and even as part of Insight Games (explored in Chapter 24).

Listening

Listening in games is as important as reading and writing, and as technology has evolved, we can hear characters in an array of accents and with emotional inclinations making them sound more human. Non-dialogue-based audio helps players too; as explored in Chapter 4, the music and sound effects are imperative in creating mood, warning of danger, or even changing the speed of how participants react within a game.

Why is it useful for researchers and research buyers for participants to be engaged in what they are listening to, or be able to listen to more content?

The multiple uses of music in games are also rooted in heuristics; fast music nudges faster, instinctual responses and slower music can nudge slower, more evenly paced behaviours and thought-out responses. The market research industry already values the automatic 'System 1' thinking because there are many cases where researchers want to discourage deliberation and encourage 'top-of-mind' participant responses.

Aside from listening to non-dialogue audio for behaviour change, there are other times that researchers would want participants to listen to content, and listen with high attentiveness:

- testing radio content, TV content, film etc;
- testing music and jingles for commercials;
- most video content will have a 'listening' component – so it's important to watch as well as listen;
- research and technology is evolving so that narration for surveys can become mainstream, which means people may listen to (instead of read) surveys;
- as research moves into virtual reality, there will also be the need for participants to listen to instructions.

When a ResearchGame got participants listening

In 2011, I designed the ResearchGame *Magazine Question Hunt* for a publisher of children's magazines. One of the objectives was to understand which songs by which artists were favourites among a small selection of children. The participants were between 7 and 10 years old.

Figure 8.9 Image from the *Magazine Question Hunt* ResearchGame – 'Boys' room'

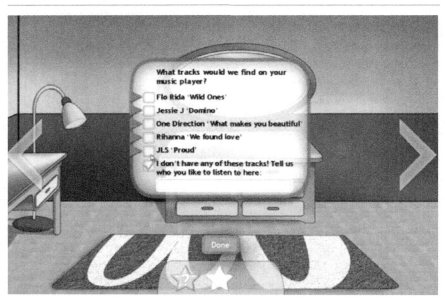

SOURCE © Research Through Gaming Ltd

We asked the participants which tracks we would find on their music player (Figure 8.9). There were five tracks to choose from, with the option to add in a track that wasn't already mentioned; 97 per cent of participants listened to all tracks and 85 per cent gave positive feedback about the platform.

Watching/observing

Watching what is going on in a game is crucial: watching out for baddies, watching for the time running out, watching out for rewards, coins and other items. At any one time during gameplay, players might need to keep their eye on several moving parts. So much so, that 'they wouldn't notice if the roof collapsed (unless it unplugged the game in the process)' (Rigby and Ryan, 2011).[26]

Digital games might task players to solve mysteries and crimes where player observation needs to be especially acute; there can be clues in the smallest of details like a raised eyebrow from another character or a momentary sideways glance, or hidden items in busy virtual rooms.

Outside of direct gameplay, watching other people play games is a popular pastime. Twitch and YouTube gaming are two of many websites that allow people to watch *other* people play games, of which the top Twitch member at the time of writing has almost 2.5 million followers – all having instant access to watching their favourite gamers playing their favourite games.[27]

At the 2014 UK Videogames industry conference in London, Mark Green the research director at Sony, confirmed that watching videogames is now more than ever a form of entertainment in itself with 32 million people having watched the *League of Legends* Season 3 World Championship over Twitch and 8.2 million watched the live stream.

Why is it useful to research suppliers and buyers that participants are engaged in what they are watching, or able to watch/observe more content?

- To recall and assess aspects of video content (like in adverts, music videos and movie trailers).

- In a simulation, participants will need to be observant of various aspects in a virtual environment in order to answer questions about different elements within it.

- In circumstances where product designs are being assessed, participants may be required to watch changes in product design closely to assess differences and preferences.

When a ResearchGame got participants watching closely

In the ResearchGame *Magazine Question Hunt* (mentioned earlier) a mini-game was included to understand which celebrities were most recognizable to the participants (7- to 10-year-old children) on behalf of our client, a magazine publisher (Figure 8.10). Rather than place the image on the screen and have participants note whether they recognized the celebrities or not (which may have been the case with a traditional online survey), this question was restyled as a guessing game.

The participants began this activity with three lives for each of the five celebrities (represented as hearts on the left side of the screen). As the tiles moved away from the face of the celebrity, the participant could write who they thought the celebrity was, but had to think fast as the countdown timer was on. The countdown timer served to encourage instinctive responses

Figure 8.10 Image from the *Magazine Question Hunt* ResearchGame – Celebrity guessing game

SOURCE © Research Through Gaming Ltd

because we wanted to replicate the short timespan that children would have, in real life, to recognize a celebrity on the front cover of one of our client's magazines.

Not only was this activity explicitly mentioned in participant feedback as 'the most fun' or 'favourite part', but also served an additional purpose in terms of insight, because even when the participants guessed incorrectly, we were still able to collect data on which *other* celebrities were top-of-mind. We also understood how long it took for audiences to recognize the celebrities, but crucially, we understood something we didn't anticipate: the importance of how the celebrity was dressed in their photos. One of the five celebrities tested was a celebrity called Dappy from a band called N-Dubz. If you search for an image of this celebrity online even today, he is most depicted wearing a woolly hat or sports cap and casual clothes like hooded jackets. The image the client provided of Dappy, however, showed him wearing dark sunglasses and a sharp suit. The participants, in their majority, struggled to recognize Dappy. This showed that the clothing of the celebrity was important in helping the young audience recognize who they were, helping the client make more informed choices about the *types* of images they use of celebrities.

Such an activity needn't be confined to just recognizing celebrities. A guessing game like this can be used for anything visual such as logo and product packaging recognition.

As we can see from these cases, game-based research encourages creativity and collaboration. But it's not just in entertainment and market research that game-based techniques are used. Other industries recognize the power of the inspiration and engagement that games and gamification offer, as we explore in the next chapter.

ACTIVITY

Check out the podcast *+7 intelligence – How Games Impact People* (http://plus7intelligence.com) and the conference *Games for Change* (www.gamesforchange.org) for stories and case studies on how games result in real-world achievements.

Notes

1 Romero, R and Adamou, B (2014) Expert interview with *Minority Media* Community Manager, Rommel Romero, on understanding intrinsic engagement behaviours with videogames, Web interview 27 May

2 Adamou, B and Newman, J (2014) Expert interview with author James Newman on understanding intrinsic engagement with videogames, Web interview, 19 November

3 Newman, J (2008) *Playing with Videogames*, Routledge

4 Kruse, K (2012) [accessed 30 December 2014] What is employee engagement? *Forbes* [Online] www.forbes.com/sites/kevinkruse/2012/06/22/employee-engagement-what-and-why

5 Pink, D (2009) [accessed 1 October 2014] *Dan Pink: The Puzzle of Motivation*, Proceedings of TEDGlobal 2009, Oxford [Online] www.ted.com/talks/dan_pink_on_motivation

6 Schlechty, P (1994) *Increasing Student Engagement*, Missouri Leadership Academy

7 Hudson, Laura (2013) [accessed 25 May 2018] How fans recreated Game of Thrones in a Minecraft map the size of LA, *WIRED* [Online] www.wired.com/2013/03/westeroscraft-game-thrones-minecraft

8 DK1 Games (2017) [accessed 25 May 2018] *Sims 4: Big Brother Episode 1* [YouTube video] [Online] www.youtube.com/watch?v=4W434lQC8YE

9 Margolis, Jonathan (2017) [accessed 25 May 2018] My flirtation with gaming has been an education, *Financial Times* [Online] www.ft.com/content/ f7dbad8c-ac02-11e7-8076-0a4bdda92ca2

10 Author's note: for more about player engagement, the paper 'The Player Engagement Process – An Exploration of Continuation Desire in Digital Games' by Henrik Schoenau-Fog is useful: http://www.digra.org/wp-content/ uploads/digital-library/11307.06025.pdf

11 Plummer, Joe, Zaltman, Gerald and Mast, Fred (2006) [accessed 25 May 2018] Engagement: Definitions and Anatomy, Proceedings of the Advertising Research Foundations workshop [Online] www.warc.com/content/paywall/ article/arfw/engagement_definitions_and_anatomy/86531

12 *Blackbar* game: http://mrgan.com/blackbar/

13 *Blackbar* and *Grayout* both by Neven Mrgan: www.mrgan.com

14 McSpadden, Kevin (2015) [accessed 28 May 2018] You now have a shorter attention span than a goldfish, *TIME Magazine* [Online] http://time. com/3858309/attention-spans-goldfish/

15 Information about the Hofstede Cultural Value scale can be found here: www.hofstede-insights.com/models/national-culture/ [accessed 28 May 2018]

16 Note: the continuation rate is indicated by the amount of survey participants who complete the first survey and begin a second follow-on survey

17 The panel company also warned that continuation rate would drastically decrease to well under 70 per cent the further apart the two ResearchGames were in their release. With a four-month gap between the release of *TESSA* and *Dubious*, the higher-than-expected continuation rate was further surprising.

18 *World of Warcraft* wiki: http://wowwiki.wikia.com/wiki/Portal:Main

19 Note: wikis are a collaboratively made online platform of knowledge, which can be about any given subject. The *World of Warcraft* wiki is one of thousands of online wikis.

20 Note: for more examples of game fan fiction, you can check out www. fanfiction.net/game/

21 https://www.mcsweeneys.net/articles/angry-birds-letters-from-the-front-lines

22 *Monument Valley* game: www.monumentvalleygame.com

23 http://monumentfriends.tumblr.com

24 Parker, Louise (2015) [accessed 28 May 2018] Artist spends 1,000 hours and £1,000 making amazing moving wings for cosplay costume, *The Mirror* [Online] www.mirror.co.uk/news/weird-news/artist-spends-000-hours-1000-6968260

25 Research study fielded in January 2016 with 2,208 participants. The case study was presented at the IMPACT MRS Annual Conference, 15 March 2017, London and as part of the proceedings of the ISPO event, Munich, 29 January 2018.

26 Rigby, S and Ryan, RM (2011) *Glued to Games: How video games draw us in and hold us spellbound*, New Directions in Media, California

27 *Social Blade* website: https://socialblade.com/twitch/

How games and gamification are used for engagement and data collection outside of research and entertainment

09

Consumers are now hungry for not just things to have, but things to do
Iain Swan, Strategy Director at Bright

There is an irony that almost every industry outside of market research has already used games and gamification for user engagement, data and insight, and yet the people working in the research industry who are best placed to understand that data, and who desperately require participant engagement, are yet to fully embrace games and gamification as research methodologies. But there is a silver lining to being a late adopter as it provides learning opportunities from the successes and failures of others before us.

This chapter will explore how game-based approaches have been used outside of research. We will:

- understand how multifarious industries are already using game-based approaches for engagement and data collection;

- understand the changing functions of games and gamification, their fluidity as media, and their applications in dozens of disciplines and industries;

- explore 'Functional Games', looking at how other industries use games outside of direct entertainment;

- explore gamification, looking at applications from various industries;

- discover how using games and gamification has been advantageous in other industries, and what market researchers can learn;

- understand the level of impact game-based approaches have already had around the world, and allow you to realize how games are part of our everyday lives. As such, the move to more game-based research approaches shouldn't be surprising to research participants and should be fully embraced by researchers as a data collection technique.

Typically, games have been an artefact of entertainment, and gamification reserved as an artefact of function. We play games for fun, but gamification adopts game-like elements to make non-game activities feel more fun for a purpose – to engage people, increase profits, save money and other commercial benefits. However, the lines between games, gamification and simply more playful experiences are becoming increasingly blurred, with these mediums being used in fluid ways.

There is now a world of fully-fledged games that are made for reasons beyond entertainment; for health and wellness, for political campaigns, for promoting awareness of causes – you name it, there is likely a game for it. Such games are a genre unto themselves. They are known as Serious Games, Persuasive Games and/or Empathy Games. Gamification, on the other hand, is being used to such a degree that it is morphing into a medium that can provide truly playful experiences, to the point where we start wondering where does a game end and gamification begin (or vice versa)? Many brands and organizations have been using playful approaches for decades, but why?

Why brands use playful approaches

Like market research, other industries recognize the commercial advantages of play and the intrinsic engagement that is inherent in game-based approaches. One of these advantages is engagement, and that is a hot commodity. Considering that games are regarded as the most engaging medium of all time, it's obvious why this medium has been a huge source of inspiration. Engagement has become synonymous with data collection and the *playing of games* has become a data collection method in itself. **Play is a data generator.**

Through watching how people play games and take part in gamified activities, people can gain all sorts of data: how emotion drives choice, how different social contexts and stimulus generate different outcomes, and the 'why' behind behaviours. If you have a loyalty card, such as the cards from coffee stores, grocery stores and airlines, you are involved in one of the most prominent forms of gamification. Your participation, your 'play', is what generates data, every time you buy something, every time you use a voucher, every time you visit. Lots of different companies are taking advantage of using games, gamification and play to do exactly what market research wants to do: **create engagement and generate data.**

The idea of using playful approaches for otherwise non-playful activities isn't necessarily new. Game-like approaches have been used for decades in sectors like education and employee engagement. Even if we didn't necessarily have the labels at the time to name them as such, they were there.

As a parent or child, you might not have heard of 'gamification', but you may very well have implemented or been part of a points/badge system to encourage good behaviour. In UK schools, such systems are ingrained in education: getting gold star stickers for good work or achieving attendance milestones. I've applied gamification in my own teaching; as founder of the *London Young Entrepreneurs Club*, I implemented a complete game-based approach to give feedback, create competitions, allow students to level up after every session, and award badges relevant for different displays of skill and effort. The course gained great feedback from the students, but from a facilitator's perspective, the gamification was a useful tool to record and keep track of the students' progress; hence the students' participation and play generated data.

Such game-based systems are just a few that have been around long before the terms 'Serious Games', 'Persuasive Games' or even 'gamification' came about. Take TV shows for example, where we see many examples of gamification. TV executives put a dozen people in a house, add in the game ingredients with some bonus features (surprise, an ex-boyfriend has *just* showed up!) and they call it *Big Brother*. For job interviews, they add the game ingredients to create a multi-level, multiplayer game called *The Apprentice*, a game where you compete with other employees for a six-figure salary. What about becoming a pop star? That's gamified too. There's *The Voice*, *X Factor* and *Pop Idol*, which utilize the competitors and audience as game players. Yes, these are game *shows*. We're all familiar with them and yet, if we look at them through a different lens, they can be a great source of inspiration for game-based research design.

The right vocabulary is yet to evolve to encompass the many things that Serious Games or Persuasive Games can be. They can be at once educational, satirical, emotional, while gaining data from your gameplay and while advertising a product or service, or even sell things to you directly.

Such games exist in commercial and non-commercial spaces. What do you call such a game that does all of these things at the same time? While we await the right vocabulary, we have given industry-specific games their own categories and labels: game *shows*, *adver*games, *marketing* games, *exer*games (games for exercise) and, of course, *Research*Games. For ease, I've provided an umbrella term to encompass Serious Games, Persuasive Games, Empathy Games and similar: collectively they are 'Functional Games' – games with function.

The Functional Game market is global. This single chapter will not cover the breadth of these types of games, so further exploration is encouraged. However, I will try to give a broad spectrum of examples to illustrate the richness and diversity of game-based approaches outside of direct entertainment, their benefits and what researchers can learn.

Engagement is now almost fully quantifiable; through likes, clicks, reads, what you are reading on a website and how long you are reading it for – your online engagement is data. Engagement is the new oil.

Games, gamification and general game-like approaches are now so much a part of modern marketing, loyalty programmes, health and wellness, the pharmaceutical industry, education, military, engineering, hospitality, employee management, politics (the list of industries is endless) that it would be quicker to explore where games and gamification are *not* used, as this would make for a far shorter list!

Functional Games

Functional Games are often made as fully-fledged games but their sole purpose is not for entertainment. Functional Games encourage play and encourage intrinsic engagement. For example, a research-game is a type of 'Serious/Persuasive/Functional Game' whereas a gamified survey is an example of gamification. Functional Games have a variety of uses and purposes.

In marketing, game-like approaches have been used to engage consumers in all kinds of campaigns, from the purposefully bonkers *Spots VS Stripes* Cadbury's campaign from 2010/2011 (a US $50 million initiative which included online games[1]) to the fun Marmite *Are you born a lover or a hater?* gene project[2] of 2017, which at its basic level is a game-like test to spread (pun intended) viral video content and encourage online conversation.

Game-based approaches have been used for more serious content such as promoting charities, as political campaign tools and fan-made political propaganda. In 2016, *CorbynRun*[3] was released: a fully-fledged digital game to promote the UK Labour Party leader Jeremy Corbyn. Such was the influence of this game, it became a televised BBC news feature the following year,[4] a platform in which games are rarely, if ever, discussed. The game *Come Wheat May* is another political-propaganda game aimed at poking fun at the UK Conservative Party leader, Theresa May, who famously said the most naughty thing she did as a child was running through fields of wheat. In the game, you can be Theresa May and do just that.

In marketing, familiar board and digital games have been reimagined for brand engagement. One of the most familiar examples of this is the McDonald's *Monopoly* game, where stickers found on purchased products can be placed on paper or digital Monopoly boards to win prizes. This use of Monopoly-reimagined-as-a-marketing-tool has been going since 1985, but that's not the only game McDonald's has repurposed. They've used a Pong-like game to engage consumers into winning food prizes as well as including a range of games on their website.[5]

But if you were to search for "McDonald's games", you are likely to come across a different type of game about McDonald's altogether; the *McDonald's Videogame* (2006). This McDonald's game is just one of many from the Molleindustria game studio, which uses dark humour, controversy, provocation, satire and even places you in the role of complicity, to educate players about serious issues. One of their games, *Nova Alea*,[6] simulates property investment and places the player in the role of real estate spectator (Figure 9.1). The game makes commentary, through play, on how gentrification changes the human landscape of cities, driving some residents out while others become richer. As a player, you are at once learning something new while becoming complicit in a simulation of a changing city. These kinds of simulations could be easily used for market research purposes.

Molleindustria also built a game to explore the harsh realities of smartphone manufacture. *Phone Story*[7] a game that went viral in 2015 and (at the time of writing) has been banned from the app store, makes players catch suicidal factory workers and mine for precious materials by using slaves. Molleindustria games do not shy away from taboo subjects but instead, use the capabilities inherent in games to simulate experiences through role-play, just as market researchers could do with games.

Feelings of complicity, guilt and shame are complex emotions that humans experience in real life. Games are the only other place where humans can experience these same feelings and battle with their moral compass. The *BigPharma* game[8] by Positech Games allows players the opportunity to cure the world's diseases, while on the other hand they can compromise such altruistic opportunities for profit.

Figure 9.1   Nova Alea game

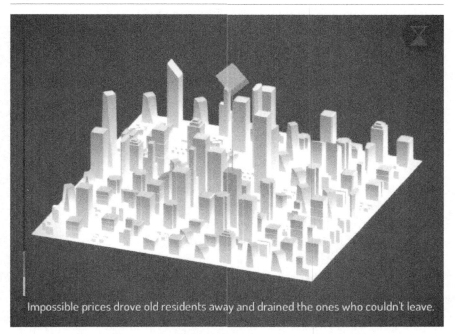

Impossible prices drove old residents away and drained the ones who couldn't leave.

SOURCE © MolleIndustria. Reproduced with kind permission from Paolo Pedercini

In health and wellness, the use of specially designed Functional Games *and* pre-existing videogames are used widely. Doctors from McGill University in Canada have used the game *Tetris* to treat people with weak vision in one or both eyes,[9] with positive results such as a dramatic improvement in vision and 3D depth perception. Patients can play a game called *Re-Mission*[10] to learn more about their cancer conditions; doctors play VR games where they are conducting surgery on virtual avatars which in turn reduces errors in the real world; another game helps patients relax before surgery reducing stress by 40 per cent,[11] and one game even places the player in the role of a mortician.[12]

SuperBetter, a game created by author and game designer Jane McGonigal, is designed to help players overcome their current health and wellness issues and go even further to become even better than they were before. Players have overcome depression and anxiety through the game mechanics of assigning goals and feeling connected to others for support by creating allies.

Nintendo Wii games, and even specially developed games, are commonplace in care homes for the elderly; they are used to do things like encourage exercise or help those who have been affected by a stroke. The results showed cognitive, memory and mood improvements, and players could do things more easily like tie their shoes or open a drawer.[13,14]

Zombies, Run!,[15] an alternate reality and audio adventure game set in reality, has been so successful that a book and board games are being developed. The premise: while you're running around in the post-apocalyptic world getting supplies and saving people, you exercise – the louder you can hear zombies, the closer they are to you, and the faster you run. A 'Virtual Race' was launched in spring 2018, with 5,000 entrants from 72 countries running a total of 30,864 kilometres.

This book explores games as market research instruments, but actually games have been used as part of medical research and even medical training for decades, where play has been the source of data generation. In a study conducted at Harvard University, teenage subjects were asked to play a game, and the data collected from how they played gave an indication as to the participants' levels of risk assessment.[16] Surgeons have been using games for training, where simulating surgery on avatars before heading to the real-life operation table has resulted in 37 per cent fewer errors and a 27 per cent increase in speed, according to a 2007 study.[17]

In employee management, specially developed games are being used across the spectrum. How prospective or existing employees play these games may result in job offers, rejections, identifying training needs and even changing company culture.

Deloitte, the professional services company[18] as well as other Fortune 500 brands, are now talking about and using games and gamification synonymously with employee engagement. Games are no longer seen as frivolous, but as powerful moneymaking or money-saving tools, and there is a lot of money to be saved in recruiting the right people. The US Army knows this all too well, having developed its own first person shooter, multiplayer videogame, *America's Army*.[19] The data collected from the way people play provide learning opportunities and abilities for recruitment (as well as playing online, it can also be played at recruiting stations). It is at once an education platform, a propaganda tool, a training tool, a recruitment tool, and a way to reduce the cost of hiring soldiers who quit in the first nine weeks of training; and with a US $15,000 price tag per soldier,[20] that's a lot of money to save.

How employees play games has also worked the other way around; instead of businesses identifying talent through gameplay, the talent is using their videogame status and achievement scores to impress prospective employers. Job seekers are showing off their leadership and problem-solving skills in the virtual world, which is carried out entirely voluntarily, on their real-world résumés.[21]

In interior design, the *Design Home*[22] app game (2016, Crowdstar Inc[23]) crosses the boundaries between entertainment and learning about interior design, with marketing *and* sales. In *Design Home*, players reimagine rooms to different style briefs. But, the little graphics of furniture and home accessories are not fake: they are real and available for purchase in real life, thus blurring the lines between entertainment, education, marketing and sales.

Such is the emphasis on sales and marketing in Crowdstar games that their other game app, *Covet Fashion* (a game about dressing up for different occasions) is proclaimed to be 'the future of mobile fashion marketing.'[24] Sounds far-fetched? It isn't. In a public review from the high street clothing brand, French Connection, they say:

> We joined *Covet Fashion* because we thought it was a unique and different way to reach mobile consumers. We've been blown away with the exposure our collections have received, resulting in significant mobile traffic and conversions. It is now one of our top sources of all e-commerce sales.

These examples of multipurpose games are a small glimpse in comparison to how many Functional Games are being played and developed. While these games are not built primarily as research tools, they are tools for research. Data are collected so that feedback like points and badges are rewarded, but also so the organizations and researchers administering the games learn through the participants' play. Companies specializing in designing such Serious/Persuasive Games (there is actually a company called Persuasive Games[25]) know the value of such data, incorporating data and analytics into their designs for clients.

Where games and data collection blur lines: the case of *Miitomo* and how games are already using research techniques to find out more about people

While data have been collected through games for decades, some games are more overt than others in doing that, so much so that they border on becoming market research tools anyway.

Miitomo, the app game from Nintendo, is one of such games that overtly collect 'market research style' data from players – in fact the gameplay is based on *answering questions*. In *Miitomo*, you can create an avatar of yourself and 'tell your story'; you can share all your likes and dislikes with friends, while Nintendo finds out more and more about players. *Miitomo* even encourages the uploading and creation of visuals – uploading photos and drawing pictures to describe your favourite things or experiences. Their opening text in the app reads 'Listen to answers and answering questions will net you a few Miitomo coins' and so, each time players reveal more information, they are rewarded. Data are collected from players, and data are collected from market research participants, except in *Miitomo* players provide information about their experiences, preferences and so on without an incentive but market research suppliers often provide incentives. Despite no incentive for the *Miitomo* player, it was still played by some 10 million people in 2016.[26] You may argue that the people behind *Miitomo* are geniuses, doing the thing that so many researchers would love to do – gain data but without the added cost of having to offer participants any financial rewards. Indeed, the *Miitomo* 'game' could be a blueprint in how research can use games to find out more about participants on a long-term basis, but there is a huge drawback.

In an article on *Polygon*, written by the *Polygon* news editor and her team, they contribute stories and anecdotes about their *Miitomo* experiences.[27] In the contribution from the news editor, she notes: 'You aren't allowed to say or do whatever you want. You have to respond to questions only.' In the same article a senior reporter for *Polygon* went on to add: 'I stopped checking it regularly a week or two ago. I just got tired of answering its insipid, vaguely market-research-y questions (like asking me to name a recent advertisement that I liked).' The *Polygon* Product Manager went on to note: 'I need more to do than just get outfits, and answering questions isn't that fun.'

It is clear from these comments, which echo the sentiments of many other *Miitomo* players online, that there was not enough 'game' to keep their engagement and too much focus on just answering questions. Such questions will include 'What did you do last weekend?', asking where your favourite holiday destination is, and other unrelated questions on likes and dislikes about all sorts of subjects. As a result, Nintendo is shutting down *Miitomo*[28, 29] due to its decline in players. However, *Miitomo*'s loss can teach researchers four valuable lessons about using games as a tool to engage people in research:

1 **People don't like taking part in research that is disguised as a game:** another reason why game-based research, developed by researchers, needs to be honest about its approach to participants and make it clear that the platform is very much still a research tool.

2 **People do not wish to simply answer random questions – especially questions that don't seem to relate to each other:** a lesson for market

researchers – to ensure that our questions within a research-game or gamified survey are linked by subject to provide clear focus and immersion in a certain context or line of thinking.

3 **A research-game or gamified survey must do more than offer coins, real or virtual, in exchange for questions**: which is why all the other elements we explore in this book are so important, like offering self-discovery and transcendent value to participants, giving them a great user experience, and creating engaging gameplay. This is the biggest lesson from *Miitomo* – you can't just engage people with the superficial aspects of games like the coins and points.

4 **Finally, that there is so much more that games, as an instrument for research, can achieve**: simply asking questions in a game-like environment does not cut the mustard. This book explores how and why game-based research can be elevated, so research participants actually take away something far more valuable than just coins or points; they take away an experience.

However much it may sound like a dismissal of Nintendo's efforts to collect market research data through a game, and indeed, I don't think anyone but Nintendo employees know what they are doing with the data, Nintendo has achieved game-like research on a mass scale – something no research supplier or buyer has been able to do before. So those concerned about or threatened by the innovations of game-based research from the research industry should also have one eye on potential competition from the games industry, as *Miitomo* clearly shows.

What about gamification? Exploring how gamification is used to create playful experiences

Gamification is everywhere. Loyalty programmes are the most used go-to examples of gamification, and for good reason because it seems every company, from the large corporations to the independently run stores, now offers stamp and points cards. By collecting points based on your purchases, you level up, you gain higher status, you gain more rewards. Some businesses even offer bonuses, like the Boots loyalty card in the United Kingdom, which may offer 'triple weekend points' or similar. Such programmes built for loyalty and data collection have now come full circle; the loyalty programmes in themselves are conversation pieces within marketing: 'this weekend come to our store and earn double points on all purchases!'. As such, gamification typically affects more than one function in a business.

But herein lies one of the biggest issues with gamification: gamification is based on the foundations of extrinsic motivation. Gamification works on a 'do this, get that' approach. As we explored in Chapter 7, these types of extrinsic motivators don't always work and certainly don't encourage the kinds of intrinsic engagement and play we see with games. After all, when you hand your coffee store stamp card to the barista, do you feel like you're playing a game? And how intrinsically engaged and loyal are you really, when you have several other loyalty cards in your wallet?

The three most prominent components in gamification are:

1 **Status** – giving the user a name or label depending on status within the gamified activity. For example, *Foursquare* (now known as *Swarm*) would name a user a 'Mayor' if he or she reached the highest status.

2 **Social elements** – being able to find your friends and connect with them, or find people with similar interests around you. This is an ingrained component in social media.

3 **Levelling up with points, badges and stickers** – the more users do and/or progress, the more points they may achieve, and unlock badges that in themselves may signify new status. Some applications make their additional badges and levels part of a 'paywall' in that you cannot progress further unless an advanced package is purchased, or similar.

While these elements are indeed found *in* games, they are the more superficial aspects of games. But, that doesn't mean they are not effective. Success stories from well-designed gamified activities are plentiful.

For example, Audible, the e-book company, has gamified the process of listening to books, offering an array of badges such as 'night owl' for those who tend to read in the evenings, to 'weekend warriors' who reserve their reading for the end of the week. Such badges and points can only be awarded when things like the day people are reading, and the time they are reading or how much they are reading, is known. As such, digital gamified activities are synonymous with data collection – in fact you cannot have a digital gamified activity *without* data collection, and those data feed into further commercial endeavours, even improving the platforms themselves.

Game companies and companies selling games have gamified the *process* of playing games. Apple and Blizzard Entertainment (producers of games such as *Diablo* and *World of Warcraft*) produced the iPhone game centre and Real ID platform respectively. These platforms award players points and badges depending on games they have bought/downloaded, how many games they have played, and even badges based on *how* they play the games themselves. Again, such points and badges can only be awarded when data are collected. The tourism game *Play London with Mr Bean* also gamifies the process of playing a game combined with marketing and tourism where users can earn awards based on their gameplay.[30]

Codecademy,[31] the gamified learning platform that teaches people how to code in a variety of programming languages, has been so successful that at the time of writing, it has 45 million 'learners'.[32]

Nike, with its various gamification activities including *Nike+* and *Nike Fuel Missions*,[33] was able to use points, badges, status and social interaction to get 30 million people running, jogging and taking up another form of physical activity.[34] Not only were new products sold in the form of specific trainers and fuel bands, but it was an effective marketing campaign in itself.

Duolingo[35] introduced a gamified way of learning a new language. It has been so successful that according to Zan Gilani, the Associate Product Manager, *Duolingo* was the most downloaded and used education app in the world, with gamification being core to its success.[36]

The world's first photography game app, *GuruShots*,[37] gamifies the experience of taking photos and encourages players to improve their skill to win badges, points and real-world rewards from brands. Klout,[38] the now bought-out company, gamified the process of understanding and increasing your social media influence by providing a Klout score and badges depending on the quantity of your retweets, social media reach, and so on.

These examples are just a handful of literally thousands of companies producing gamified activities that are synonymous with engagement and data collection. The next chapter discusses experiential research approaches as part of the Triple E Effect – engagement, emotion and experience, exploring research experiences further using games as simulations to observe behaviours in context for untapped insight.

ACTIVITIES

- **Play and take part in some of the games and gamified activities mentioned in this chapter**

  Download *Zombies, Run!* Start a *SuperBetter* account. Play *Design Home, America's Army* and learn to code (even a little) with *Codecademy*. Pick at least five of the game or gamification examples noted in this chapter and explore them as a player but also as a researcher; you're on the hunt for inspiration.

Take notes: Are there any specific capabilities in these digital platforms that can cross over as effective research tools? Could you borrow, for instance, some of the role-play ideas in these games as projective techniques, or could you reflect the ways that some platforms illustrate progress or use narrative in your online community or tracker study? Take screengrabs of anything and everything that inspires you; create a **concept board** and keep referring to it next time you're designing a research experience.

- **Search for gamification and Serious Games**

  Look at how gamification is truly all around us. Make a list of gamified activities/websites/apps and so on that can act as sources of inspiration later on. What sort of activities have already been gamified? What activities have not been gamified yet?

Notes

1 www.campaignlive.co.uk/article cadbury-65m-spots-v-stripes-campaign-takes-off/1057390

2 https://tasteface.marmite.co.uk/

3 *CorbynRun*, developed b' Games for the Many: http://corbynrun.com/

4 The news item was also reflected in this article: http://www.bbc.co.uk/news/av/uk-politics-42215453/can-gaming-change-the-face-of-politics

5 http://www.happymeal.com/#games

6 http://molleindustria.org/nova-alea/

7 http://phonestory.org/

8 http://bigpharmagame.com/

9 McGill (2013) [accessed 21 May 2018] Lazy-eye disorder – a promising therapeutic approach, *McGill* [Online] www.mcgill.ca/newsroom/channels/news/lazy-eye-disorder-promising-therapeutic-approach-226011

10 Tiemann, Amy (2008) [accessed 21 May 2018] Re-Mission is a video game with a vital purpose, *CNET* [Online] www.cnet.com/news/re-mission-is-a-video-game-with-a-vital-purpose/

11 Blunden, Mark (2018) [accessed 21 May 2018] Medical marvels: this virtual reality game is helping young patients having surgery, *Evening Standard* [Online] www.standard.co.uk/tech/virtual-reality-game-young-patients-surgery-anxiety-a3791741.html

12 D'Anastassio, Cecilia (2017) [accessed 21 May 2018] One of 2017's Best Games Is About Being a Mortician, *Kotaku* [Online] https://kotaku.com/one-of-2017s-best-games-is-about-being-a-mortician-1819509818

13 Hung, Ya-Xuan, Huang, Pei-Chen, Chen, Kuan-Ta and Chu, Woei-Chyn (2016) [accessed 27 May 2018] What do stroke patients look for in game-based rehabilitation? A survey study [Online] www.ncbi.nlm.nih.gov/pmc/articles/PMC4839901/

14 Coulter, Michael (2015) [accessed 27 May 2018] Stroke rehabilitation study finds Nintendo Wii an effective treatment, *The Sydney Morning Herald* [Online] www.smh.com.au/national/stroke-rehabilitation-study-finds-nintendo-wii-an-effective-treatment-20151008-gk4bkh.html

15 *Zombies, Run!* game is available from: https://zombiesrungame.com/

16 Hamzelou, Jessica (2017) [accessed 28 May 2018] Teenage brains can't tell what's important and what isn't, *New Scientist* [Online] www.newscientist.com/article/2154884-teenage-brains-cant-tell-whats-important-and-what-isnt

17 Rosser, James C Jr, Lynch, Paul J, Cuddihy, Laurie *et al* (2007) [accessed 25 May 2018] The impact of video games on training surgeons in the 21st century, *JAMA Network* [Online] https://jamanetwork.com/journals/jamasurgery/fullarticle/399740

18 White, Sarah K (2016) [accessed 28 May 2018] How to know if workers are engaged (don't ask them), *CIO* [Online] www.cio.com/article/3126302/leadership-management/how-to-know-if-workers-are-engaged-don-t-ask-them.html

19 *America's Army* game: www.americasarmy.com/

20 Kenny, Brian (2002) [accessed 28 May 2018] Uncle Sam wants you (to play this game), *The New York Times* [Online] www.nytimes.com/2002/07/11/technology/uncle-sam-wants-you-to-play-this-game.html

21 Tassi, Paul (2014) [accessed 28 May 2018] Should video games go on your resume? *Forbes* [Online] www.forbes.com/sites/insertcoin/2014/08/14/should-video-games-go-on-your-resume

22 Hellyer, Isabelle (2017) [accessed 28 May 2018] 'Design Home' has completely taken over my life, *Vice* [Online] www.vice.com/en_au/article/53jp7d/design-home-has-completely-taken-over-my-life

23 www.crowdstar.com/

24 www.covetfashion.com/brands/

25 http://persuasivegames.com/

26 Lee, Tyler (2016) [accessed 28 May 2018] Miitomo has 10 million players, *Uber Gizmo* [Online] www.ubergizmo.com/2016/04/miitomo-10m-players-worldwide/

27 Frank, Allegra (2016) [accessed 28 May 2018] Here's why we've stopped playing Miitomo – and how Nintendo can win us back, *Polygon* [Online] www.polygon.com/2016/5/13/11671370/miitomo-review-nintendo-mobile-app

28 Byford, Sam (2018) [accessed 28 May 2018] Nintendo is shutting down Miitomo, *The Verge* [Online] www.theverge.com/2018/1/24/16930822/nintendo-miitomo-closing-down-date

29 Nintendo (2018) [accessed 30 May 2018] Miitomo end of service announcement [Online] http://en-americas-support.nintendo.com/app/answers/detail/a_id/28226/~/miitomo-end-of-service-announcement

30 *Play London with Mr Bean* by Pointvoucher Limited: www.play.london

31 *Codecademy* website: www.codecademy.com

32 Codecademy (2017) [accessed 28 May 2018] Codecademy's 2017 Retrospective, *Codecademy* [Online] https://news.codecademy.com/2017-retrospective-great-reeducation

33 Streams, Kimber (2012) [accessed 28 May 2018] NikeFuel Missions make daily exercise into an exciting game, *The Verge* [Online] www.theverge.com/2012/12/18/3780898/nikefuel-missions-exercise-game

34 Hoffman, Elizabeth (2015) [accessed 28 May 2018] Nike: Creating a digital ecosystem (and leaving hardware to the other guys), *Harvard Business School* [Online] www.hbs.edu/openforum/openforum.hbs.org/challenge/understand-digital-transformation-of-business/why-digital/nike-creating-a-digital-ecosystem-and-leaving-hardware-to-the-other-guys/comments.html

35 https://www.duolingo.com/

36 Draycott, Richard (2017) [accessed 28 May 2018] Gamification is the key to Duolingo success says product manager Gilani at Canvas conference, *The Drum* [Online] www.thedrum.com/news/2017/10/26/gamification-the-key-duolingo-success-says-product-manager-gilani-canvas-conference

37 https://gurushots.com

38 Russell, John (2018) [accessed 21 May 2018] RIP Klout, *TechCrunch* [Online] https://techcrunch.com/2018/05/10/rip-klout/

The Triple E Effect

10

Games as engaging, emotive and experiential simulations for research and insight

This chapter explores:

- why evoking emotive experiences is important in market research;
- benefits of the Triple E Effect: engagement, emotion and experience in game-based surveys;
- benefits of replaying simulations in 'alternate realities' to understand context effect and develop predictive models.

Four reasons why evoking emotive experiences is important in market research

1 **Emotion and context influence choice and behaviour.** Emotion and the contexts that form experiences *drive* choice and behaviour. Contexts like how much time consumers have, how much money they have to spend and how they feel (as well as other factors) not only impact what people purchase, but also how they physically move and occupy a space – their behaviour. Researchers know this already; this understanding about context and behaviours that arise with different limitations, opportunity and emotion is what has spurred deprivation studies, ethnography, conjoint studies and other methodologies where context is crucial.

2 Researchers want to understand what emotions and contexts influence choice and behaviour. From the literature on behavioural economics and psychology, researchers understand that context is crucial. Research buyers use this information to support their product development endeavours, pricing models, marketing campaigns and more.

3 We need to understand emotion to *create* emotion with brands. 'We think very rationally in the market research industry, but the fundamental premise of marketing is to generate emotional reactions. It's why marketing and design exist. It's often why consumers pay more for a product than it costs to make.[1] The ways in which research buyers want to apply insight is often to engage with consumers on an emotive level. Thus emotion is important to understand not only when thinking about context, but in how brands develop meaningful relationships with consumers.

4 Explaining behaviour and choices isn't always accurate. Research tells us that humans are bad at articulating the reasons why we do things. Asking participants to post-rationalize their decisions doesn't always answer the 'why' accurately. As Jeffrey Henning, market research expert, recounts of a presentation by Aaron Reid and Stephen Springfield of Sentient Decision Science: 'Traditional surveys uncover rationalizations, not reasons. We cannot reliably evaluate, anticipate, nor communicate the impact of emotions on our behaviours.'[2] Creating digital environments in which researchers can plug in different stimuli, limitations and opportunities can allow researchers to watch the participant play (remember, we already discussed play as a data generator). Using this 'plug and play' approach, researchers won't even need to ask questions, but set up a narrative with some instruction and observe how participants respond.

Where digital games are proven to:

- evoke emotion – and a wide range of complex emotions;
- provide experiences – and even conceptual experiences;
- spur players to replay a game time and again;

this means games are uniquely placed for use in market research to allow participants to act through any constructed emotive landscape, rather than having to explain their behaviours and choices, as well as allowing participants to replay a variety of simulations so that researchers can understand the true mindset of consumers in any given context.

The benefits of the Triple E Effect

Intrinsic engagement, emotion and experience are synonymous with each other. Indeed, anything experiential evokes emotion.[3] So much so that emotive experiences in digital content are encouraged to increase engagement and 'enrich interactions and communications'.[4] Because we have already extensively explained the role of intrinsic engagement in market research by borrowing from games, this chapter focuses on emotive experience through simulations in game-based research.

In market research, what I call the Triple E Effect is a triple-win, where researchers can explore game-based surveys to their full powerful potential, beyond increasing engagement, in order to:

- evoke desirable behaviours from participants that hold commercial value for market researchers;
- go beyond intrinsic engagement to provide emotive, experiential platforms that get to the heart of how participants think, feel and understand what they are likely to do in a variety of scenarios that can be observed through simulations;
- use data collected from such simulations to help to generate predictive models on outcomes; anything from likeliness of user behaviour and purchases, to how people might react to changes in product design and even governmental policies.

Through the Triple E effect researchers can also:

- evoke relevant emotions to allow for state-dependent recall and more detailed and rich imaginings of past, present and future contexts;
- create empathy when using role-play techniques to immerse participants in the role, especially roles that participants may have never experienced before, like running a bank or even a country.

Emotive experiences

Emotional memories can be activated by images, thoughts or words. 'Somatic markers'[5] allow us to anticipate how it would feel if we took an action or a decision, making humans experts at vividly experiencing 'future emotions' and recalling past emotions. This is useful in market research as research buyers often task participants to imagine future scenarios and recall the past, for example: 'why did you buy this laundry detergent?' to 'if you managed a political party, what policies would you prioritize'? Future scenarios are uncertainties that the participant couldn't possibly foretell. The somatic marker hypothesis proposes that emotions play a critical role in the ability to make fast, rational decisions in complex and uncertain situations. Emotions motivate every human action and intention,[6] therefore if researchers want to understand the motivations of intent, then evoking emotion is the way to gain such insight.

Games simulate emotive experiences, even with low-fi graphics and just text-on-a-screen

Games are uniquely able to place players in emotive simulations of experiences, more than any other medium like music or film. So much so that many Serious Games prioritize the emotive effects of simulations to maximize engagement[7] and big organizations want a slice of this lucrative pie. For example, McGraw-Hill Education, a learning science company and educational publisher, is planning to produce 50 simulation environment games in 2018. They say: 'The simulations and scenarios provide opportunities for students to apply their learning in experiential situations that mimic "real-life" work scenarios.'[8] In the simulation of emotive experiences, market research will feel more meaningful to participants and provide value beyond financial incentives.

For a game-based survey, emotive experiences can be constructed as long as the words and semiotics of the visual components, narrative and other elements work in harmony with the research content to support participant immersion; there must be internal consistency in the 'game-based survey world'. We see this kind of internal consistency working to great immersive effect in videogames all the time. As James Newman, game expert and author, writes in *In Search of the Videogame Player* (2002): 'in recounting their play, videogame players talk of "inhabiting worlds" and the experience of "being there" rather than remotely controlling or manipulating icons or characters.'[9] As such, if a game-based survey is well-designed with internal consistency, participants can too feel that they experience 'being there', whether that 'there' is in a past, present or future context, or in a realistic or conceptual environment. Emotions are so strong in videogame players that there are real psychophysiological responses – where the body and mind physically react, from sitting on the edge of your seat to an increase in heart rate and sweaty palms. The emotive experiences in games are therefore felt in the real world – they are *real emotions* being experienced. Even the use of 'I' with game-players is telling, where players may say 'I won!' or 'I died again!'.

The game ingredients, game components, game elements and game values all play their roles in evoking emotive experiential simulations, especially considering that each of these aspects evoke emotion on their own: narrative, music, the emotional connections with an avatar, the aesthetic of the game, the use of timers, being able to 'live and breathe' through others in a game world and so on.[10, 11]

If you were concerned that a game-based survey wouldn't be fantastical or exciting enough to benefit from the Triple E Effect, you would be mistaken. Games also immerse players in realistic (bordering on the mundane) experiences and are just as emotive and engaging. For example, in the game *Cart Life* (Richard Hofmeier, 2013), players understand what it is like to run a street stall. They embody characters that try to balance multiple life aspects while making money. The designer interviewed street vendors to ensure he got the details about their lives correct, much like a game-based survey designer is encouraged to create a Participant Profile and deeply research the objectives before they embark on their design. As a result of Hofmeier's research and the design, the game 'masterfully evokes in players the feeling that there is never enough time ... [and] succeeds in creating feelings of struggle and triumph and connection'.[12] Thus the role of the designer, and the role of the game-based survey designer, **is directly and instrumentally significant in the emotions that can be constructed in a research-game or gamified survey.** Games journalist Colin Campbell notes how game designers manipulate emotions: 'the men and women who are tinkering with our interactions in order to make us feel what they want us to feel, and what we have volunteered to feel' involves letting go of yourself to a certain degree 'to the desires and goals of the designers'.[13]

While mediums like music or film evoke emotion, some emotions are unique to games. For instance, where a player may experience shame, guilt or feelings of complicity when playing a game. Such intense feelings are not necessarily experienced when, say, reading a book. And why? Because games have the uncanny ability to place us in a character's shoes and/or to experience a new narrative as ourselves; to be so deeply immersed in another world that when forced to make certain decisions in a game, players feel the emotions as if they, in real life, were making those choices, where they can sit and deliberate those choices because they know their decisions will have consequence. **The choices in a game have meaning.** As such, games as an instrument for market research can evoke emotions and experiences that are unattainable via any other media, making GbRM unique in gaining untapped insight.

But why is the experiential nature of games important in research too? If life is experiential, and market research seeks to uncover conscious and non-conscious opinions, feelings and aspects of our lives, then research must be experiential too.

We are all experience seekers. The rise in experiential activities to engage consumers has been felt the world over; from novelty gyms to ball-pit night clubs and sleepovers at museums, everyone wants something experiential. The game *Hunt a Killer* allows people to solve fictional mysteries in the real world through deciphering messages and objects they receive in the post. *The Mysterious Package Company* does the same. *Confidential*,[14] the theatrical participatory experience, lets you 'live a night as a secret agent'. *Secret Cinema*,[15] the immersive movie experience, builds a 'movie world' in the real world, often recreating small versions of the towns and cities depicted in film. The *Back to the Future* experience of 2015 included real stores where you could purchase 1950s-style clothes, get a 1950s-style haircut and eat in 1950s diners. Prior to entry, customers are given a character name and told what costumes to adopt (and your costume can represent your status, character type or level). As such, the *Secret Cinema* experience begins months before attendance, creating inspiration, curiosity and intrigue.

In marketing, the 2010 *Catch-a-Choo* campaign from the Jimmy Choo brand used London as its game board.[16] Brought about by marketing company FreshNetworks to help create a buzz about Jimmy Choo's new trainer collection, the focal point was that social media was used, for one of the first times in this context, in marketing. In three weeks, 4,500 players went on a treasure hunt to catch hidden Jimmy Choo shoes,[17] and if you caught them, you kept them. Not only was this an effective experiential marketing campaign and did indeed create a buzz, it also raised sales by 33 per cent daily during this campaign.

These experiences are popular and commercially lucrative. As hundreds of brands move towards experiential approaches for consumer interaction, we see more interest and adoption in games and gamification as these approaches lend themselves so easily to providing experiences, and experiences like engagement and emotion are a hot commodity.

What these brands have in common is that by using games and gamification for experiential interactions, it means they are also providing *unique types* of engagement. So as well as gaining and growing engagement from new and existing audiences and collecting data, they are standing out from the competition. If your brand is producing engaging, experiential forms of marketing, training, recruitment and, in our case, market research, then you can be a step ahead of your competitors.

Exploring text-adventure games: harnessing experience and emotion with simple graphics and/or just text on a screen

But what if you don't have the time or money to create visual research-games or gamified surveys, complete with narrative and music for a 360-degree immersive and emotive experience? You can adopt the 'text-adventure' style simulations we see in many engaging games. If you're a game-based survey designer on a budget, you can still evoke and benefit from the Triple E Effect, and allow participants to imagine different situations with nothing but text-on-a-screen. The power of narrative, even if that narrative is articulated just as text, can place participants in relevant emotional contexts. **Surveys are just underdeveloped text-adventure games.**

Case in point: observe the screengrabs (Figure 10.1) from the text-adventure game *Grayout* (Mrgan LLC, 2015).[18] *Grayout* puts the player in the role of being someone at the heart of a conspiracy. The black text at the top of the screen is words that are spoken to you, and the white words underneath are words you can choose to reply in the conversation. With just text-on-a-screen, *Grayout* completely places you in the emotional context of being under heavy-dose medication where it is a frustrating struggle to form even simple sentences. As you struggle to find the words, your own actions as a player simulate the struggles of the character you are embodying who is also finding it hard to remember the appropriate words to speak. Be inspired by how we can use interactions of a similar ilk from text-adventure games like *Grayout* (and *Zork*, *MetaHuman Inc* and *A Wise Choice of Time*, both from Choice of Games LLC,[19] and many others) to transport participants into someone else's shoes, place them in relevant contexts, and encourage emotion through just text-on-a-screen. Again, these capabilities are possible using existing survey software. It's our imaginations that can make the text in a survey dull or evoke the Triple E Effect.

Figure 10.1 *Grayout* game, published by Neven Mrgan

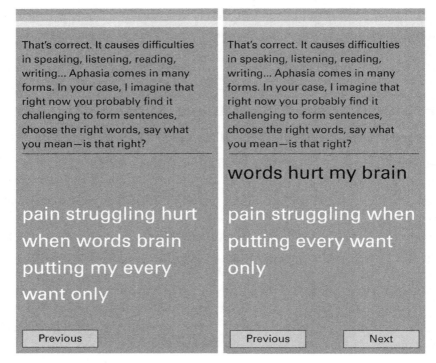

SOURCE © Neven Mrgan

A text-based research-game example

Borrowing from text-adventure games, on the next page is a simple example of a simulation with two scenarios: the participant is busy with limited time and money; the participant has plenty of time and no set financial budget.

While this is a very simple emotive and experiential simulation, it tasks participants to imagine aspects of their lives in a way traditional surveys do not. Coupled with actual music and visuals, these text-based simulations can become more emotive and immersive with just a little more effort. This text-adventure asks participants to *imagine* these different scenarios – but what if, through digital game-based simulations, we could *show* them instead?

START

MONDAY MORNING. Round 1.

You're in a supermarket.

It's busy and crowded with people. It's very noisy.

You only have 15 minutes to get your groceries or you'll be late for your doctor's appointment.

Your baby is crying, and your phone is ringing, but you need to get some supplies right now otherwise you won't have much in the house later.

How do you feel?

I FEEL _____

You try to make it through the crowds while trying to calm the baby and ignore your phone. With only 15 minutes, what are the essentials you need to buy for your home? (Add more lines if you need to.)

Your 15-minute timer begins now. Press finish when you're done.

1. _____ Approx. price $ _____

2. _____ Approx. price $ _____

3. _____ Approx. price $ _____

TOTAL PRICE (*calculated from participant response above*) $ _____

Oh no. You've just realized you only have $10.00! Does this change what you keep on your list? If so, remove an item by simply putting a line through it.
If not, proceed to Round 2.

FINISH

MONDAY MORNING. Round 2.

You're in a supermarket.

It's empty with just the sound of a few people talking and the store music. You're so pleased you've been able to find time to do some much needed grocery shopping. You could spend over an hour in here if necessary, buying everything you need for the home. Your baby is with a sitter, who has been paid to stay as long as needed. Someone is giving out free cake samples, yum! You take a bite, why not?

How do you feel?

I FEEL _____ (revealed: earned 10 points)

You begin down the first aisle, ready to start shopping. What are you buying today?

(A timer will begin – take as long as you need. Press finish when you've done your shopping and add more lines if you need to.)

1. _____ Approx. price $ _____

2. _____ Approx. price $ _____

3. _____ Approx. price $ _____

TOTAL PRICE (*calculated from participant response above*) $ _____

Nice surprise! Just found $15.00 in your pocket. You decide to treat yourself to a luxury item.

What's the luxury item? IT'S A _____ .

How much is this? IT'S $ _____ .

FINISH

Welcome to the Supermarket Simulation!
A text-adventure game where researchers understand how
emotion and context drives behaviour and choices.

Simple 'story games': visual but narrative-led and text-based simulations

Download *Episode* (Episode Interactive LLC, 2016) and have a play of the game to get a feel for it (available in the App and Google Play stores, or search for gameplay videos online). *Episode* is essentially a narrative and role-play led questionnaire, where the player is asked questions and has a range of choices that may or may not impact how the game unfolds. In *Episode*, your character interacts with other characters, making the conversations feel more personal as you are able to contribute to the conversations using your own choices, rather than watch a narrative unfold (which is common in many games).

There is much researchers can borrow from this game to inspire game-based survey design as 'online qual'. In this game, we have characters with different personalities to feel connected with, as well as our own character that we can build (through an avatar maker) in our likeness. This, coupled with the fact that players are placed in relevant and context-based virtual environments, is what helps to engross them in the story. The 2D images of 3D environments depicted in this game (for example, chatting on a street or in a college classroom) are absolutely within the capabilities of existing survey software. Researchers could also use 2D images of 3D environments in a research-game or gamified survey. Also look at how these background images work in harmony with asking questions, or setting up scenarios and giving the player options of choices. *Episode* is one type of blueprint in how researchers can use existing survey software to create observable 'conversations' with participants that feel more natural, and are much more akin to how we communicate in everyday life, rather than the 'anonymous' voice of traditional online surveys.

Telltale Games is a games studio that has been producing story-led games since 2004. I was first introduced to their games some years ago now, after watching my husband play *The Wolf Among Us* (2013) in which, like the *Episode* games, you are placed in different scenarios and are offered choices that will have different outcomes. The key with these Telltale games is that they are episodic, so players may download the game which, say, comes ready to play with five episodes (or levels) and you might need to wait some time before more episodes are released. This in itself can inspire the way researchers approach long-term online studies. Game-based tracker studies could be episodic like Telltale games where we can build engagement and anticipation among participants.

Similar games, where players make choices to shape the narrative, are *The Stanley Parable* (Galactic Cafe), *Life Is Strange* (Square Enix) and *Mass Effect 2* (Electronic Arts) among many others.

Replaying simulations in 'alternate realities' to understand context effect and develop predictive models

I remember being in a science class at school and we were given a machine that had one program: a simulation for fox and rabbit populations. There were no fancy graphics – this was just coloured squares on the screen. One colour represented foxes and another the rabbits. You would program how many foxes and rabbits you wanted, press play, and then watch what might be a complete horror-show of foxes annihilating rabbits, or a harmonious balance of both animal populations. As a child, of course, you would try all the extremes: one fox to a million rabbits, one rabbit to 1,000 foxes. Eventually, you would find a balance so both populations could thrive.

I thought, how could we use this kind of simulation in research? Could we have the same sort of rudimentary program in which people could input the various conditions for which they would buy a specific product, be it fabric softener or a can of beans? What about social and political research? Could researchers use simulations like this in their work with government and other non-profit organizations to see how department-specific expenditure would impact their cause and the future? Could people input how much money the government spends on various projects in a simulation, press play, and watch an alternate reality unfold? Crucially, the data and insight we could gather from such simulations would be instrumental in shaping everything around us.

The fox and the rabbit simulation is partly what inspired the *Designer for a Day* ResearchGame I designed on behalf of a Fortune 500 apparel portfolio brand.[20] In the ResearchGame, participants could input different aspects of activewear bottoms like the length of their pants, the rise, shape, colour and so on, then see what the pants look like in real time, and see the price of the pants increase or decrease depending on their choices. Who would have thought that the fox and rabbit 8-bit simulation I played in the 1990s would have been an inspiration many years later? This is why researchers should play *all* kinds of games; you never know what inspiration will resonate for a future game-based survey design.

Conjoint studies, the projective techniques we use in focus groups and online research, and the ways we might ask participants to imagine completely new products – all these methods are ways that researchers immerse participants in alternate realities. We ask: 'what if this wine bottle had a larger label – would you buy it? What if we used this colour instead of that, would you buy it now?' We are already asking them to replay, just as players do with games.

Being able to die in a game and become respawned, or restart from a certain point in a level, has been a feature of digital games since games were created. When players replay games, they change their behaviours for a result – that is, to finish the level in a certain amount of time, or to overcome a specific obstacle in the 'correct way', or to earn a certain quantity of points and so on.

You may wonder 'would any participant replay a research-game?' The answer is 'yes'. Not only have participants replayed my ResearchGames (despite no additional incentives) but, of course, we know that players replay games and enjoy doing so; they literally relive the same scenarios over and over again, albeit changing their behaviour and choices until an ideal outcome is reached.

Researchers could include replay opportunities to allow participants to interact with (potentially countless) simulations of the same event, but with incremental changes to existing stimuli and/or different stimuli. As long as participants were as intrinsically engaged as players are with games, asking them to replay a game-based survey wouldn't seem like a chore as participants will be experiencing the joy and flow that comes with play. Researchers can completely gamify the conjoint survey while taking advantage of replay capabilities. This can help researchers build predictive models.

Predictive modelling uses AI and automation to allow past data and probability to determine potential future outcomes. If game-based surveys are used as simulations of various events and to test a variety of stimulus material, gain enough data and that can allow researchers to forecast the future; for example, if X happens, then Y is likely to occur. Predictive modelling can also be used as a simulation in itself, much like the fox and rabbit simulation, which used existing data from research and probability to shape the populations depending on different conditions like the type of environment, size of environment, and the number of foxes and rabbits and so on. Predictive modelling can help research buyers become proactive instead of reactive, and even help spur the development of products and services that were previously unimagined. (More about future forecasting and predictive models through game-based surveys is noted in Chapter 24.)

Five places to start on creating emotive, experiential simulations in game-based surveys

David Freeman, game designer and author of *Creating Emotion in Games: The craft and art of emotioneering* (2003), has identified 1,500 ways to create emotion in games including building chemistry between players, giving the game narratives interesting plots, and including 'true to life' principals, among many others.[21] In *How Games Move Us: Emotion by design* (2017)[22] the author Katherine Isbister also takes us through concrete ways games induce emotion with examples. These two books, and many other papers, conference talks, research studies, videos, show that inducing emotion in games (and thus game-based surveys) is not something that can be covered with a few quick tips. It is a *huge* area of study and so further reading is wholeheartedly encouraged. However, these pieces of advice are good places to make a start:

1 **Think like a 'Brand Experience Curator'.** Imagine your sole job was to make the research experiential through the lens of the six vital states (as explored earlier in Chapter 7). Would you approach the game-based survey design differently? Yes.

2 **Evaluate how your participants feel about the research content *before* you design.** Look at your research objectives through the Triple E Effect lens: how do your participants already feel about the research content, product or service being discussed? What about if you're placing participants in future scenarios or 'alternate realities', how might they feel given the choices available to them? Would they feel a sense of urgency, frustration, pride, joy? Can you (safely and tactfully) build the relevant emotive landscapes (through using the game ingredients, components, elements and values) to understand how those emotions drive behaviours and choices?

3 **Experiment with the game ingredients, components, elements and values to evoke emotive, experiential simulations.** Narrative, the use of timers, the aesthetic of a digital interface, the relationships people build with their avatars, the use of role-play, music and so on can all be used as tools to generate emotive experiences. The best way to understand how these game techniques do that is to play a wide range of Serious Games and Emotional Games. Only through having these kind of play experiences can researchers understand the nuances and intricacies of how games do this.

4 **Ensure the choices in the game-based survey have impact to create meaning.** Games referenced throughout this book like *Episode* (Episode Interactive LLC), *Choices* (Pixelberry Studios), *The Wolf Among Us* (Telltale Games), *The Stanley Parable* (Galactic Cafe), *Life Is Strange* (Square Enix) and *Mass Effect 2* are engaging because the choices made in the game have narrative weight and meaning. These games have a 'if this, then that' quality. To produce meaning means there needs to be a tangible impact – perhaps this is why traditional surveys are unengaging because participants usually never get to see the impact of their choices. In games, impact is crucial. Gordon Calleja, game designer, who also created the Player Involvement Model, has identified six dimensions that relate to each other that generate emotional involvement with games, from 'narrative involvement' (engagement with the game story) to 'ludic involvement' (where players are engaged with the choices they make in a game). He writes: 'Without repercussions, actions lose their meaning and thus the emotional excitement (affective involvement) generated by their execution (kinaesthetic involvement).'[23]

This is easily translated into a game-based survey environment; how can you ensure that participants, who might be tasked to make choices on product design, product name and prices, see impact? You can allow them to see the changes visibly and let them see what kind of effect that might have on other sales, profit margins and so on in a simulation (like the foxes and rabbits program). This also provides a learning opportunity (knowledge value) that is enjoyable for participants.

5 **Take part in anything experiential.** Go to a *Secret Cinema* experience and immerse yourself between the borders of film and reality. Dine in complete darkness in the *Dans Le Noir?* concept restaurant. Buy tickets to an immersive theatre experience. Keep tabs on the experiential marketing on offer from your favourite and not-so-favourite brands. You never know how someone else's experiential and playful approaches to products and services will open your eyes and mind to how you curate emotive and experiential research-games or gamified surveys. Take notes: write down the key things that evoked emotion and elevated your experience; think about the common themes or patterns you can employ in your game-based surveys.

Notes

1 Henning, Jeffrey (2017) [accessed 4 June 2018] *Putting Emotion into the Equation* [Blog] Recounting a presentation delivered at The Market Research Event (TMRE), Orlando, Florida by Aaron Reid and Stephen Springfield of Sentient Decision Science [Online] https://blog.mrii.org/putting-emotion-into-the-equation

2 Henning, Jeffrey (2017) [accessed 4 June 2018] *Putting Emotion into the Equation* [Blog] [Online] https://blog.mrii.org/putting-emotion-into-the-equation/

3 Plummer, Joe, Zaltman, Gerald and Mast, Fred (2006) [accessed 25 May 2018] Engagement: Definitions and Anatomy, Proceedings of the Advertising Research Foundations workshop [Online]

4 Grimes, Seth (2015) [accessed 25 May 2018] Faces, Emotions, and Insights: Q&A with Affectiva Principal Scientist Daniel McDuff, *Breakthrough Analysis* [Online] https://breakthroughanalysis.com/2015/06/29/mcduff/

5 Somatic markers are feelings in the body that are associated with emotions, such as the association of rapid heartbeat with anxiety or of nausea with disgust. More can be found at: Damasio, Antonio R (2008) [1994] *Descartes' Error: Emotion, reason and the human brain*, Random House

6 Markus and Kitayama (1991) cited in Perlovsky, L (2014) [accessed 4 June 2018] Mystery in experimental psychology, how to measure aesthetic emotions? *Frontier in Psychology*, 5 [Online] www.researchgate.net/publication/308866844_Mystery_in_experimental_psychology_aesthetic_emotions

7 Campbell, Colin (2016) [accessed 25 May 2018] Emotion, manipulation and the future of game design, *Polygon* [Online] www.polygon.com/2016/3/30/11319406/emotions-video-games

8 McGraw-Hill Education (2018) [accessed 25 May 2018] *McGraw-Hill Education delivers new game-based learning simulations in higher education course materials*, McGraw-Hill [Online] www.mheducation.com/news-media/press-releases/new-game-based-learning-simulations-higher-education.html

9 Newman, James (2002) [accessed 25 May 2018] In search of the videogame player: The lives of Mario, *SAGE Publications*, 4 (3), pp 405–422 [Online] http://journals.sagepub.com/doi/pdf/10.1177/146144480200400305

10 Frome, Jonathan (2007) [accessed 25 May 2018] Eight ways videogames generate emotion, Proceedings of DiGRA 2007 Conference [Online] www.digra.org/wp-content/uploads/digital-library/07311.25139.pdf

11 Isbister, K (2017) *How Games Move Us: Emotion by design*, MIT Press, Cambridge, MA

12 Isbister, K (2017) *How Games Move Us: Emotion by design*, MIT Press, Cambridge, MA

13 Campbell, Colin (2016) [accessed 25 May 2018] Emotion, manipulation and the future of game design, *Polygon* [Online] www.polygon.com/2016/3/30/11319406/emotions-video-games

14 *Confidential The Game*: www.confidentialthegame.com [accessed 22 May 2018]

15 *Secret Cinema*: www.secretcinema.org [accessed 22 May 2018]

16 WGSN (2010) [accessed 22 May 2018] To Catch a Choo [Blog] [Online] www.wgsn.com/blogs/to-catch-a-choo/#

17 FreshNetworks (2010) [accessed 22 May 2018] Campaign management & long-term strategy, *Slideshare* [Online] www.slideshare.net/freshnetworks/jimmy-choo-pep-foursquare-web-4667255

18 *Grayout* game: http://mrgan.com/grayout

19 *Choice of Games*: www.choiceofgames.com/category/our-games [accessed 22 May 2018]

20 Research study fielded in January 2016 with 2,208 participants. The case study was presented at the IMPACT MRS Annual Conference, 15 March 2017, London, and as part of the proceedings of the ISPO event, Munich, 29 January 2018

21 Freeman, David (2004) [accessed 25 May 2018] Creating emotion in games: The craft and art of emotioneering™, *ACM Computers in Entertainment*, **2** (3), July 2004, Article 8a [Online] www.skynet.ie/~ogami/notes/year%204/writing/Freeman_emotioneering04.pdf

22 Isbister, K (2017) *How Games Move Us: Emotion by design*, MIT Press, Cambridge, MA

23 Calleja, Gordon (2011) [accessed 25 May 2018] Emotional involvement in digital games, *International Journal of Arts and Technology*, **4** (1) [Online] https://www.inderscienceonline.com/doi/abs/10.1504/IJART.2011.03776

Case studies and results from game-based research

11

This chapter explores:

- limitations and opportunities of case studies on game-based research methods (GbRM) to date;
- the benefits of game-based online research methods by looking at 10 years of papers and presentations;
- five case studies from my own designs through Research Through Gaming Ltd (RTG).

Limitations of case studies on game-based research methods (GbRM)

Games and gamification have been applied in online research for over a decade with some favourable, unfavourable and mixed results. These results (even the good ones) are problematic to interpret because we must unpack:

- the research designers' understanding of the definitions of games and gamification;
- whether their design approach adhered to those definitions (even when there are good results, was gamification actually being used, or is there another approach with a better-suited term that can help more researchers take advantage of the beneficial technique?);
- the levels of game play and game design experience the research designer has had in the past.

Often the researchers designing the game-based approaches may not necessarily have digital UX design, game design or other related design experience. Through personal discussions with these peers, some admit to having minimal experience playing digital games. By contrast, it would be hard to find a game designer who has never played a game; playing games is recognized as one of their most important resources. For a game-based survey designer, playing games and experimenting with game design prior to embarking on game-based research design is as crucial as having research knowledge and experience.

There has also been design and labelling confusion, for instance:

- What some researchers have constituted as gamification in their case studies would have been better suited as case studies on surveytainment.

- What has been labelled as a game in some case studies is not a fully-fledged game, but a survey that has been gami*fied* – a gamified survey.

- The terms 'game' and 'gamification' have been used interchangeably in research papers and presentations, leading to confusion around design and its links to impact.

- Some case studies that have used GbRM have had little to no internal consistency; where graphics and gameplay are not related to the research content. This has, in some cases, created detrimental results such as distracted and confused participants, and actually lowered data quality, completion rates and participant engagement.

- Some case studies are only focused on using rudimentary aesthetic and interaction techniques common in some games, like 'shooting' the answer to questions or changing the aesthetic of the cursor.

It is difficult to unpack the results, as there are several moving parts. However, there are commonalities in the ways that market researchers have designed their approach to gamified surveys:

- **Rewording questions** to sound more playful but without a surrounding game-framework. For instance, using a less formal tone and making each question sound like a challenge.

- **Using a single game component or game element with a couple of game ingredients,** such as the use of feedback and rules with a timer and narrative (but in some cases, the narratives used are unrelated to the research content).

- **Only changing the aesthetic elements and using dynamic question types** such as 'drag and drop' functions and using pictures, where again, visuals may or may not be unrelated to the research content.

In the situations where game-based approaches have not worked well, there could be a number of reasons. While pitfalls might be due to design, we must remember that with no formal design guidelines in place to date, many researchers attempting to improve research through using game-based techniques have been 'shooting in the dark', therefore every experiment is important, and has provided education in this space.

Opportunities of case studies on game-based research methods

The silver lining is that the efforts made represent a huge turning point in market research; it's potentially the first time in a long time that, when considering these techniques, market researchers have consciously reassessed the aesthetic, layout, language and overall enjoyability of their surveys, essentially carrying out a 'UX overhaul'. This has contributed to an industry-wide re-evaluation of general survey design. As we know, there is no reinvention without trial and error.

Rather than spend time unpacking why previous case studies showed unfavourable results, this chapter will focus on where game-based research has performed well so we can take these learnings with us into the future. We'll also look at five case studies from RTG to look at the results and impact. Where available, information and results pertaining to each case study will be included.

What we know: benefits of using game-based research methods

Even when case studies have only used rudimentary game-like techniques, like the three common approaches noted earlier, there have *still* been positive results. Below is an accumulated list of benefits noted in the case study based publications that used the three most common approaches, and from my own case studies using ResearchGames through Research Through Gaming Ltd. These results are a mix of outcomes that have been both compared with other research methodologies (like traditional and flash-based online surveys) and through analysis as 'standalone' studies. The papers and other publications that were studied to produce these lists of benefits are included in this chapter's Notes.[1–18]

The benefits are divided between benefits to research suppliers and buyers, benefits to the participants, and benefits to the industry at large.

Benefits to research suppliers and buyers

- Lower drop-out rates.
- Decreased straightlining.
- Increased response rates.
- Increased completion rates.
- Increased continuation rates (where a single study may have multiple touchpoints, ie more than one survey).
- More focused respondents.
- Richer data are provided in open-end verbatim questions through more descriptive responses.
- Increased word count in open-end responses.
- Higher levels of responsiveness.
- More 'work' being carried out, such as participants evaluating more items and taking part in voluntary activities.
- Less time in field due to increased response and completion rates.
- Time (and money) saved due to less time in field.
- Increased likelihood that participants will take part in more game-based research through self-reported enjoyment and requests to participate in more.
- Answer time in both open-end verbatim response fields and 'tick box' answers can be longer (when there is no sense of urgency, such as a time limit).
- More likely to provide accurate and complete answers, thus data quality and validity are improved, and we find out more about the 'true mindset' of participants.
- Through the capabilities inherent in games, researchers can capture data that traditional online surveys cannot gather, such as data from the behaviour of a participant-controlled avatar in a simulated environment.
- Stimulate memory and simulate contexts in a way traditional survey techniques cannot do.
- Better nationally representative sample.
- When designed specifically for instinctive answers (for example, with an on-screen timer), game-based approaches can discourage deliberation for more 'System 1' thinking.

- Can bridge the 'empathy gap', where we bring participants in a 'hot state' to replicate the feelings and contexts that they would during the decision-making processes in real life, rather than the 'cold state' of traditional online surveys.

Benefits to the participant

- Increased engagement (self-reported, and seen through increased completion rates, as well as from analysis on richness of responses).
- Increased enjoyment (self-reported).
- Continuation desire (again, self-reported and seen through replaying the survey despite no other incentive offered, and continuing to a follow-up survey).

Benefits to the market research industry at large

- Pushed boundaries in technology and design application. Researchers have experimented with new design and new applications of existing survey software and in the case of Research Through Gaming, created new software for the purposes of building and executing ResearchGames.
- Introduced new skills and talent to market research; game design professionals and graduates have been hired to work with me on game-based research studies. Approximately 500 people to date (students and market research professionals) have attended my workshops to learn new skills in game-based research techniques.
- Increased client engagement – where clients have taken cameo roles in ResearchGames, are more invested in the research process, and by their own admission have had their wider team interested in the study and its outcomes more than when traditional surveys have been used.
- Increased market researcher engagement; market researchers attending my workshops and presentations have said they are more interested and engaged with market research as a result of understanding more about game-based techniques.
- Increased engagement among the next generation of market researchers; where students have said they are more engaged with market research and research careers as a result of understanding more about game-based methods.

Through the use of GbRM *everyone* involved in market research stands to benefit.

Case studies from Research Through Gaming Ltd

These case studies provide an overview of the results from using Research-Games produced by Research Through Gaming Ltd (RTG). Through eight years of designing and using ResearchGames as a research instrument, I have seen consistent displays of intrinsic participant engagement and research impact through insight. The five case studies below are different in terms of research objectives and participant demographics to show the plasticity in which game-based approaches can be applied.

PRE-TESTING CASE STUDY Testing the concept of using games as research instruments

In a study I conducted as part of a research paper for the CASRO Las Vegas 2010 conference,[19] I collaborated with sample company SSI to test the 'readiness' of using games as research instruments among 16- to 30-year-olds in the United Kingdom. The results were encouraging:

- When asked: 'You're playing a videogame on your (*insert participant's device*). Imagine that while you were playing a videogame, data were being collected on how you play the game and what you do in the game itself. Let's call this kind of videogame a 'Research Game'. Would you be happy to play this kind of game where data were being collected and used for genuine research purposes?' 78 per cent of participants answered: 'Yes, that would be fine with me'.

- When asked: 'Would you consider playing a game for free if it meant you were asked to give your opinion on a brand, product, service or advert?', 73 per cent replied: 'Yes, I would be happy to play a game for free and give my opinion on these things'.

- 84 per cent said they would recommend a ResearchGame to their friends or family if they were fun and /or educational. As ResearchGames can include four different types of value (such as self-discovery value, transcendent value and so on) this was important to understand as that value can be fun and educational, and by sharing public surveys, this can help increase response rates for public studies, such as polling or census surveys.

- 68 per cent said they would expect a reward or incentive for playing a ResearchGame, which was lower than I had anticipated, given that many people in the market research community attribute low participant engagement to low incentives, and try to increase them.

This study gave me confidence to begin exploring the game-based research approach.

CASE STUDY 1 Product development through preference testing and ideation for a new-to-market food product

Research buyer: Fortune 500 food brand

Audience: 'Millennial' (classed as 18- to 24-year-olds) and older (25 to 34), based in the United States

ResearchGame title: *Mission: Marketing. Journey into Product Development*

Research objective: To gain insight into the preferred product name, packaging and flavours of a new food product, and gain fresh ideas from the audience.

Business need: The target audiences were not engaging with the brand as much as the brand's more established audiences. The brand wanted to engage 'the next generation' of soup lovers; young people who could 'buy in' and remain loyal for years to come. A new food product was one way to engage them.

ResearchGame concept

RTG created two parallel running ResearchGames with implicit data collected on reaction times. Both were identical except that one ResearchGame used an on-screen timer, which gave participants a 30-second window to answer specific questions. If the 30 seconds ran out, a new set of 30 seconds would kick in. The other ResearchGame allowed participants to take as long as they needed to respond. The response times were recorded in both.

The timer element was included to encourage more instinctual responses and discourage deliberation. By having two versions of the ResearchGame, this would replicate how different groups of people make choices about a new food product. Some people would take time deliberating, while for others the decision is instinctive. Understanding that instinctual decisions can be made in as little as a third of a second,[20] we implemented this element to understand whether this new product could be attractive on an instinctual basis, or if this was a product that needed a specific marketing approach to provide more information.

The participants were able to make an avatar of themselves to begin with, which informed us of the participants' ages and gender, and were also used as part of the initial onboarding and motivation process. The participants' avatars were then placed in a 'general style' kitchen environment, which could easily have been a home kitchen or office canteen, to help place the participants in the mindset of food-related themes such as food preparation and cooking (see Figure 11.1).

As the study was related to product development and marketing a new food product, participants were placed in the role of Marketing Intern, and through their decisions, could level up as President of Marketing. A simple reason was given: the Head of Marketing had retired.

Through bestowing a sense of responsibility and collaboration about the product development with the participants, this helped to create a vested interest. We applied elements of self-discovery, narrative and transcendent value through seeing how the story of their journey as a marketing employee evolved, and letting them know that the product they helped to develop 'might even hit the stores'. In their role, they could 'hire' and 'fire' ideas from in-game 'characters' who put forward ideas for product names, as an alternative way to rank preferences.

Figure 11.1 Level 1 of the ResearchGame. The real product names have been replaced with 'Product name x'

SOURCE © Research Through Gaming Ltd

As a bonus feature, the participants got to play an 'egg smash' game at the end, which was specifically designed for this study as the food product in question was related to (potentially) adding an egg to make the product.

At the end of each level, the participants would be congratulated for completing the level, and given an on-screen badge to highlight their 'promotion' to the next role. At the end, the participants could see a summary of their badges and how long it took them to make decisions in each level, and see how long it took them to complete the ResearchGame overall. If they chose to play the egg-smash game, they could also see a summary of the points they earned.

The ResearchGame was split into three levels so each level could allow the participants to focus on one specific element of the product (see Figure 11.2).

The ResearchGame asked the participants if they were hungry 'right now' to see if feelings of hunger would contribute more or less to self-reported likelihood of purchase. We also used 'light' projective techniques, asking participants what they think other people their age would like (in terms of packaging and product name).

Results

- We achieved more completes than the client needed, in half the time allocated. The study was completed early, with a week left in field. The client required 600 interviews. The third-party panel company hired to supply the

Figure 11.2 The research objectives were restyled into three distinct levels so that the participant could focus on each element

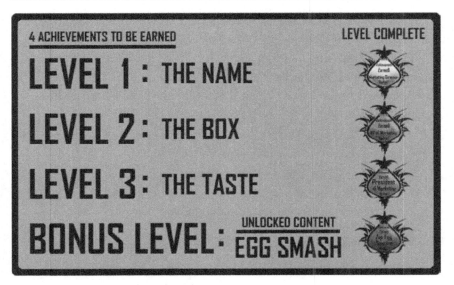

SOURCE © Research Through Gaming Ltd

sample predicted two weeks to gain the desired quantity of completes among this age group. When we reached 631 interviews in one week, the study was stopped early as we had more completed ResearchGames than were required.

- This saved time and cost both to RTG and the research buyer.
- We were able to move on to the Insight Reporting stage a week earlier.
- We understood audience preferences on all key objectives: product name, packaging and flavours.
- We understood the reasons behind the preferences through participant explanations.
- The participants shared innovative ideas for product names, package design and flavours. An example: 'maybe make the apron (worn on the model on the packaging) a flap that comes off with cooking instructions'.
- Feedback from participants was just over 90 per cent positive.
- 74 per cent of participants said they were hungry at the time, and 77 per cent said yes, they would want to buy the product they had designed if it hit the stores.
- Insight drove product development less than one year after the study was completed. A product range aimed at the target audience was launched with six different flavours. The product is still available and is sold in stores around the United States and online.
- The product brand continues to gain engagement on the brand's dedicated social network pages.
- The product, which has a look different from most food items in the brand's portfolio, has its own dedicated website.
- The product drove further marketing: from tasting 'roundtables' with their target audiences[21] to specific social media communications, sponsor launches of app games, advertising on Spotify, and developed shareable content on BuzzFeed.
- The company has stated that the range of food products 'represents the next generation of products' from the company.
- From the invisibly timed ResearchGame, 93 per cent said 'yes' to the question 'Would you like to play a ResearchGame in the future?' and 92 per cent said 'yes' from playing the visibly timed ResearchGame.

Participant responses

The voluntary feedback from participants was positive with participants reporting to enjoy the experience, thanking us for a fun game, and asking for more surveys of this type in the future.

In addition, one participant who happened to be a writer for game blog *Game Skinny*, voluntarily (unbeknownst to me at the time) wrote about the ResearchGame experience in a blog titled: *Video Games! Science! Research! Having Fun (Officially) Makes Things Better.*[22] The writer noted: 'I could not possibly be more thrilled to find similar game-based research opportunities in my inbox in the future' and 'I can say with absolute certainty that I was significantly more invested in this process than I have **ever** been in market research.'

CASE STUDY 2 A study on advertising trust and advertorial preferences

Research buyer: UK children's magazine publisher

Audience: 7- to 10-year-olds in the United Kingdom

ResearchGame title: *Magazine Question Hunt*

Figure 11.3 The fonts used in this ResearchGame were typically larger than I would design for older age groups, and much more basic sentence structures were used

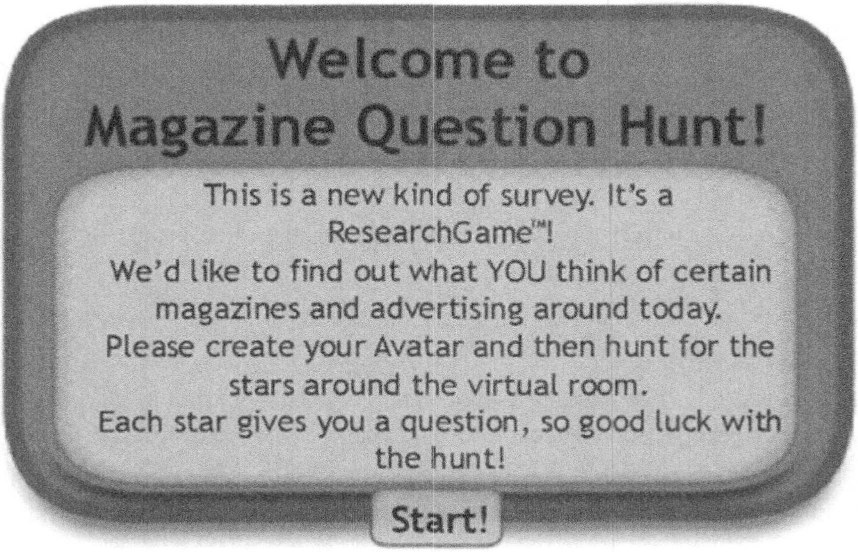

Welcome to
Magazine Question Hunt!

This is a new kind of survey. It's a ResearchGame™!
We'd like to find out what YOU think of certain magazines and advertising around today.
Please create your Avatar and then hunt for the stars around the virtual room.
Each star gives you a question, so good luck with the hunt!

Start!

SOURCE © Research Through Gaming Ltd

Figure 11.4   In Level 1, the stars in the room were easy to find, and became progressively hidden to add a layer of challenge

SOURCE © Research Through Gaming Ltd

Research objective:

- Understand if 7- to 10-year-old children were more responsive to interactive print advertorials (using quizzes, mazes or similar) than traditional magazine promotional inserts or adverts.

- Understand if such advertising was trusted by children.

- Understand what, if any, preferences the audience had for interactive print advertorials.

- Understand if advertorials were obvious as promotional tools, and how this may have affected brand trust.

- Understand which celebrities were the most recognizable to the audience.

Business need:

- Increase sales through selling more advertising space and potentially advise their ad buyer on effective and engaging interactive print advertorials.

- Increase sales from understanding which celebrities to put on the front cover of their publications.

ResearchGame concept

I hadn't conducted research among children with RTG or in any of my previous roles as a researcher at that time. However, in reading the survey from the client that I was commissioned to turn into a ResearchGame, I knew instinctively that the vocabulary used and some of the complex sentence structures would not have been suitable for young audiences, particularly as it was important in this study that the children participate without the help of their parent or guardian (even though permission and consent from parents and guardians was gained).

To test the hypothesis, and as part of my SIMC process (Smart Intuition and Meaningful Creativity which you'll read more about in Chapter 16), I conducted two focus groups among 7- to 10-year-olds to better understand how to communicate with them. I discovered significant differences in the reading and writing abilities in this age group. This told me that the ResearchGame needed to be challenging enough to hold the attention of the 10-year-olds but not 'babyish', and not too difficult for the 7-year-olds. In addition, it was clear the wording had to be updated from the original survey. For example, one of the original questions was: 'Do you trust advertising?' This became: 'When you see adverts, do you believe what they say?'

The children would make an avatar of themselves at the beginning to personalize the experience while helping engagement in the onboarding process. In building their avatars, the participants shared their age and gender. This was important in understanding if the participants were eligible to participate and provide them with specific questions about specific magazine titles relevant to their gender. Note: while it may seem old hat to distribute magazines by gender, this is a way that many magazine publications work, even though it's common for boys to read 'girls'' magazines and vice versa.

If the participant was male, he would enter a 'boys' virtual bedroom', complete with posters on the wall, a TV, a shelf with books, a dresser and other typical things that might be found in an average British child's bedroom. If the participant was female, she would likewise enter a 'girls' virtual bedroom' with the same items, albeit different colour palettes were used. From there, participants were challenged to treasure-hunt for stars hidden around the room. Each time a star was found, it would open up into a question or activity. This star-hunt gameplay was created to fit with some of the advertorials being tested, which were mostly advertising platformer-style videogames, where the collection of coins and stars is common – the theme was relevant. Plus, this gameplay wasn't going to be too difficult for the different spectrums of learning abilities. When the ResearchGame began, the stars were obvious to find in the virtual bedroom. As the ResearchGame progressed, the stars became increasingly hidden, in virtual drawers or behind other items in the room, using the 'Increases in difficulty' game element.

A mix of question types was used. The main focus was making the print advertorial quizzes digitized and available to interact with on the screen, so we could ask questions about the particants' enjoyment and brand perceptions and trust afterwards.

We also included a Celebrity Guessing Game activity so participants could tell us if they recognized the given celebrity or not. Not only did this help the client understand which celebrities were the most recognizable, but also how long it took participants to recognize the celebrity. This is important when we consider the limited window of time that magazines on a shelf can attract audiences and give them the impulse to purchase. The Celebrity Guessing Game activity also allowed us to know who else was top-of-mind when the children didn't guess correctly. In one example, the UK celebrity Dappy was used; however, he is normally seen in a hooded pullover and woolly hat. In the stimulus material, he was dressed in a suit and sunglasses, so this prompted participants to wonder if he was another celebrity. This let the client know not just which celebrities were recognizable, and how long the recognition took, but how the celebrity should be pictured in order to be recognizable (for example, wearing clothes that are typically linked to that person's overall 'look').

Results

- The research buyer was provided with insight that answered the research objectives.

- Client allocated two weeks to gain 500 completes. This was considered too short a window by the panel organization that was hired to provide the participants. They recommended three to four weeks in field, after assessing the length of time of the survey, and considering that we wanted the children to take part without the influence of a parent or guardian. However, due to time limitations from the research buyer, two weeks in field was the time allocated. We gained 700 completes in just under seven days from a slightly wider age group (data records from 6- to 16-year-olds were included in the raw data). When non-relevant data records were removed, we had 565 completes from the target audience, showing that we could gain more completes than the client required in just under half the time we were allocated, and a third to a quarter of the time predicted by the panel manager.

- 86 per cent of participants provided voluntary positive feedback.

- Response rate noted as 'a miracle' by the then panel manager, who also noted 'especially as the game was typically longer than what we would normally give to this age group'. This supports the fact that the ResearchGame methodology can hold engagement for longer.

- The ResearchGame provided untapped insights that couldn't be gathered from traditional online survey methods: this is especially seen in the Celebrity Guessing Game activity.

- The client and panel company anecdotally noted they had 'never seen children engage in research in this way before'.

- A handful of participants replayed the ResearchGame, twice and even three times in some cases, despite no further incentive offered.

Some participant feedback, which is reflective of the overall sentiment

- 'SO MUCH FUN'

- 'Loved it!'

- 'Good fun!'

- 'This was actually really enjoyable!'

- 'I really liked that, thank you!'

CASE STUDY 3 Preference testing and ideation study on identity and authentication

Research buyer: IMPRINTS Futures – a multidisciplinary research project, funded by the Engineering and Physical Sciences Research Council (ESPRC) which ran for three years

Audience: 18 to 65+ year-olds in the United Kingdom

ResearchGame titles: *TESSA Undercover Agents* (shorthand as *TESSA*) and *Dubious*

Research objectives:

- Test current and future forms of identification and authentication tools to understand preferences, desires, dislikes and taboos around certain designs.

- Understand in what contexts certain forms of ID are used.

- To help design forms of identification and authentication tools that can be used among the UK public in the future.

ResearchGame concepts

ResearchGame gameplay footage can be viewed online at:
www.koganpage.com/gamesandgamification using the access code DUBTES2 when prompted.

To answer the research objectives, two ResearchGames were developed so that the participants could focus on the 'present day' and the 'future' separately.

The first ResearchGame, *TESSA*, was based in the present day. Participants were placed in a role of an undercover agent and challenged with overcoming an enemy hacker through four missions. The role-play of undercover agent was used because this deals with themes of identity, which related to the themes of the study.

The second ResearchGame, *Dubious*, was based in the future in 2030. The participants were told that they had travelled to 2030 but their time machine had broken in three places, so they couldn't get back home. The participants could get help from three people to fix their time machine, but those people would only help to fix the time machine if they truly believed the participant was from the future, otherwise they would remain 'dubious'. How could the participant convince the people of this? By answering their questions about the future. The three people represented different aspects of the research content:

- a doctor represented questions about medical data and information storage;
- a friend represented questions about thoughts around future data privacy and data storage on things like social network accounts;
- the choice of a teacher or colleague represented questions around education and work.

In *Dubious*, I evolved the design of our basic Avatar Creator Tool using stimulus material required by the client, such as futuristic modes of identity, authentication, and other gadgets like GPS footwear and augmented reality glasses.

Both ResearchGames used a variety of question types, including digital diary-entry style questions, and 'simulated conversations' with other people in places like a doctor's waiting room. We included, as with other ResearchGames, 2D images of 3D environments to simulate scenarios, such as entering a 'hideout', and being in a time machine with a friend. We also used 'basic' question types like open-end verbatim questions, Likert scales, single and multiple response questions – but these could also be highly dynamic, such as 'removing items from a safe', which stylized preference ranking.

Results

- The IMPRINTS Futures project as a whole, including our study using ResearchGames, was selected as a *Big Idea for the Future* by the research councils and the universities of the United Kingdom, expecting that the research will 'have a profound effect on the UK future'.

- From the jury report of the Novay Digital Identity Award (2013): 'IMPRINTS is a unique and very-user-centric research approach on how people perceive identity systems, which will make it possible to develop better solutions, with a higher public acceptance.'

- We gained a better nationally representative sample compared with our client's previous experience with traditional surveys, with the eldest participant aged 89 years old – results as analysed by the client.

- 19 per cent took part in the voluntary Diary activity.

- 27 per cent of the participants who played *TESSA* left voluntary feedback (N=376) and 13 per cent left feedback after playing *Dubious*. One hypothesis is that fewer people left feedback after playing *Dubious* as they may have already left a comment after playing *TESSA*, explaining the lesser percentage of feedback after the second ResearchGame.

- Words most commonly used to describe *Dubious* were (again, most to least frequent) 'fun', 'good', 'interesting', 'great', 'enjoyable', 'different', 'enjoyed' and 'brilliant'.

- 91 per cent of the voluntary feedback was categorized as positive, reporting to enjoy the experience.

- 91 per cent of participants answered 'yes' to the question 'Would you be interested in playing a ResearchGame like this again?' after playing *TESSA*. To see a continuation rate of 81 per cent then, was encouraging.

- The most frequently used adjectives to describe *TESSA*, from most to least frequent, were fun, interesting, different, enjoyed, great, good, enjoyable, unusual and novel.

- 19 per cent of participants filled in both the morning/afternoon and evening sections of a non-mandatory digital diary, and 21 per cent filled out just the 'morning/afternoon' section. The responses were often detailed and lengthy.

- Of the 115 participant feedback statements, 19 per cent of those made reference to the previous ResearchGame, *TESSA* (which they would have played four months earlier). Some participants recalled specific information. In the voluntary feedback about *Dubious*, one participant thanked us for including a mute button (referring to *TESSA's* lack of a mute button).

- Some comments were negative about the background music in *TESSA Undercover Agents* – in hindsight a mute button on this ResearchGame would have been useful. A mute button was included in *Dubious*.

- The continuation rate between *TESSA* and *Dubious* was at 81 per cent, which was 11 percentage points higher than the estimated continuation rate of

70 per cent. The estimated continuation rate was provided by the third-party panel companies that were used to provide the respondents. We were also warned that the continuation rate would be significantly lower the longer we left the gap between the completion of the *TESSA* study and the launch of the *Dubious* study. With a four-month gap between the two ResearchGames, we were surprised to see a higher-than-estimated completion rate.

- 12 per cent of participants asked (in their voluntary verbatim feedback) to play more ResearchGames.

- One participant emailed me directly to thank me for the ResearchGame experience, while providing constructive criticism on things like loading times. This additional voluntary effort is a sign of engagement.

- The client noted: 'The whole team and I couldn't be happier. Our respondents clearly loved this format of research which is fantastic.'

Some participant responses

- prob one of the best and inventive surveys I done, if only more were like this. Interesting and enjoyable to participate. would participate in these again.

- Amazing way of conducting a survey, Very interesting and fun to do. I wish all the survey's are like this. Feels like I am playing a game. Hats off to who evey has come up with this unique idea.

- Great idea – more surveys should be like this!

- very enjoyable way to do a survey well done to whoever thought of it thank you really enjoyed this

- it was good fun and if you have any more in the future please do not hesitate to send me a request to complete it I have really enjoyed this survey

- really liked this survey probably one of the best I have taken as so unusual and far more interactive than most

- I really enjoyed this fun game and I really hope the information gained will be beneficial in making everyone's IDs safer

- i really enjoyed doing this survey like a game it was different

- such fun! i wish all surveys were like this. what a refreshing change to the tickboxes, thank you!

- it was a very interesting concept wasn't sure if I was actually doing a survey or playing a game!

- Definitely different!!! And less time wasted too.

- Thank you very much, this survey was new and different and kept me on my toes!! it didnt feel like a survey which is often boring, very good way to keep me alert!! thanks!

- really great experience, made it more real and involving

- That was the best survey I have ever done. Really imaginative and engaging. great fun and an enjoyable way to do a survey as some can be rather staid or even downright boring, wish more were like this!!

- this was pretty cool and interesting also very exciting and i would love to fill out another survey like this one. also just imagine if all surveys were like this or even most of them i be doing surveys alot more often than i do them now.

- I really enjoyed this type of survey thank you for inviting me EXCELLENT

One participant wrote: 'I enjoyed playing this game very much. I am not a gamer and neither do I use smart phone or phone apps but I also learned from this gaming experience'. What's interesting is that this person, aged 72 at the time, didn't use the term 'survey' at all, and despite not being tech savvy, was able to use the ResearchGame, indicating that when designed well, ResearchGames can also help onboard older audiences with greater ease and interest than traditional surveys. This is perhaps one of the elements that contributed to a better nationally representative sample.

CASE STUDY 4 Apparel product development and preference testing

Research buyer: Fortune 500 apparel portfolio brand, for one of their US-based athleisurewear brands

Audience: 20 to 45+ year-old females living in the United States

ResearchGame title: *Designer for a Day*

Research objectives: Learn about the leisure activities that the client's customers, and non-customers of the same demographic, partake in; learn about customers' preferences and desires for ideal activewear bottoms.

Business need: Use the insight to help inform the next collections of activewear bottoms sold through the client's brand.

ResearchGame concept

A three-level ResearchGame was developed, placing the participant in the role as 'designer' for the day. Through three levels, participants were promoted in their designer status as a reward for completing activities, working their way to create their own ideal workout pants. In the final level, the participants could personalize their certificate for achieving 'Super Designer' status. As the ResearchGame progressed, the design choices became more challenging. For example, in Level 1, participants were tasked to choose the basic 'foundations' of their activewear bottoms, such as style, rise and length. In Level 2, participants could make more complex choices around pocket quantity, logo design, colour, print, fabric texture and other elements. In the final level, participants used an in-built calculator to make further choices that impacted price. The participants would finally view a summary of all their choices (see Figure 11.5).

Results

- 81 per cent completion rate.
- Understood more about the activewear consumers' preferred activities.
- Learned what the style, colour, print and texture preferences were.
- Learned which design combinations were most popular.

Figure 11.5 Participants could see all their choices and the final price of their ideal self-designed activewear bottoms

SOURCE © Research Through Gaming Ltd

- Understood what design 'upgrades' the customers desired and would be willing to pay for.
- Understood willingness to pay for final design.
- Of 161 women who left voluntary feedback, 99 per cent of the comments can be categorized as positive with the most frequently used words being fun, awesome and cool.
- 82 per cent said they would like to play a ResearchGame again.

Research buyer feedback

- 'More enjoyable for customers to fill out (it's fun and engaging in a way most surveys are not)'
- 'Motivates internal clients to be more involved in the research process'
- 'Serves as a great platform for co-creation versus purely evaluating/validating our own thinking'
- 'They (the team, including head of design and head of marketing) were so grateful for the insight and found it highly actionable for future product development, and indeed are already putting much of the learning to use in new product designs.'
- Anecdotally, the client added that it was the first time the Head of Marketing and Head of Design were so involved in the research process and came to the insight reporting meeting, and not just for the free candy!

Participant responses

- Great, first time experiencing this innovative way to get feedback!
- I enjoy it because it was interactive. It is not the same questions over and over that you see in a lot of research surveys.
- I thought it was fun! and different! it made doing a survey a lot more enjoyable and I would like it if more surveys like this one, followed their model!
- THIS IS AN EXCELLENT IDEA, I LOVE IT! YOU ARE WONDERFUL, YOU ARE THE PEOPLE WHO CARES ABOUT US
- I liked that its interactive. Was a topic I love and was glad to help.
- I actually really enjoyed this research game. Having the ability to help brands design a product that we, the consumers, want is always worth it. The only thing I would have like to of seen is the pockets show up on the design. I noticed I could not really see the design with the pockets which made it a little difficult to decide. However, I thought this was a great way for the brand to reach out to its target market.

- This was the best survey I have taken in a while. The time involvement was nice and short too.
- I loved it! I would definitely do this again if given the chance!
- This was fun and original. Instead of asking endless questions, you make a game out of it and make it lots more fun and we can show you what we want or don't want much easier this way.
- It was so much fun I wish I could do it again! Thank you.
- This was the best research I've participated in, it was very entertaining and creatively fun!
- It was a fun activity - not like the typical survey.... I liked it!
- The research game was fun and easy
- I actually like this survey. it was fun and noninvasive .
- I thought this survey was extremely creative, loved making my own workout pants. Thank you
- It was super fun! I Really Enjoyed making the leggings, i just wish there was more to choose from! :) I had a lot of fun, thanks!
- This was awesome

CASE STUDY 5 Segmentation research on behalf of a UK university

Research buyer: The University of Surrey

Audience: Prospective university students in and outside the United Kingdom

ResearchGame title: *What type of student are you?*

Research objective(s): The research buyer had created a segmentation of six different student types in a previous study and wanted to use the segmentation algorithm developed from the previous study to find out about the different types of prospective students who were engaging with the university. Specifically, the objectives were to:

- collect information about prospective students and test the segmentation model;
- allow the university to segment students at face-to-face events and online via their website homepage;
- communicate why the university would be a good place to study (specific to their segment).

Business need: To use the insight gathered about the student segmentation to help evolve future marketing endeavours, which would engage future prospective students.

ResearchGame concept

Participants would initially answer demographic questions before responding to '17 golden questions'. The responses to these 'golden questions' would determine the participants' profile result. There were six profile results, each relating to a student 'personality' type. The design was purposefully developed in a quiz-like fashion, as our research showed this age group enjoyed online quizzes, such as those often circulated on social networking sites. Once the participants gained their profile results, they could see a text-based description of that result with an accompanying profile image, and a description of how the University of Surrey would fit their profile type. The students could also click relevant links to order a prospectus, arrange a visit to the university, download their app, and look at the other five profile types. We wanted to create social currency for this audience, so allowed them to share their profile result on social media, or download it, and share any of the six profile types to friends to recommend they take part in the survey.

Results

- Participants self-reported to enjoy the experience, with 95 per cent of the voluntary feedback categorized as positive.
- Completion rate among prospective students was at 83 per cent, and non-prospective students at 69 per cent.
- 72 per cent of participants who pressed 'start' on Screen 1 of the ResearchGame got their profile result. This varied between non-prospective students and prospective students.
- In an initial version of the ResearchGame design, 97 per cent of participants who had started the 'golden questions' went on to receive a profile result. In a later version of the design, the percentage dropped slightly to 91 per cent.
- 28 per cent responded to non-mandatory questions around their university life interests and values.
- The study was nominated for an award at the University Insights Conference in the United Kingdom, where the university was awarded a 'highly recommended' certificate.
- The client and I were invited to give a presentation based on this case study at the IIeX conference, which we did in February 2018, titled *Game design: engaging students to evolve university marketing*.

- Participants self-reported to look upon the university favourably, by praising the university for recognizing that there are different types of students, and applauding the innovative approach.

- The ResearchGame itself became a mode of marketing, having been used to engage prospective students at the university's stands at UCAS fairs and other student recruitment events.

- At the time of writing, the ResearchGame is being redesigned to become a lead-capture tool, thus becoming a tool for insight, marketing and student engagement.

- The study, which at the time of writing, has been running for almost a year, continues to gain high levels of engagement wherever it is promoted – via the university's social media pages, newsletters and on the homepage of the website.

Participant responses

- It was very interesting almost accurate and I had fun doing it lol. Bravo ☺
- I like the quiz and information I get in the end of it. Thank you ☺
- This was really fun! Not only that but it was accurate too. It's good to see that you acknowledge students and have a way with dealing with each and every type.
- cool! amazing! Do more!!
- Wow really love the quiz and the results. Kudos
- it was really amazing, i didn't thought it could be so accurate loved it
- it was very helpful, thank you
- I believe (the university is) listening to each student very carefully. And I believe the survey help me to understand more about myself why I want to apply (to the university). Thank you !
- It seems interesting and a good effort from the uni management team
- It was a good quiz. Having to answer such questions that I have been avoiding in my head has cleared to me what exactly I want. I feel more confident. Adding a few more questions could improve it some more.

These case studies illustrate enjoyment and engagement from participants, and I've received consistent positive feedback from our clients on the value of the ResearchGame methodology.

Before utilizing game-based research methods, there are five important things to consider, which the next chapter explores.

Notes

1 Adamou, B (2017) Fashion Design and Sustainability through ResearchGames, Proceedings of the MRS Annual Conference, 15 March, London

2 Adamou, B and Birks, D (2013) [accessed 25 May 2018] ResearchGames as a methodology: The impact of online ResearchGames upon participant engagement and future ResearchGame participation, Proceedings of the Association of Survey Computing Conference, University of Winchester, UK [Online] www.academia.edu/9487108/ResearchGames_as_a_Methodology_ The_Impact_of_Online_ResearchGames_Upon_Participant_Engagement_and_ Future_ResearchGame_Participation

3 Adamou, B and Gray, M (2018) Game design:Engaging students to evolve university marketing, Proceedings of the IIeX Conference, 20 February, Amsterdam

4 Bailey, P, Kernohan, H and Pritchard, G (2013) [accessed 25 May 2018] The Role of gamification in better accessing reality and hence increasing data validity, Proceedings of the Association of Survey Computing Conference, University of Winchester, UK [Online] www.asc.org.uk/events/previous-events/ september-2013/presentations

5 Bailey, P, Pritchard, G and Kernohan, H (2015) [accessed 25 May 2018] Gamification in market research: Increasing enjoyment, participant engagement and richness of data, but what of data validity? [Online] www.mrs.org.uk/ ijmr_article/article/103651

6 Cape, P (2017) [accessed 25 May 2018] Gamification: The challenge of rules, Proceedings of NewMR webinar conference, 21 June [Online] http://newmr.org/ presentations/831a398c

7 Harrison, Peter (2011) [accessed 25 May 2018] The researchification of games, Proceedings of ESOMAR 3D Digital Dimensions conference, Miami [Online] www.esomar.org/uploads/public/library/news/ESOMAR-3D-2011_ Conference-Papers.pdf (page 28)

8 Koenig-Lewis, N, Marquet, M and Palmer, A (2013) [accessed 25 May 2018] The effects of gamification on market research engagement and response [Online] http://marketing.conference-services. net/resources/327/3554/pdf/ AM2013_0291_paper.pdf

9 Malinoff , B and Puleston, J (2011) [accessed 25 May 2018] How far is too far? Proceedings of ESOMAR 3D Digital Dimensions conference, Miami [Online] https://www.esomar.org/uploads/public/library/news/ESOMAR-3D-2011_Conference-Papers.pdf (p 41)

10 Mavletova, A (2014) Web surveys among children and adolescents: is there a gamification effect? *Social Science Computer Review* [Online] DOI: 10.1177/089443931454531

11 Puleston, J (2013) [accessed 25 May 2018] Rewarding the truth, Proceedings of the Association of Survey Computing Conference, University of Winchester, UK [Online] www.asc.org.uk/events/previous-events/september-2013/presentations

12 Puleston, J and Sleep, D (2011) [accessed 25 May 2018] The game experiments [Online] www.esomar.org/uploads/public/publications-store/papers/The-game-experiments_Puleston-Sleep.pdf

13 Puleston, J and Rintool, D (2012) [accessed 25 May 2018] Can survey gaming techniques cross continents? Examining cross cultural reactions to creative questioning techniques [Online] https://www.esomar.org/web/research_papers/ Concept-Testing_2357_Can-Survey-Gaming-Techniques-Cross-Continents.php

14 Van Leare, S (2013) [accessed 25 May 2018] Using gamification to increase participant engagement and data quality in Online Research Communities, Proceedings of the Association of Survey Computing Conference, University of Winchester, UK [Online] http://www.asc.org.uk/events/previous-events/ september-2013/presentations

15 Van Zoonen, L, Turner, G, and Adamou, B (2013) [accessed 25 May 2018] Research through gaming: Public perceptions of (the future of) identity management, *SAGE Book of Methods* [Online] http://srmo.sagepub.com/view/ methods-case studies-2013/n39.xml

16 Van Zoonen, L and Turner, G (2013) [accessed 25 May 2018] Taboos and desires of the UK public for identity management in the future: Findings from two survey games, Proceedings of the 2013 ACM workshop on Digital identity management [Online] https://dl.acm.org/citation.cfm?id=2517887

17 Warnock, S and Gantz, J (2017) [accessed 25 May 2018] Gaming for respondents: A test of the impact of gamification on completion rates, *International Journal of Market Research*, **59** (1) [Online] http://journals. sagepub.com/doi/pdf/10.2501/IJMR-2017-005

18 Yagi, F, de Siqueira, L and Rodrigues, L (2013) [accessed 25 May 2018] Let's go game!: Borders of advantages and gains for gamification compared to in-depth-interviews [Online] www.warc.com/content/article/ lets_go_game_borders_of_advantages_and_gains_for_gamification_compared_ to_indepthinterviews/100592

19 Adamou, B (2011) [accessed 25 May 2018] The future of research through gaming, Proceedings of CASRO Online conference, Las Vegas, 3 March [Online] www.academia.edu/9487174/The_Future_of_Research_Through_ Gaming

20 Milosavljevic, Koch and Rangel (2011) [accessed 25 May 2018] Consumers can make decisions in as little as a third of a second, *Judgment and Decision Making*, **6** (6), August 2011, pp 520–530 [Online] http://journal.sjdm.org/11/10420a/jdm10420a.pdf

21 Campbell Soup Company (2012) Campbell's Go™ sets the table for millennials with communal table events in New York City and Chicago, Press release [Online] https://www.campbellsoupcompany.com/newsroom/press-releases/campbells-go-sets-the-table-for-millennials-with-communal-table-events-in-new-york-city-and-chicago/

22 Billings, HC (2013) [accessed 25 May 2018] Video games! Science! Research! Having fun (officially) makes things better, *GameSkinny*, 12 February [Blog] [Online] www.gameskinny.com/8987d/video-games-science-research-having-fun-officially-makes-things-better

Five things to   12
consider before
using games and
gamification for
market research

Understanding whether or not to apply game-based research methodologies to a study should undergo the same rigorous research and thinking that you would apply to any other research methodology, with the same level of sense-checking of the time and budget you have, and the objectives for data outcomes. Therefore, deciding to use game-based online research whether applied as a research-game or gamified survey needs its own consideration process.

This chapter explores five things to consider before designing a game-based online survey:

1 The strengths and limitations of existing survey software.

2 Is it worth your time and effort?

3 What project do I start with?

4 Your design approach will be completely different from someone else's.

5 How creative can I be?

The strengths and limitations of existing survey software

In the market research industry, it is commonplace for researcher suppliers who administer surveys to use the survey software licensed from another organization than it is for each agency to have developed and deployed their own survey software. Therefore, any market research agency wishing to 'update' the look and feel of the surveys is at the mercy of the limitations and strengths of the survey software it is using.

You may, for instance, simply want to change the background colour of a survey from white to blue. You may want to ensure the 'next' button is on the right, and not the left side of the screen. But how do you do this? Market researchers wishing to make simple changes like these often have to seek the assistance of a colleague with the technical know-how of the survey software being used, or go to the source: get help from the survey software company itself. Granted, you may know how to make such simple changes yourself, but what if you want to have a complete design overhaul? Where should you start?

Survey software has come a long way. Researchers can now produce more modern looking surveys and with customizable elements. But even with the evolution of survey software, designers who want to implement a game-based design will find themselves at a roadblock.

Let's say you would like to implement a simple 'diluted gamification' design. You want to divide your survey into three levels. You have 21 questions in your survey, and so with three levels, you can have seven questions per level (or five questions in Level 1, seven questions in Level 2 and nine questions in Level 3 – however you wish to divide your questions). Let's imagine you want to assign points for each question answered, where those points can add up to different rewards and achievements to unlock at the end of the survey. You may wish to have a screen that pops up at the end of each level showing participants how many points they have earned so far, and how many points are available for the remaining level(s). Even for this rudimentary approach to gamified surveys, implementation can be complex if your survey software doesn't allow for this type of customization. You could speak to your survey software suppliers and ask for their own developers to implement this for you, but this could take time and money.

For many researchers, this makes gamifying a survey almost impossible; your budget doesn't stretch to customization options and you have zero time to put such gamification ideas in place for your survey. Therefore, it is important that you speak to as many game-based research suppliers to assess which company's capabilities suit your needs best, and if they have the capabilities at all. If not, you may want to consider suppliers that specialize in game-based surveys or even build your own 'game-based survey engine'.

Is it worth your time and effort?

Designing and then creating a gamified survey or research-game, unsurprisingly, will take longer than designing and implementing a traditional online survey. In Chapter 18 we see that generating an idea and design for your game-based survey can take as little as 20 minutes. But graphically designing each element of your design and then putting those graphics through for programming, and then playtesting can take days, if not weeks and months.

While GbRM can and has been used for ad-hoc studies, you need to consider if the commercial rewards for this process are worth your time. If you are a research buyer, you may want to consider applying game-based research to an ongoing study, thus benefiting from economies of scale as well as knowing that your initial investment is going to go a long way.

What project do I start with?

Game-based research is a tool to solve low levels of participant engagement, and to gain the benefits we see from the six vital states, as well as the game techniques from intrinsic engagement and play, increased productivity, focus, creativity, problem-solving and more. You *don't* need to use GbRM if you are already gaining useful insight that is proving successful to the research buyer. In short, if it ain't broke, don't fix it.

But, if there is a study that needs help, then begin with a small-scale study and preferably with an existing project that has already been 'live' via a traditional online surveying method to provide points of comparison. Beginning small means a project that is aimed at a small pool of participants, in just one country, in one language and a maximum of 20 minutes as the length of interview (how long it takes the participant to complete your game-based survey). If the data analysis shows that the game-based survey you have designed has been effective, use the learnings to embark on using GbRM on further studies. Where possible, continue to make comparisons between the results of the traditional survey and the game-based equivalent.

Your design approach will be completely different from someone else's

Game-based surveys are a creative medium. Even if two researchers are provided with the same research objectives, survey questions, participant profiles, quotas and so on, they are likely to design their game-based surveys differently.

Designing and creating a game-based online survey is just like designing and creating any other media. Other media have their rules and forms to follow, but it is the creativity that makes the difference. Take film, for example. Films have a form where there is a beginning, a middle and an end. Characters have conflict. There are obstacles to overcome in the story. But how Kathryn Bigelow (*The Hurt Locker*) uses the form of film versus that of David Lynch (*Eraserhead*) is entirely different, even when the same processes and rules apply.

Because of creative differences, game-based survey design is almost incomparable as there are too many variables that are changeable, from the use of music to virtual environments, narratives and other elements. This is something to consider when using game-based survey design.

How creative can I be?

You might ask 'How creative am I?' or 'How creative do I need to be?' as a game-based survey designer. But sooner or later you will need to ask 'How creative am I allowed to be?'.

You will need to test your ideas with the research buyer in terms of what is acceptable. For almost all research buyers, it is the first time they will be embarking on using gamification and games for research. This is where research-games and gamified surveys differ even more from digital games: while game designers tend to work collectively from a creative brief on a game-as-product to sell to players, the game-based survey designer will present the idea to the client and colleagues for feedback, often with lots of different opinions to take on board.

You may have a client who might say something like 'I don't want anything too "out there"' or 'Can we have a "mild" game approach?' Ultimately, while you need to take on board your client's requirements, you must also design what is going to be the most effective game-based survey. A balance must be struck. As we explore in the next chapter, you should show your client examples of different kinds of digital games that are similar to the design you have in mind, or better yet, show the client a storyboarded version of your idea to test the receptiveness of the design before going into build-mode.

If you have considered these five items, level up to Part Two: World of Design.

PART TWO
World of Design – overview

The design of your game-based survey is the key that will unlock the potential of your study in terms of participant engagement, emotional, and experiential immersion. While it may seem that the design process is not the job for a market researcher, they are the best people to be involved in or even create the design as they will understand the research buyers' objectives and business needs, and as such, can create a coherent design that drives those objectives.

But the process of design is not without its pitfalls; it is a craft, there will be trial and error, and there are ethical principles to abide by. Rather than let this worry you, enjoy the process of mastering the new skills of research-game and gamified research design. In this world, you will learn about the steps to take to develop engaging designs, and even get to design your own game-based survey. You will also take a look into my own design work, learning from some of the errors I have made through dissecting my own game-based surveys, with tips on how to build solid design foundations.

In guest lectures and workshops I have carried out, I have watched people design, from scratch, their own research-games to a project brief with impressive results. These were people who didn't necessarily consider themselves creative, but given the right space and guidelines, were able to produce designs that would have been much more engaging and effective than traditional surveying techniques. Let this inspire you as you embark on Part Two: World of Design.

Fifteen ethics guidelines for designing and making game-based surveys

> The overwhelming ethical principle should be that 'just because you can do something doesn't mean you should', and in general ethical design is the same as good design, and good business as well.
>
> Jane Frost, CBE, CEO of Market Research Society (MRS)

The following manifesto is a set of ethics and design guidelines based on my practice and experience in the field. These guidelines should be used as a self-monitoring system for game-based survey designers to boost a relationship of transparency and trust between you and your stakeholders. While these guidelines are certainly applicable today, they will still be applicable and just as important when game-based research evolves with technologies like augmented reality and virtual reality. Many of these guidelines will apply to other research methodologies as well.

The choices in your design will *directly impact* how people interact with your game-based survey and the research results. Therefore, the designer is responsible for handling all design choices with great care and consideration of the audience, whether that is your choice of music and sound effects (if needed), or the narratives created. As celebrated game designer and researcher Gordon Calleja writes: 'The cognitive, emotional and kinaesthetic feedback loop formed between the game process and the player makes games particularly powerful means of affecting players' moods and emotional states.'[1] Participants *will*, lightly or heavily, emotionally engage with your game-based survey, so being mindful is crucial.

The guidelines should help you develop these ethical approaches as habit, and help you to help participants have better research experiences.

1 Use transparent labels: never 'disguise' your research-game or gamified survey as anything else but research

Games and gamification are tools to inspire participation and engagement, not a means to dupe participants. The fact that some researchers are tempted to rename 'surveys' as 'quizzes' to inspire participation is in itself a warning that surveys need to be more engaging, otherwise we wouldn't be tempted to mislead participants. If you have read anything encouraging the disguise of surveys as quizzes, these should be disregarded. It will never, *ever* be okay to disguise your game-based survey to be something other than what it is. This point is so important; it is the cornerstone of good ethics, research and business.

You could, and are encouraged to, use labels that combine terms that let the participant know that the research experience will be a game, or playful, or as gamification, or a quiz *but is still a piece of research* in which data will be collected. Terms like quiz-style survey, game-style survey, survey game or survey quiz would be helpful in terms of clarity and consent.

It will also help to manage participant expectations and help to get them in a game-play state of mind. As game designers and researchers Espen Aarseth and Gordon Calleja point out in their paper *The Word Game: The ontology of an indefinable object* (2015): 'for the object or system to become a game, a player needs to think of it as such. That is, she needs to actively interpret the activity as a game for it to be considered a game at all.'[2] This is what is known as a 'lusory attitude', which is the psychological attitude required of a player entering into the play of a game.[3] To adopt a lusory attitude is to accept the arbitrary rules of a game in order to facilitate the resulting experience of play.[4]

We also need transparent labelling so that game-based surveys aren't confused with non-market-research-related online quizzes, like the ones often seen on social media, for example: 'what's your spirit animal?' or 'what super hero are you?'. While game-based surveys and social-media-based quizzes have value in their own right, they are different, and that difference needs to be reflected in the labelling.

2 Get the survey basics right – create a solid foundation

As we explore in this World of Design, it is important to get the basics of your survey design right before thinking of applying gamification or developing the survey as a fully-fledged game. Laying a solid design foundation means doing things like making sure your survey is device agnostic, and that the question language is simple and clear. Seemingly small things like font size and font style can also impact engagement, so be sure to get these basics underway before embarking on the rest. Chapter 15 provides 10 tips on designing for your audience's limitations and strengths.

3 Prepare the participant for the experience

Whether your approach is to send participants a link to your survey via an email invitation, or whether the survey is available on a company website homepage, researchers should prepare participants for what to expect at the earliest stage of interaction, particularly if the look and feel of the game-based survey is radically different from the 'traditional' surveys that participants are familiar with.

Managing participant expectations will help researchers build relationships of trust and transparency, and participants can make an informed choice of whether they want to take part. Some people with particular needs may find the change in format stressful or confusing, so by managing expectations *before* participation, you will also help people with special requirements to feel more comfortable and respected.

Managing participant expectations is simple. Text saying something like 'you are about to take part in a survey designed more as a game/quiz for your improved research experience' or similar is helpful, with perhaps some screenshots of the gamified survey or research-game. By doing this, you are reinforcing that it is a research study while also articulating the reason and value for the difference in design.

In RTG ResearchGames, a section on describing what a ResearchGame is, and why there is a different look and feel compared to some typical surveys, is included. While our data tell us that small quantities of participants look at this information, it is important to those people to have that information available.

4 Conform to GDPR guidelines – articulate what kinds of data will be collected through the game-based survey, and what the data are for

Will you collect paradata and/or metadata from participants who play your game-based survey? What about personally identifiable data? Will data be collected on what actions participants take within the research-game and how long they take to carry out those actions? If the answer is 'yes' to any of these, it is important to let participants know. You can provide such information in the initial email invitation, or through a 'Data usage and privacy' section that is easily accessible in the game-based survey itself. In describing the kinds of data that will be collected, it is important to keep the language jargon-free and clear, and provide examples. If you say something like 'We will collect paradata', elaborate with examples like: 'which includes data such as the time of day you are taking part in the survey, and how long it might take you to complete it'. Again this transparency takes researchers closer to building stronger relationships of trust *and* is a legal requirement with the implementation of EU General Data Protection Regulation (GDPR) guidelines. More information about GDPR can be found here: www.eugdpr.org.

How you choose to articulate this information is up to you – you can even gamify it if you want to or use text and video. In fact, making this kind of data privacy text engaging is encouraged by GDPR professionals because the more engaged participants are, the better they will understand the consequences of their consent and participation.

5 Give participants the option to leave the game-based survey whenever they wish, and give them simple options to do so

Some participants may feel apprehensive about exiting your game-based survey, so provide clarity on what will happen to their data and/or incentive (if you are providing an incentive) if they leave the survey early. For example, will they still be invited to take part in future studies? Will they still receive their incentive? Will the data they have already provided be used or discarded? This information can be made available through an FAQ section on a relevant company website, or an 'About' section in the survey itself, or described in the survey invitation.

Ideally, your game-based survey is so engaging, participants will want to complete it, but there could be many causes for early termination, so assurances as well as guidance on what participants can do (like simply close the browser window, or press an 'exit' button) will help make things clearer.

6 Give the option to provide non-mandatory feedback about the experience

At the end of the research experience, it's always worth asking a few questions about what the participants thought of the platform. Ask things like what worked well, and what could have been better? Would they like to take part in a similar format of research in the future? Add an open response field so participants can 'say what they like'. The open-end feedback is by far the most useful in my experience because it has given me confidence as a designer when the feedback is positive, and made me aware of any errors I've made, for instance, if there's feedback like 'there was a typo in Level X'. Allowing for feedback will also help you see if you have particular audiences that don't enjoy this kind of survey.

Bear in mind that if you have an audience who say they did not find the game-based survey engaging, assess your design *first* and try out an improved or different version *before* telling yourself that they were too old/too young/too distracted to be engaged and 'get it'. It is your job as a game-based research designer to design *for* your audience, so if it looks like it hasn't worked out for a particular group of participants, it is probably to do with the design and not with them. After all, there are videogames played by 3- to 75-year-olds – and why? Because the design is on-point.

Giving opportunities for feedback is the only way you can understand *why* a design didn't work so you can work on a solution.

7 If you are using music and/or sound effects, say so at the beginning

Using audio in a game-based survey can have many benefits, and if you have decided to take advantage of background music and/or sound effects, make a clear note of this in the survey invitation *and* on the first screen of the survey. Ensure you include a mute button (don't just rely on the ability of participants to control volume from their device) and let participants know they will have the option to turn off or lower the audio, with a quick guide on how to do this.

If sound is crucial to the research experience, politely encourage participants to use headphones. This way, if they are in an open-plan room and want to hear the sound, they have the choice to go somewhere less public.

You should also consider the emotional effects of using audio; overwhelming evidence shows that music and sound effects have the ability to change human emotion and even the speeds in which we react to different stimuli. In short, audio is a powerful tool: research how different audiences might react first.

8 Provide a reminder of realism in the fantasy

If you expect participants to engage in a game-based research narrative in which they play a role, for example an undercover agent or a fashion designer – remind audiences that they will still need to respond to questions and/or react to scenarios with their true opinions and beliefs. The purpose of role-play is to give participants an opportunity to share ideas and opinions on things that they wouldn't normally do in everyday life. Even though 'humans are built with psychological checks and balances which help us acknowledge the differences between reality and fantasy'[5] you can always provide a small prompt if you think participants might get carried away; remind them that the study is about what *they* think and about what they would do given the chance, not about what they think *someone else* is likely to think/do/want. A simple pop-up explaining this, or a few lines of text in an 'About' section should suffice.

9 Practise mindful design – design with care, courtesy and empathy

Whether you are designing a game-based survey for children or an elderly audience, consider their reading, writing and cognitive abilities. Do not produce, for instance, a game-based survey with difficult and convoluted challenges, while using complex vocabulary and long sentence structures for an audience of 7-year-olds. While being mindful enough not to make your game-based survey too complex, you should find the right balance so that a game-based survey that is 'too easy' doesn't feel childish, boring or patronizing.

Striking the right balance between simplicity and challenge to engage participants can take time, particularly if you have a single game-based survey that requires participation from a wide range of people. But with good initial audience research, a single game-based survey can engage everyone you need. Indeed, in the digital games industry, some games have vastly wide-ranging audiences. It is not uncommon for me to see a child play a game like *Monument Valley* (UsTwo games) but also see the same game played on the London Underground by people in their fifties.

It is not just the challenges that need the right balance, but also the rewards and the punctuation used. For instance, an audience of artificial intelligence (AI) engineers is likely to find it a bit daft if exclamation marks are used in every other sentence in a survey, and gold stars are awarded for answering basic questions. These sorts of things also make for an 'overexcited' tone which might not be in line with certain types of research, for example in sensitive healthcare studies.

You should also consider how fast- or slow-paced the game flow should be. For instance, would it be appropriate to have a 30-second 'quick fire round' of questions for audiences over 85 years who may need more time to read and understand questions than younger people? Similarly, too slow a pace can become cumbersome. Again, it is about striking the right balance for your participants.

You should also consider that some participants experience digital content in different ways. For instance, the Colour Blind Awareness organization[6] tells us that colour blindness affects approximately 1 in 12 men (8 per cent) and 1 in 200 women in the world. In Britain alone, this means there are approximately 2.7 million colour-blind people (about 4.5 per cent of the entire population), most of whom are male. You can (and should) search for websites like Vischeck to see how your game-based survey looks to a colour-blind person.

Consider also that some participants might be hard-of-sight or hard-of-hearing. My dad was deaf in one ear and blind in one eye, and things like hearing aids and vision-loss friendly signage in shops clearly made life easier. But what does that kind of real-world support look like in the digital space in your research?

Digital support like narration and voice recognition for various types of surveys is absolutely possible. Improved accessibility, for all participants, will help them feel valued and could increase engagement. A win-win all round.

By designing with care, courtesy and empathy, you won't alienate your audience by using games, you'll *improve* the research experience. For more on improving digital experiences, check out the Web Content Accessibility Guidelines (WCAG), which can be found at www.gov.uk/service-manual/helping-people-to-use-your-service/understanding-wcag-20.

10 Playtest

It is crucial to playtest any survey, especially game-based surveys, for two reasons:

To ensure the game-based survey works on a technical level

Test elements like audio, accessibility via different browsers and devices, question routing and so on. Playtesting helps weed out bugs and other technical issues. It is a procedure you will be familiar with as you become a game-based researcher designer. For those of you unfamiliar with the term playtest, this is where someone may play your research-game or gamified survey repeatedly from start to finish, or in some cases the same section over and over again to troubleshoot bugs – (errors in the code) which can be caused by both human error and sometimes through web applications doing something they shouldn't.

Playtesting must be carried out using multiple devices, browsers and browser versions. The process should also involve load testing: assessing whether your survey can handle high quantities of participation at any given time.

Playtesting with a game-based survey, just as with traditional surveys, also ensures that the data are coming through as needed (so, for instance, you don't see multiple choice data for what is meant to be a single response question). It is a crucial step in the development procedure and should absolutely be scheduled ahead of time. Depending on the length of the survey, and how many errors are found, playtesting could take as little as a couple of days to a couple of weeks. A good developer will tell you upfront how much time is ideal for playtesting once he or she has seen your design and understands the capabilities/user flow and so on.

To ensure the game-based survey is as engaging/effective/ accessible/easy to follow as you hoped it would be for your intended audience

In the world of developing apps and other digital content, a core group of initial testers who encompass the target audience are asked to take part and do things like generate content and give feedback. This isn't playtesting, but an opportunity for a core group of users to give their perspective on the product.

Researchers using game-based surveys could do something similar. If the confidentiality agreement between you and your research buyer allows it, ask people you know, who are similar to your true target audience, to take part in the game-based survey. This is a different type of playtesting; it is not necessarily about finding bugs or other errors, it is more about understanding if your audience is going to engage with your game-based survey as much as you planned. The closer your playtester is to your target audience in terms of age, region, life stage, attitudes, job and so on, the better.

For example, if your target participants are C-level executives, before launching, why not see if there is a C-level executive you know who can take part and give his or her thoughts? If you can, observe them taking part in your game-based survey in real time, and assess how easy or hard he or she finds it. Ask what were the most engaging elements. Did they feel patronized or encouraged by this effort in the survey design? Was it easy to interact with and access?

Improve your design to reflect the feedback you've gathered and keep on with feedback and improvement iterations as long as your schedule and budget permit.

For more on playtesting, see Part Three: World of Making.

11 Conform to the market research codes of conduct relevant to your region, the region of the research buyer and the region(s) of participants

Using game-based research doesn't exempt researchers from complying with national codes of conduct. Compliance in how researchers collect data (using any methodology) is not just the law but good practice. Each professional body of market research, such as ESOMAR (www.esomar.org) and the Market Research Society (MRS – www.mrs.org.uk) have ample content to help in the do's and don'ts of data collection. If you're unsure about the professional body that caters for your region, check out this handy website from MR Web: www.mrweb.com/guide/guide-assocs2.htm.

12 Do not include any visuals, narratives or other content in your game-based research that is violent in nature, non-inclusive or disturbing

Part of my work as a ResearchGame Designer is teaching others how to design ResearchGames, and I have heard some suggestions like 'you can shoot the answer!' or 'you have to free a person who is held hostage!' or 'you have to stop the ticking bomb!'. And who can blame anyone for generating such storylines? These are familiar narratives in TV, film and games. But even though we see violent narratives elsewhere, it doesn't mean they are appropriate for game-based research.

Where possible, avoid other content that might be sensitive and/or taboo in nature: subjects like politics, sex and religion. If you are designing a game-based survey that requires information on how people feel about politics, sex or religion, then see the ninth guideline: do so with care, courtesy, empathy, as well as respect and sensitivity.

13 Safety and fairness

When children play together, there are unsaid but nevertheless crucial rules they (mostly) abide by. Things like 'not hurting each other' and 'not snatching toys' are commandments in the invisible rulebook of play. Translated as something more sophisticated, these unsaid rules are primarily about safety and fairness.

The sense of safety and fairness we have valued in play as children is still with us all as adults. As such, providing a safe and fair environment for participants to be themselves in a game-based survey is paramount, even if metaphorical narratives or seemingly far-fetched scenarios are used. A way to encourage safety and fairness is to provide assurances of confidentiality and ensure all participants are treated equally.

14 Do not use other people's intellectual property

I saw a presentation at a European conference showcasing the research results from a gamified survey, and all the avatar characters were the intellectual property of one of the largest media companies in the world. I watched the presentation part enthralled by the level of work and the positive results, part wincing at the thought that this was, however innocently done, an infringement of IP. (The research study itself was not on behalf of the media company in question, nor any of its affiliated companies.) Not only was this worrying from a legal perspective, but the media-company-owned characters themselves had little, if any, relevance to the research content.

However, the temptation to use the characters, or storylines, of other people's work is understandable; there is an existing engagement already there. But, while being inspired is great (and if you are bereft of ideas then please, please seek inspiration for all the different kinds of sources noted in Chapter 14), you should not copy the IP of anyone else. It is an infringement of other people's creativity, and dampens your *own* creativity. You can produce something far more effective for your game-based survey, and you know it.

15 Non-addictive design

Use your great design powers for GOOD. The significant effects of research-games and gamified research have not yet been fully realized. Indeed, there is more expansion to come and gaps in knowledge to fill. It can be tempting to toy with the idea of making game-based research as addictive as some games. Indeed, in my work I have heard such quiet muttering from others: 'but what if… what if taking part in research got addictive'?

There are ethics between great, intrinsically engaging design and addictive design. You are the ethical designer. Knowing the difference between making something engaging and making something addictive requires intuitive design skill and a moral compass.

Notes

1 Calleja, G (2011) Emotional involvement in digital games, International Journal of Arts and Technology, 4 (1)

2 Aarseth, E, and Calleja, G (2015) [accessed 27 May 2018] The Word Game: The ontology of an indefinable object, FDG [Online] https://tinyurl.com/yb5zceep

3 Salen, K and Zimmerman, E (2004) *Rules of Play: Game design fundamentals*, pp 97–99, MIT Press, Cambridge, MA

4 Suits, B (2005) *The Grasshopper: Games, life and utopia*, pp 54–55, Broadview Press

5 Jenkins, D (2018) The world is not enough: Or can movies save the world, *Little White Lies*, 75 (May/June/July), p 6

6 Colour Blind Awareness (no date) [accessed 27 May 2018] What is Colour Blindness? [Online] http://www.colourblindawareness.org/colour-blindness/

A vocabulary of play for game-based research   14
Game terminologies and inspiration

This chapter covers:

- game terminologies for your game-based survey;
- how to build on your vocabulary of play and inspire other aspects of game-based survey design.

The linguistics and tone used in game-based research are crucial in engaging participants and helping them understand the research content. Words are the most powerful tool you have as a research-game or gamified survey designer. Indeed, the semiotics of visual aids alter when words are involved – this is just as relevant in game-based survey design as it is any other media. As such, the linguistics should be carefully crafted. Get it right and you have increased your chance of participant engagement. Get it wrong and participants will switch off. And for participants to perceive your survey as a game, it has to feel like one, and that can involve using more game-like language.

Transitioning from the vocabulary and tone of traditional online surveys to a 'vocabulary of play' can take time as you research and discover terminologies that are more fitting to a game or gamified experience. For example, in a game-based survey you might not want to use a word like 'task' or 'activity' but a term like 'quest' or 'mission' so that the vocabulary is in keeping with the intended tone. This vocabulary of play is a shortcut guide to game-like terms.

While taking advantage of this mini-dictionary of terminologies, you should also spend time playing games and looking to other media to build a vocabulary of play and design to suit your research needs. Notes on inspiration and where to find it follow the vocabulary of play.

Terminology

General vocabulary

- Play, Start or Go (When you want participants to begin taking part, words like 'play', 'start' or 'go' instead of the usual words found in traditional surveys like 'begin' could be useful.)
- Competition
- Clues
- Hidden (Hidden items in a game-based survey can be things like clues to solve a puzzle or reach the goal, hidden prizes or points.)
- Secret (similar to a word like 'hidden' such as secret levels, points, opportunities to level up)
- Cast (a spell, cast a condition, could be a term used instead of 'make' or 'create')
- Boss level
- Strategy
- Character (In role-play, you could describe other 'people' in the game-based survey as 'characters' or explore the characteristics of a brand or product.)
- Combos (Combos, or combinations, are often referred to in games as various moves, which when combined together may progress the player in some way. 'Combos' or 'combinations' can be terms used in things like conjoint studies to describe the combination of elements to design the ideal product packaging, for example.)
- Game over!
- Life or lives (to give opportunities to replay the same event. By offering 'lives' you can include an illusionary win/lose state in the game-based survey.)
- Status (Players' status as they progress through a game can often be seen on some kind of leaderboard. In the game-based survey, where a participant may only be playing against the time or the narrative or a fictional character, you can still include a leaderboard to give feedback on the participants' status through the study.)
- You win!
- Time attack/countdown timer (Timers can be used to discourage deliberation and encourage top-of-mind responses. Where relevant, you can tie in a 'limited time' activity with the narrative to create a sense of urgency.)

- Stealth or being Undercover
- Sharing (sharing points, achievements, social media sharing)

Gaining something

These terms can be anything from winning downloadable certificates, progressing through a narrative, gaining points etc.

- 1-up (A '1-up' is a bonus feature found in games, often referred to the bonus of an extra life. A 1-up in a game-based survey could be gaining an extra life through taking part in an additional activity or extra questions.)
- Achievements
- Accumulating – gathering, storing, stockpile, hoard, stash, save
- Bonus (could be bonus questions, bonus activities, bonus rewards etc)
- Easter egg (a bonus feature otherwise unexpected in the game-based survey – easter eggs can also be hidden or secret)
- Level up
- Farming/harvesting/mining/uncovering (as in, farming or harvesting information, mining insight, uncovering questions etc)
- Mission complete! (or 'Quest complete' or 'Operation successful' etc – often found in games and can be used in game-based surveys to make it clear that the participant has finished a task or activity)
- Reward
- Prize
- Power-up (Is there something you can offer participants that might help them through the narrative somehow, or help them take part in activities? A power-up is often used in games to do anything from making the character more powerful or moving through a game faster.)
- Unlocking (Unlocking is a term often used in games, such as 'unlock an achievement', or 'unlock a secret level'. In a game-based survey, participants can unlock questions, activities, even other surveys, as well as rewards.)
- XP (short for experience points. Participants can gain XP for answering questions, or be rewarded with higher rates of XP for certain types of questions.)

Doing something

Such words could be used instead of words like 'task' or 'activity'.

- Adventure
- Challenge
- Expedition (similar meaning – voyage, trek, pilgrimage)
- Experience
- Hunt or Investigate (can be used instead of 'search' – such terms are often used in treasure-hunting games)
- Journey (can be used instead of the term 'going through a process')
- Mission
- Operation ('Operation: Improve the Product X flavour!')
- Pursuit
- Puzzle
- Quest

To describe 'sections' or 'areas' of your game-based survey

- Levels
- Zones
- Sectors
- Episodes
- Worlds

Evolving your vocabulary of play

A vocabulary of play is not just limited to words, but the visual vocabulary you build after playing many different types of games where you can observe, for example, how avatars are used and designed in different games, how role-play is constructed, how emotion is developed and so on. You want to become fluent in the many languages of play to ignite inspiration when embarking on game-based survey design. This is why it is important to engage with different content that you wouldn't normally engage with as it can unlock new ideas. (See what I did there? 'Unlock'?)

Inspiration has struck me from some of the weirdest and seemingly irrelevant of places; picking up a leaflet for a music festival has prompted the exploration of different aesthetics for ResearchGame graphics, and playing an app game aimed at teens has given me inspiration for a ResearchGame aimed at C-level executives. If you are going to be a designer, you need to build up a body of inspiration and knowledge about design – from games and beyond.

Having go-to places for inspiration when it doesn't strike immediately is crucial. This list is a handy start.

Play games for inspiration

While it is obvious that someone designing game-based surveys should play games, I can tell you from experience that being busy means you don't always get the chance to do so. Even seasoned game designers have confessed they can become out of touch just because they are so busy with their job, families and so on. But, it is crucial to play games as a designer because it provides opportunities to understand technological advancements, a chance to be inspired by and view trends in artistry/creativity, and a chance to take a look at the mechanisms and interactions that might very well be relevant for your own game-based research design. Play lots of different kinds of games: board games, app games, games for children, games for health and wellness, VR games and take part in an array of gamified activities – the broader the range the better.

Take part in anything 'experiential'

As mentioned in Chapter 10, go to immersive movie experiences, go for the experiential and even the gimmicky dining experiences. Check out any experience-based marketing campaigns. Also check out the experiential narratives of *Hunt a Killer* (www.huntakiller.com) and *The Mysterious Package Company* (www.mysteriouspackage.com). Get involved; take notes; be inspired. You never know how someone else's conceptual and playful approaches will inspire your game-based survey designs.

Read magazines you wouldn't normally read

These are good sources of inspiration for content, and for layout and aesthetic ideas. The magazine *Little White Lies* is about film, and while

I'm not necessarily a film buff, its strong aesthetic and bold patterns look completely different from the aesthetic of other magazines, which I find inspiring. Magazines like *New Scientist, Wired* and *Edge* keep me informed of technological developments but also new research into human behaviour that prove useful in developing data collection techniques. Consume media outside your regular habits to open your mind to ideas!

Read graphic novels

Graphic novels, or comics, where narrative meets art and human interaction are great places for storyline ideas, aesthetic inspiration and character development. Some of my own ResearchGames can be described as digital comic books – where each screen pushes the narrative along in a 2D space. Graphic novels are now more varied than ever before so finding a range of graphic novels to inspire you should be easy.

Explore weird and wonderful websites

Jennifer Dewalt, founder of project management platform Zube, made 180 websites in 180 days. They are not your conventional sites – they are quirky and illustrate ways in which websites can be used a little differently to engage users. In Dewalt's *Hello World!*[1] website, we discover that clicking a graphic of a piece of rope while simultaneously looking at raining bacon has never been so much fun. We also see how Jennifer makes words engaging by making users scroll to reveal full text on the *Secret Message* site.[2] Other websites, like *Patatap* by computer programmer Jono Brandel provide an audio and visual interactive experience, making the act of tapping on your keys addictively fun. These 'left field' websites will encourage you to think differently and get creative juices flowing.

ACTIVITIES

- What words/terms/phrases do you most frequently use when scripting a survey? Can any of these words be swapped for a 'game word' like the examples in this vocabulary of play? Could terms like 'take part', or even phrases like 'please tell us' or 'please indicate' be replaced by terms such as 'join the mission' or 'create the right combination to unlock …'? More importantly, are these game-like words entirely appropriate or do you need to build an alternative vocabulary better suited to your research content and participants?

- **Make a list of five new games, magazines, books and playful experiences** that you can get involved with in the coming weeks. This content should be outside of your habitual media consumption, ie content you wouldn't normally engage in.

- **Think about how the new experiences have shaped your thinking** – have they introduced you to new concepts, interaction ideas and engagement techniques you wouldn't have known about otherwise? Which new mediums have you discovered that are more inspiring than others?

- **Save content:** in the next chapters, you will see how concept boards are a key part of the process for game-based research design. Find ways of saving inspiring content that works best for you. Try to put everything in one place so it is easy to access when you are designing a game-based survey.

Notes

1 *Hello World!* website: https://jenniferdewalt.com/node/hello_world

2 *Secret Message* website: https://jenniferdewalt.com/secret_message.html

Game-based research design   15

Ten tips for building the right foundations

Before getting started with game-based survey design, there are important design principles to explore. In this chapter, we visit design concepts and processes on an introductory level that will help construct how participants 'read' your research-game or gamified survey. As such, further study is recommended (check out 'Recommended reading' at the end of this chapter) to understand various design principles more deeply.

Game-based survey design is a craft. The process combines all the intricacies and challenges of designing a game, designing a questionnaire, designing an engaging digital experience and designing a platform for data collection, and where that data needs to generate insight in which businesses can make decisions. The process combines knowledge from multiple disciplines including but not limited to semiotics, user experience design, behavioural economics, linguistics and play. Needless to say there is a lot to think about.

Perhaps because it is such a unique process, some things I describe in this section are a little more conceptual and can't necessarily be explained on an academic level. However, I hope to have shared enough of the guidelines and processes (which I personally use) to give structure to what can be an abstract process.

The direction in this chapter will not only help with game-based survey design but with general survey and even online community design.

Ten common-sense tips for good game-based survey design

1 Never undervalue design because design impacts data

How you design your game-based survey will directly impact the data and the insights gathered. And better design – even improving answer options in basic ways through dynamic design – leads to engaged participants and improved data quality.[1]

Let this be your mantra: DESIGN IMPACTS DATA. Tattoo this on yourself!

2 Ensure concise and clear game-based research design

- Avoid convoluted storylines.
- Avoid too many in-game characters.
- Keep text on the screen to a minimum, not because of engagement concerns, but because all surveys should be concise.
- Keep language simple.
- Keep the fonts simple.
- If you are in a face-to-face setting, keep instructions brief and easy to understand.

You get the idea.

3 No more than three different fonts

The fonts you use should be easy to read (even if they are more stylish fonts with flourishes) and should harmonize with your research content, storyline (if you are using one) and game structure. You should also avoid using too many different font styles. My general rule is to use one 'novel' font type (something that stands out a little more – something that has more of a flair if needed) and two standard font types. You also want to test that your chosen fonts can be viewed on most popular browsers. The Google Fonts site lets people download fonts for free, and also shows the popularity of different fonts: https://fonts.google.com.

4 Composition and being device agnostic

Ensure you give enough space for all the text and/or images to be easy to read and test this on various devices. (Your game-based survey doesn't have to be live and fully coded to test this – you can see how the game graphics look before the development process by opening the graphic files on different devices.) It would be frustrating to see your research-game or gamified survey looking beautiful on a laptop screen, but having text and images cut off, or overlaid, on smaller screens. Even digital games made for entertainment, with all their fixtures and trimmings, can bomb miserably if not fully device agnostic. If your game-based survey *isn't* available on lots of different devices, make it clear to participants; let them know they would be better off viewing it on a laptop, tablet and so on.

5 Mind the rag

Related to the tip on good composition, the 'rag' (a largely US term used in typesetting and typography) describes how and where words are laid out. The rag of text can either make it easy or cumbersome to read. For example, someone might write:

> Hi everyone! Welcome to
> this gamified survey where you'll be asked to cheer-
> lead a group of scientists in discovering the latest inn-
> ovations in medicine. Please
> try to take part in all the
> activities.

A better 'rag' would be:

> Hi everyone!
> Welcome to this gamified survey
> where you'll be asked to cheerlead a group of scientists
> in discovering the latest innovations in medicine.
> Please try to take part in all the activities.

Keep an eye on the rag when you design and playtest your game-based survey with various devices.

6 Nudge and anticipate the participants' journey

Good design will not only help a user 'flow' through a website, application or survey, but anticipate where the eye 'wants' to go next. For instance, on a website we anticipate that contact information will be on the top right of the screen so we will look there to find a button. To go to the next question in a survey, users may look to the bottom right. You can use the design of the game-based survey to manipulate the participants' journey so they can focus on key information. Design your game-based survey in a way that supports the users – don't make them have to look for basic things to progress in their experience. Of course, if an activity specifically asks participants to look for/collect items, as in a treasure-hunt style game, then of course this approach is different, but instructions and the logistical information about the activity should be easily accessible.

7 Create an appropriate tone

Semiotics tells us that everything has meaning with some signs/symbols/other visual cues more ingrained than others in evoking meaning. Font styles, font sizes, even how we use punctuation, can affect how people consume any text, so certainly impact how traditional surveys are consumed, and game-based surveys. As game-based surveys can be much more visual than traditional surveys, the designer must tread more carefully even with basic design choices and how they develop the text. Too many exclamations points, and the tone becomes overexcited!!! **<u>Too many bold words and underlines adds strong emphasis to everything</u>**.

Here are some mini-experiments to show differences in tone. Look at these examples of the same text in different fonts.

What genre of story is Figure 15.1 compared with Figure 15.2?

Figure 15.1

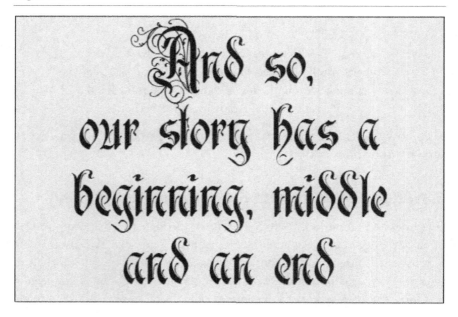

Figure 15.2

In several workshops, delegates have said Figure 15.1 looks like it's from a medieval story or a fairytale, while Figure 15.2 looks like it's from a horror story. The associated genres affect how the 'media' is consumed and the tone.

Now, what if we give the words a face? A personality?

Figure 15.3

"And so,
out story has a
beginning,
middle
and an end"

SOURCE   Photograph courtesy of Christian Newman on Unplash.com

Figure 15.4

"And so, our story has a beginning, middle and an end"

SOURCE Photograph courtesy of Tyler Nix on Unplash.com

How did you read the words in these figures? Was the pace slower for Figure 15.3 compared to Figure 15.4 because the lady in the photograph is older? Was the pitch of your inner voice lower or higher for Figure 15.3 or Figure 15.4?

What if we swapped the photos for pictures of Morgan Freeman, the acclaimed actor, and a photo of Sir David Attenborough, the science and nature documentary narrator? Both have very distinctive voices. If the consumer of the media knows how they speak, the timbre of their voices, consumers can mimic their tone in their own inner voice.

How we use visual aids, especially those with human faces expressing emotion, can significantly impact how we consume meaning in the accompanying text. This also happens vice versa; how we use text can impact the meaning of visual aids. Think of a picture showing a lovely sunny day in a park with people having picnics, surrounded by flowers and trees. The accompanying text reads 'and one of them had just escaped prison'. Suddenly our pleasant image takes on a sinister tone.

Let's now experiment with font style and size.

Figure 15.5

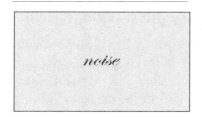

Figure 15.6

Did you whisper the word in Figure 15.5, or read it as a squeak? Did you read Figure 15.6 loudly?

These mini-experiments show that there are a myriad of possibilities in how visuals can impact the tone and consumption of your game-based survey, but the more you know about your clients, their research objectives, their business objectives and the target audience, the faster you will make design decisions and the more those design choices will narrow down.

For instance, when creating a ResearchGame for very young audiences, I am highly unlikely to use fonts like Times New Roman. Similarly, if a ResearchGame is aimed at a global audience, but in English only, I would avoid using difficult-to-read script fonts (where the fonts are typically in a joined-up handwriting style). So in understanding even just basic facts about the target audience, I eliminate specific design aspects and leave myself open to make design decisions that are more effective to engage participants.

8 Consistency

Have you ever watched a movie or TV show, where an aspect of what you see on screen is completely unbelievable? Even if the world is filled with dragons, magic or set on an alien planet, we find it unbelievable if even the smallest thing seems unrealistic, despite the fact that we are looking into an unrealistic world. This is when our 'suspension of disbelief' is broken and this can disengage audiences.

Narrative unity is important in film and TV, in games and in game-based surveys. As Dan Calvert, Character Art Director at Guerilla Games described in a conference presentation, the game world you design needs 'internal consistency – nothing to detract from the functional narratives'.[2] As such, the narrative you choose (if any) must relate to and harmonize with the research content, and any rewards you provide should be narrative- and research-relevant.

9 'Don't let great get in the way of good enough.' No!

To say I really dislike this phrase is an understatement. If everyone took this advice, we would be living in a different world. What joy is there in any craft if you are not aiming for a high level of polish? Start with the mindset that you are really going to engage your participants in the best way possible and with the best design possible. Only if pushed for time/budget should compromises be made. There are too many 'just good enough' surveys out there that aren't good enough. You will be in a different league of designer.

10 Does the game-based design need your client's branding?

Your research-game or gamified survey certainly doesn't need to be visually heavy or graphically detailed but if that's your design direction, then you need to check with your client (or whoever is commissioning the study) if they need it to be designed with their branding in place. And you need to check this *before* designing.

A ResearchGame I designed for a Fortune 500 technology and consultancy company saw the ResearchGame as an extension of their brand, and had very specific brand guidelines; they extended these to the kinds of fonts I could use, the font colours, whether I could or could not use italics, and a very precise colour palette as HEX codes. (HEX codes are the six-figure digits – a mix of numbers and roman characters – that inform digital colour. For example, 'ffffff' is white, '000000' is black, and I'll let you use Photoshop to figure out what 'f6ff00' is.)

They also wanted the ResearchGame to feel authoritative to match with their brand tone. As the designer, you need to ensure that you check and work with this information *before* designing your research-game and gamified survey.

These tips, embedded in learnings from UX, UCD, semiotics and linguistics are basic but set solid foundations for game-based research design. Check out the recommended reading to find out more about key design principles.

Recommended reading

Books

Don't Make Me Think (2005), a book on web usability and design by usability consultant Steve Krug.

Principles of Gestalt Psychology (2014) by Kurt Koffka, psychologist and one of the founding fathers of gestalt psychology.

People Aren't Robots: Tips for creating questionnaires that people want to answer by Annie Pettit, author and thought-leader in the market research industry provides great advice for designing better surveys – even for the veteran researcher. Her webinar with the same title is available on the NewMR.org website here http://newmr.org/presentations/a5310250/.

Conferences

UX.Live (User Experience) – based in the United Kingdom: http://ux-live.co

UCD conference (User Centred Design) – based in the United Kingdom: http://ucduk.org

AIGA Design Conference – based in the United States: http://designconference.aiga.org/#!/

Other

Check out the Better Surveys project (https://bettersurveys.business.uq.edu.au/) for guidance on better traditional survey design. The Better Surveys project ran for three years to understand how different design components affect survey data and participant response rates.

Notes

1 Dolnicar, Sara, Grün, Bettina and Yanamandram, Venkata (2013) [accessed 22 May 2018] Dynamic, interactive survey questions can increase survey data quality, *Journal of Travel & Tourism Marketing*, **30** (7), pp 690–699, DOI: 10.1080/10548408.2013.827546

2 Dan Calvert, Character Art Director at Guerilla Games speaking at the Parallel Worlds conference, October 2017, Victoria and Albert Museum, London

Introducing Smart Intuition and Meaningful Creativity (SIMC)

16

This chapter explores:

- combining instinct with evidence for successful game-based survey design and ensuring that design links to research impact;
- the process and mindset of SIMC for game-based research design;
- SIMC in action – how SIMC was applied to develop a ResearchGame design;
- how you can heighten your Smart Intuition;
- using the SIMC process to prepare four important items that you will need to play '20 for 20' in Chapter 18.

What is SIMC?

Chris Crawford, veteran game designer, notes in his book *Chris Crawford on Game Design* (2003)[1] that the process involves 'a great deal of expertise, some rules of thumb and strong intuition'. He is right.

Smart Intuition and Meaningful Creativity (SIMC) is a term I've coined to describe both a mindset and a process that supports effective research-game and gamified research design. Smart Intuition and Meaningful Creativity are two aspects of a whole process that work together harmoniously. This process was created to give structure to an otherwise abstract workflow with many moving parts.

While 'intuition' may sound like delusion more than science, the process of Smart Intuition is grounded in instinctive design and research. Valerie van Mulukom, research associate at Coventry University in the United Kingdom, notes in her article 'The secret to creativity, according to science' (2018) that there are two phases to creative imagination; one of them is Divergent Thinking. This is the ability to 'think of a wide variety of ideas, all somehow connected to a main problem or topic, which is fast and automatic'.[2]

As game-based survey design requires a researcher to think of lots of creative ideas to solve a particular problem, but the researcher doesn't necessarily have lots of time to do so, this style of thinking is ideal. After all, having an idea pop up from our unconscious for an effective research-game or gamified survey design doesn't 'just happen' (unfortunately). As much as we would like the light-bulb moment to come spontaneously, it won't, *unless* the SIMC process is applied; it is what will drive your creativity. There is evidence to support this approach as well. As science journalist and author of *Override* (2017) Caroline Williams notes, you should 'build up a good store of information so that the unconscious has something to work with'[3] to get into a creative mode and inspire ideas.

So while the SIMC process may seem like a lot of work just to help generate ideas, it is exactly what will drive the functional creativity required.

Smart Intuition

Smart Intuition is a 'research first' approach that allows a game-based survey designer to use existing evidence to support and help engineer an effective design. For clarity:

1 How one approaches game-based survey design will be driven by the research objectives. However, it is important to bear in mind that even with functional design, many researchers will be embarking on practically unchartered territory in terms of design process and understanding how design affects research results. As such, new game-based survey designers will likely rely on, and require, strong intuition.

2 This approach is not to be confused with user-testing; game-based survey designers are unlikely to have time to create various iterations of a research-game or gamified survey and then test that on participants, gain results, make changes and put the survey live in field once again. Game-based survey designers will be working in unique conditions in that they have only 'one shot' to make the design effective from the start.

The fact is, every research-game or gamified survey that people create for the foreseeable future is going to be new – no single research-game or gamified survey will be exactly like another. Even for 'pre-made, off-the-shelf' game-based surveys, the design (and results) will be different every time because the audiences will be different, the research buyer needs will be different, and the research content will be different. There are too many variables to conclude that an '*x* or *y*' design approach is going to be 100 per cent effective.

A game-based research designer will be doing her or his job in completely unchartered territory, borrowing from a myriad of disciplines, and with the option of using a cornucopia of techniques and technologies. So our game-based survey designs are likely to be approached by instinct rather than holistic concrete evidence.

But, what designers can and must do is build a tapestry of evidence that supports and ignites confidence in *specific aspects* of their design ideas. Game-based research designers (including myself) have no way of knowing for certain that our design will resonate with the intended audience or will garner the results that help the research buyer. This is where *Smart Intuition* has real impact; if your instinct inspires a particular narrative, background music, colour palette and so on, you can validate those hunches through research and evidence *first* to provide you (and your client) with increased confidence in the design approach.

However – a warning. Gathering evidence to support specific aspects of an instinctive design (this applies to all sorts of design – websites, apps, logos etc) can be time-consuming. In a *New York Times* article discussing the work of Marissa Mayer at Google, we understand just how specific and arduous the process of making a choice about an exact design facet can be, with the article noting that in one instance, 41 shades of blue were tested and there were many discussions on the use of the words 'view' and 'invite' for different Google products.

You need to ask yourself: How many aspects of the design should be researched to validate your intuition-based (but functionally driven) design approach? How much time and resource can you realistically allocate to do this?

The answers depend on two more questions:

What 'margin of design error' can be afforded?

If thousands of people around the world take part in a game-based survey, then any non-effective design choices will be felt more widely across participant engagement and data quality. The larger the 'design fault' the bigger the repercussions, like a larger stone creating wider ripples in a pond. However, this is still the case with a smaller sample. Consider that a study of several doctors can be just as efficacious as a study with 10,000 consumers across several markets. As such, you must understand the time and financial investment/impact for the research buyer. This will help determine the length of time you invest in finding evidence to support your design approach as a whole, and if that's not possible, then focusing on specific design aspects.

How 'out there' is your design, honestly?

Is your design fairly 'low key' – perhaps using the four game ingredients with just 'text on a screen'? Or are your intentions to develop a fully-fledged research-game with simulated experiences, where participants can create an avatar and engage in a role-play-based narrative? If the former, then we can argue that less extensive initial research is required than the latter approach. As such, a designer creating a more novel design with many different components functioning together to make a whole experience should research and validate those components.

Meaningful Creativity

Meaningful Creativity means 'design with function'. All the aspects of your creativity – your design – must have meaning – function. **Never design for design's sake**. As Stephen King said on writing: kill your darlings. If a design aspect looks pretty but doesn't add anything of value – get rid. If you're going to use music and sound effects, if you're going to use a pastel colour palette, if you're going to choose Impact font instead of Trebuchet, you need to articulate how those design decisions support participant engagement and the research objectives.

Every pixel in your game-based survey needs to be justified. The narratives must harmonize with the research content; the reward systems must have relevance to the overarching narrative. The design is what unifies the 'game aspects' of your survey with the research content as one – the harmony and synchronicity will help to engage participants. The opposite will cause confusion: for instance, if you are encouraging participants to imagine their shopping experiences in the future, it might not feel coherent to use a piece of classical or country music in the background (unless, of course, these genres of music are relevant to the narrative you are using). Every design aspect must be backed by function.

This is how Meaningful Creativity works harmoniously with Smart Intuition. While Smart Intuition is a process that encourages validation of design choices, Meaningful Creativity ensures the design choices are functional.

I make it part of my deliverables to produce a 'Why Guide' – a document I present to clients to show the reasons and research that support and explain the design choices – ie, why is the ResearchGame designed THIS way? As we explore more in Chapter 19, the Why Guide is great not just as a means to explain your thinking as a designer, but a great way to get the client on board. It is during my presentation of the Why Guide that clients have the 'aha' moments.

SIMC in action

In designing two ResearchGames for an academic study, I thought that a more personalized experience for the participants would be effective; specifically, to add an additional layer of engagement to encourage participants to feel at ease enough to 'speak their mind' when prompted to imagine future-based scenarios by talking to 'in-game characters'.

I was inspired by personalized experiences at the time – in the way my nephews had personalized Father Christmas video messages and the way that new children's books included the reader's name and the names of their friends. I wondered if this kind of personalization could translate as engagement for research participants. I applied personalization in three ways:

1 Participants could name their avatar.

2 Participants could name the other in-game characters – naming the characters of a doctor and a friend, thus building a 'relationship' with them (although we didn't measure if participants used the real names of their friends or doctors or if any kind of emotional connection developed between the participant and these characters. In hindsight, I wish I had measured these things).

3 Participants could dress a 'friend' character in futuristic clothing so they could accompany the participant to the year 2030.

Not only could these types of personalization engage the participant, but I thought potentially, participants might be more comfortable answering conceptual questions about the future if they felt they were 'talking to' characters they named and built a relationship with – however brief or 'faux' that relationship was in the ResearchGame.

The hunch prompted further research into personalization: in games and across other digital and non-digital media. While there was no evidence to confirm that the *exact* design approach I wanted to take would be effective, there were huge quantities of evidence to support aspects of these design choices. For instance, how personalization increases engagement in almost all digital media with examples across social networks and companies like Netflix, in product design where people's names are printed on Coca-Cola bottles and other food products[4] and how in games, players can develop emotional relationships and trust in shared virtual environments (SVEs) with other players who they didn't previously know[5] and even with non-player characters (NPCs)[6] – even marrying them.[7] It is well documented that significant efforts are being made in the games industry to create more realistic and dynamic NPCs through artificial intelligence because this increases player engagement.[8]

With the evidence, the client had green-lit the design. This was Smart Intuition – intuition backed by evidence. And it paid off – the participants were engaged and left rich responses in imagining the future[9] through 'conversations' with other characters and an optional online diary study. The quality of responses led us to believe that participants felt comfortable to imagine the future and give intricate details – they imagined sensory information: smells, sounds, living conditions, taste of food and other aspects. Of the participant feedback, 91 per cent was positive about the ResearchGame platform, with the most frequently used terms being 'enjoyable', 'fun', 'novel' and 'great'. The client informed us that the data derived from the verbatim response elements (that were not included in the original survey outline) provided some of the most interesting insight and talking points among their peers.

Ways to support and improve Smart Intuition

It would be impossible to intuit what an effective research-game or gamified research design would be without understanding your audience. If you are going to create something engaging, for anyone, you have to find out what's going to make them tick.

Research the participant audience until you know them as well as possible

By researching your audience first, you can create a game-based survey design that is much more catered for them; catering for their age, lifestyle, what they already think about the research content and so on. So the first step, even before putting pencil to storyboard, is to understand as much about the participants and the research content as possible. This is the stand-ard information researchers should seek before embarking on any study:

- What does the client intend to do with the research findings?
- What are their business objectives?
- How will the results shape decisions?
- Are there allocated personnel in place, or time and budgets, to action the research findings?
- How do participants already feel about the research subject, and are there any similar related topics in the news and other popular culture?

Spend time with your research client to answer these questions, and see what information they already have about their participants that they can share without breaking any confidentiality or privacy agreements. The more you know about the study and the participants, the more effective your design will be because the research objectives, business objectives and knowl-edge about participants will inform the design. I absolutely can't design a ResearchGame without such information – and where there are gaps in the client's knowledge about the participants, I will research the audience myself.

How to research and understand the participants: building Participant Profiles

By consuming the media your participants consume, you are likely to under-stand them better – what is going to make them engaged and any emotions/attachments/discussions they might already have that relate to the research subject. This research will help to build a 'participant profile'. Again, many research buyers are already likely to have such information, but if they don't have detailed segmentation or consumer type information, then try to research and understand:

- Demographic data, for example:
    - their age(s);
    - country of residence and regions;
    - gender(s);
    - the kinds of jobs/careers they have;
    - ethnic background;
    - language(s) the participant is most comfortable using;
    - income.

- Media consumption, for example:
  - the magazines and newspapers they read, if any;
  - TV shows or films they watch;
  - books they read;
  - their hobbies and interests;
  - the music, radio shows, podcasts they listen to;
  - the celebrities, organizations, thought-leaders, influencers they are likely to follow on social media.

Being that game-based surveys can include narratives, I also typically look at literature, film and online content that the audience could be engaged with.

Why look at media consumption? Answer: because it's cheating

Magazine publishers know their readers. They design content and layout to engage them, right down to font types, colour palettes, the people they interview – they know what will resonate with their readers, which is why different companies advertise with different magazines. Consuming the same media as your participant audience is a cheat – it's the fastest way to get to know them and what's going to engage them, which is especially effective if you have time constraints.

Designer –> Participant Empathy and Emotion Transference (DPEET)

When you are building the participant profiles, you will be 'placing yourself in their shoes' both from a **practical perspective** (for example, where are the participants most likely to be when they play my research-game? And what sort of devices can I expect them to use?), and also from an **emotional perspective** (for example, how do the participants already feel about the research content? Is there an existing emotional relationship that might be useful to understand?).

Much in the way that method actors truly immerse themselves in character roles, what I call Designer –> Participant empathy and emotion transference (DPEET) describes how the game-based survey designer can understand the participants' mindset, and reflect that in the design. As a result, he or she can design with more empathy. If the participants feel that they are understood, they are more likely to be honest and transparent. If games can prompt creative and self-expression in players, then game-based survey designers can engineer conceptual, or imitate real, relevant emotional contexts in the design to view how emotions drive behaviours and choices. But as a designer, you must understand profoundly the participants and their relationship with the research content in order to design with high degrees of empathy.

ACTIVITIES

Prepare and take these four quest items with you to Chapter 18. You will need them as you design your game-based survey while you play '20 for 20'. The items to take are in bold.

- The **map of Research Objectives** – prepare a document detailing your client's research objectives. Within this, write details on how the research objectives help the client with their business needs/goals. Explore what actions the research buyer wants to, or is willing to, undertake from the research results.

- Your **log of the related, Broader Themes** (if any) – try to uncover: is there anything happening in politics, economics, pop culture or elsewhere that relates to the research content that can help to inform the way questions and/or simulations are shaped? For example, if the research seeks to uncover the frequency and behaviour of visits to a particular store, could there be other, broader, themes to explore such as the concerns over diminishing retail in the high street?

- The **Participant Profile(s)** – allow the demographic information you have about the target participants to spur your research into building a participant profile (or profiles). Consume the same media. Research how the participants might already feel about the research content; for example, if a research study is aimed at reviewing a company's interview process, it might be worth looking online on sites like Glassdoor. com or Great Place to Work to research what the general feedback might be. Your participant profile can be a written document or something more visual – whatever you feel comfortable with.

- Your game-based survey design **Concept Board** – when consuming the same media as the participants, and/or looking elsewhere for inspiration, cut out/save/print anything that is inspirational in terms of design/layout/colour/copy and create a concept board. How you create this is up to you – it can be digital, printed – even if this is just items pinned to a wall (as per Figure 16.1) then that's fine – whatever works for you, as long as this is something easily accessible in the physical place where you are likely to embark on creating the design.

Figure 16.1 From inspiration wall to Concept Board: before designing a ResearchGame I build an 'inspiration wall', which is later streamlined as a Concept Board. This helps identify ideas, themes and patterns in aesthetics, and interaction ideas. This wall consists of printed screengrabs from games, interesting websites, tear-outs from magazines and newspapers, photos I've taken of related content – anything that inspires ideas for the Concept Board

Notes

1 Crawford, C (2003) *Chris Crawford on Game Design*, New Riders Publishing, Indiana

2 Van Mulukom, Valerie (2018) [accessed 27 May 2018] The Secret to Creativity, According to Science, *The Conversation* [Online] https://theconversation.com/the-secret-to-creativity-according-to-science-89592

3 Williams, C (2015) The human brain, *New Scientist: The Collection*, 2 (1), p 119

4 Roderick, Leonie (2015) [accessed 22 May 2018] Personalization: A short-term fad or long-term engagement strategy?, *Marketing Week* [Online] www.marketingweek.com/2015/11/10/personalization-a-short-term-fad-or-long-term-engagement-strategy/

5 Yee, N (2006) The psychology of massively multi-user online role-playing games: Motivations, emotional investment, relationships and problematic usage, in *Avatars at Work and Play: Collaboration and interaction in shared virtual environments*, ed R Schroeder and AS Axelsson, Chapter 9, Springer, Netherlands

6 NPCs are characters in games, also known as 'synthetic agents', that are not controlled by a person but by the game itself

7 Meyers, Chris (2009) [accessed 22 May 2018] Japanese man takes video game character as wife, *Reuters* [Online] https://www.reuters.com/article/us-japan-videogame/japanese-man-takes-video-game-character-as-wife-idUSTRE5BJ1XX20091220

8 Harth, J (2017) [accessed 25 April 2018] Empathy with non-player characters? An empirical approach to the foundations of human/non-human relationships, *Journal of Virtual Worlds Research*, **10** (2) [Online] https://journals.tdl.org/jvwr/index.php/jvwr/article/viewFile/7272/6407

9 Adamou, B and Birks, Dr D (2013) [accessed 22 May 2018] ResearchGames as a methodology: The impact of online ResearchGames and game components upon participant engagement and future ResearchGame, Proceedings of 'Critical Reflections on Methodology and Technology: Gamification, Text Analysis and Data Visualisation' conference, the Association of Survey Computing (ASC), University of Winchester, UK, 6–7 September 2013 [Online] www.academia.edu/9487108/ResearchGames_as_a_Methodology_The_Impact_of_Online_ResearchGames_Upon_Participant_Engagement_and_Future_ResearchGame_Participation

Overcome these 17 four concerns about game-based survey design

You may have reservations in starting your own game-based survey design process. Here are the top concerns I have heard from my workshops and lecture delegates, so let's smooth out these worries.

'I'm bad at drawing'

You are not expected to be Frida Kahlo or Vincent Van Gogh. There are plenty of great designers who aren't great at drawing. In the context of game-based survey design, your drawings (Figure 17.1) don't necessarily matter as long as your ideas can be translated into graphical content (Figure 17.2), a board game, or whatever medium you are using. When you are designing, stick people are okay.

'Design ideas are slow to surface'

Game-based survey design is a craft. The longer you are at it, the better and more confident you will become. Plus, over time, you will build experience on what kinds of rewards, narratives, simulations and so on work better with some types of research or some audiences over others. If at first it might feel as if it takes forever to come up with ideas, don't fret, but keep at it. You will find it increasingly easier to catch the creative ideas that will work to support research objectives while simultaneously engaging your audience.

Figure 17.1   Photograph of my own concept drawing. The drawing conveys the concept that participants can see inside the graphic of a building. It's no work of art! But these initial design ideas help me streamline the overall design direction and later on, I can polish the ideas for the graphic design process

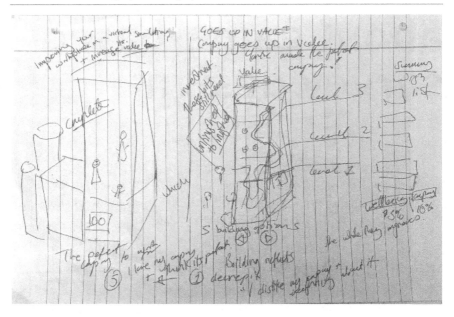

Figure 17.2   You can pass your designs to a graphic designer to create a polished, useable file for developers, and to use in your storyboard

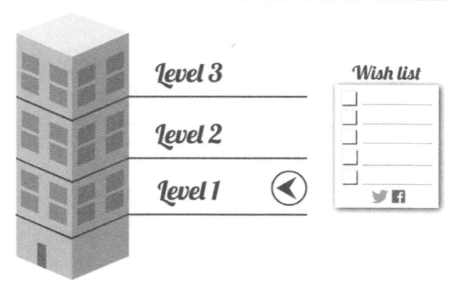

SOURCE © Research Through Gaming Ltd

'Someone else has a different game-based design approach to the same research project'

While this book introduces processes and guides on game-based survey design, we must remember that it's a creative endeavour; how one person designs a game-based survey will be different from how someone else does. It is for this reason that, from an academic perspective, it is hard to make comparisons between how some game-based capabilities gain certain results compared with others. There is no wrong or right in the design, but there is *better*, that is, the most effective design.

'I got the design wrong'

Remember that even highly paid game designers can lose player engagement. *Pokémon Go* (Nintendo) was arguably the most popular game in 2016. The game had everything going for it: easy access through mobile, new technology through the use of augmented reality and a nostalgic, existing fan base.

But within a few months of launching, *Pokémon Go* lost 10 million players. Why? Through lack of engagement. The main gripes from players were that the game became repetitive and didn't seem to ever have an end-point.[1] Game-based research designers and even traditional survey designers can learn from this; create clear purpose, and avoid repetition. If the team at *Pokémon Go* can get it wrong, you bet you can too.

Don't pressure yourself in thinking that you will become a game-based survey designer overnight and get everything perfect; rather, think of yourself, at least for the moment, as a *play* designer, or an *experience* designer, an *emotion architect*, for which the tools you use just so happen to be games and gamification.

So take a deep breath, don't be nervous, and remember that you will be better at this than you think. Creativity is a muscle that can be exercised to become strong. So, go work out.

Note

1 Butler, Mark (2016) [accessed 22 May 2018] Why people are giving up on Pokémon Go, *iNews* [Online] https://inews.co.uk/culture/gaming/people-giving-pokemon-go/

Design your game-based research

18

Play '20 for 20'

A thousand factors make a great game; it's impossible to evaluate them separately when they all sing together in perfect harmony

Chris Crawford[1]

In this chapter you will:

- apply the game ingredients, game components, game elements and four game values to design an effective game-based survey;

- choose the research study that you would like to reimagine as a research-game or gamified survey – it doesn't matter if this is a past or a present study, just one you feel comfortable working with;

- use the four quest items from Chapter 16 to drive your research-game or gamified survey design – for reference, the items are your **Research Objectives map, Broader Themes log, Participant Profile(s)** and **Concept Board**;

- use the **vocabulary of play** from Chapter 14 to inspire different terminologies that might better fit the game-based research experience;

- play a game to design a game-based survey: '20 for 20' is a game where you will take 20 minutes to design what would be a 20-minute research-game or gamified survey;

- explore the advantages and drawbacks of your design.

Why play a game to design a research-game or gamified survey?

Researchers must undertake many tasks and solve problems:

- communicate with people they've never met before;
- ensure those people feel comfortable to be honest and open about some realistic and conceptual things;
- stimulate those people to be creative and problem-solve;
- ask those people to imagine future scenarios, products and services that don't exist yet;
- stimulate those people's memories;
- engage people to complete surveys to the end.

To encourage these kinds of creativity, productivity and problem-solving in participants, researchers need to be creative, productive and problem-solve themselves. Playing a game, as we saw in Chapter 7, encourages these abilities,[2, 3, 4] and designing (anything) *is* problem-solving that requires creative solutions. Play stimulates the mind to do so.[5]

In addition, research shows that more creative ideas come when our unconscious mind has material to work with.[6] Hence, this is why you will be using the four quest items from Chapter 16 to work with during the game.

In playing 20 for 20 you will be involved in 'serious play'; a play experience with a serious goal, with a time limit of only 20 minutes. While this may seem very mean to put you under pressure, the limitation of time will induce 'eustress' – good stress! Eustress helps us to overcome challenges[7] and gain a sense of achievement.[8]

I am a believer in learning-by-doing; by experiencing what it is like to be engaged in a playful task to inspire creativity and problem-solving, you will have first-hand experience of what that process could feel like for participants.

Before you play 20 for 20: four steps

Step 1: assess technology

What technology are you using? What kind of overall design are you looking to create? Depending on whether you are using augmented reality, virtual reality, using a highly visual and dynamic game playable on PCs and mobile devices, or just using text-on-a-screen, this will determine the direction of your design.

If this is your first time designing a game-based survey, you are recommended to try designing for 2D (flat) interface that will be used on PCs and mobile devices. As you gain confidence, you can move on to design game-based surveys for other platforms like VR, AR and so on.

Step 2: apply the game ingredients, game components, game elements and four game values

When designing a game-based survey, you must create all your game ingredients first and think about the game values; this builds the foundation of your research-game or gamified survey before you add any game components or game elements.

As a researcher embarking on game-based survey design for the first time, applying these aspects can be overwhelming: what sort of goals do I offer to bring value to the participant? What rules should I create? What will the feedback be? How can I offer autonomy opportunities beyond how the participant answers questions or interacts in simulations?

As a game-based research designer, your job is already halfway complete in that we already have rules and autonomy opportunities in our surveys:

- **Examples of rules**: you can't go back in a survey. You must answer with 200 characters or fewer. You must select only one answer option etc.
- **Examples of autonomy**: participants can answer the questions however they wish.

Although a game-based research designer can apply more in terms of rules and autonomy opportunities, the fact that this is largely taken care of by the structures inherent in surveys means you can focus on the other two ingredients: the goals and feedback. When all these are applied, we know that researchers are capable of encouraging the six vital states of inspiration, motivation, intrinsic engagement, play, flow and enjoyment.

Step 3: use a narrative to tie everything together

You will need something to tie your game ingredients and game value together – this is why I recommend thinking of a storyline to help harmonize the research content with the game techniques. When you are trying to think of the storyline that will guide your participants through the research content and six vital states, it can take a while for the 'eureka' moment.

You may go hours, even days, without making the connection between 'story' and 'research objectives'. But the moment you do, all the game ingredients fit into place. For instance, the goal of the narrative becomes the goal of the game, the rules become part of the story, the reward systems become part of the story progress, and in some cases, those rewards can even be used to help participants advance in the storyline in the game.

Step 4: 'group' research content together in levels

Tie together questions that relate together so there is a seamless flow from one subject to another. For example, in product development research you will want to group together questions about packaging, flavours and price separately so the participant can give full focus to each area. If using a

Figure 18.1 Prompts to design a game-based survey

Narrative

Why should your participant take part? What's the trouble to overcome? How can the participant become the hero or heroine in the story? The narrative must be relevant to the research content.

Goal(s)

Create incremental goals to perpetuate motivation, leading to the ultimate end-goal. Ensure goals have internal consistency in the game world or game narrative.
If using a narrative, the solution in the story should be the goal.

Autonomy opportunities

What are the opportunities for freedom and movement?
Can the participant answer which categories of questions they want to answer first? Can they explore or build an environment to their liking? Can they do things like share their own ideas & opinions, even when they don't have to?

Rules

How is the participant limited in their autonomy? Can they go back to change previous answers or behave differently in previous simulations?
Can they skip ahead? Do they have to complete a question, simulation, level or the entire experience in a limited time?

Feedback

How is the participant doing in the story? Can you design achievements and feedback that relate to the research content, other game ingredients, and help the participant achieve goals? Is there an ultimate-value piece of feedback once the end-goal is reached?

simulation where behaviours are observed in context, you can gain data on all areas at the same time, but there should still be consideration to the user flow when trying to gain data on separate elements.

But what if you don't have the time, software capabilities or money to create beautifully designed research-games or gamified surveys? Often, a research supplier is already paying a licence for survey software and can't deviate from that. As such, all the game-based survey designer can toy with is the text on the screen and basic visuals (like inserting a photo in a survey). But even with these rudimentary capabilities, you can still borrow from games to increase your chances of gaining intrinsic participant engagement. Because actually, no matter what time or budget you are on, all game-based research designers will start with the same question: why would anyone want to begin, and complete, my game-based survey? In essence you are asking 'what value can I offer participants'? This is where you can start with the four game values (discussed in Chapter 4) to your research-game or gamified survey design. For ease of reference, these are:

- **Self-discovery value** – where participants are able to take part and discover something about themselves.
- **Transcendent value** – where the study makes it clear that the participants are part of something bigger than themselves. This can be offered as part of a story in narrative value, and with the other values too.
- **Narrative value** – where a story guides the participants through the research content.
- **Knowledge value** – where the participants can unlock knowledge about the research content, or information related to the research content.

These values act as both a goal *and* a feedback system for the participants. It's the feedback they get about themselves that becomes the goal in 'self-discovery value' and it is learning about how a narrative unfolds that becomes the goal in 'narrative value'.

Once you have thought about your game ingredients and game values, you can use these checklists to prompt ideas. Remember that these components and elements have benefit for market research as we explored in Chapter 4, but should be used only where required.

For game components (CABIN), don't forget about using:

☐ Collaboration;
☐ Aesthetic;

Table 18.1 Fill the gaps

Client objective	Narrative in summary	Narratologically relevant reward	Overall goal
An athleisurewear brand wishes to understand consumer preferences for activewear bottoms (price, design, fit etc), among women aged 25–45+ in the USA.	The participant is invited to be a designer for a day. Through making different design decisions, the participant then levels up to make more creative and complex design choices.	The user is given three certificates for completing their challenges as a designer, one for completing each level. The certificates are awarded to the participant in achieving basic design status, advanced design, and super designer status.	Goal is to level up to the super designer status level.
A university wishes to understand how their current students perceive the university, such as their likes, dislikes and areas for improvement. The client also wishes to understand student commitments outside of university life so they can better understand their lifestyles and other non-related university priorities.	The participant has a friend who's also interested in coming to the university in the future, and wants an honest guide about what to expect. The friend visits the participant 'on campus' to get the (digital) tour.		
A technology and innovation focused magazine wishes to understand how satisfied their readers are with the magazine, as well as content likes and dislikes. Consumers are majority male aged between 30–50 with an HHI of $75k+.	The reader must stand in for the regular magazine editor, and must develop their version of the 'perfect edition'. In doing so, data is collected on preferences and desires.		

☐ Bonus features (and novelty);

☐ Increases in difficulty;

☐ Narrative.

For game elements (ATARE), don't forget about using:

☐ Avatars;

☐ Timers;

☐ Audio;

☐ Role-play;

☐ Environments (virtual or otherwise).

I have used this flow for designing games for seven years; it has never failed me and it won't fail you. Table 18.1 contains some examples of research objectives and their storylines to show how the above chart works in action. This illustrates how important starting with a *relevant* narrative really is. Look at how the reward systems become narratogolically relevant, and help to create an overall goal to the game in a seamless way.

Your challenge, as a way to 'dip your toes in the water' is to **complete Table 18.1**. There are no right or wrong answers – only what you think will be the most effective.

Did you notice how the storylines have an element of trouble to over-come, or the participant is encouraged to think 'in someone else's shoes'? In *The Storytelling Animal: How stories make us human* (2013) by Jonathan Gottschall,[9] he tells us that all stories have an element of trouble to overcome. And in *The Grasshopper: Games, life and utopia*,[10] the author Bernard Suits defines games as 'the voluntary attempt to overcome unnecessary obstacles'. So both games and stories have obstacles to overcome. With this clear over-lap, this is why narrative is a great place to start because it allows the game ingredients to fall into place naturally as the 'story' unfolds.

Now you have been able to 'dip your toes' into thinking about game-based research design, let's play the 20 for 20 game.

How to play the 20 for 20 game: design your game-based survey through play

Overview

In just 20 minutes, fill out the activity sheet and begin to develop a story-board of your research-game or gamified survey. The storyboard should show exactly what your participants will see from the very first screen, through to the final screen of the research experience. Remember, stick people drawings are okay!

Logistics

You can have **one or two players,** or you can play in **a team or competing teams.** Preferably, work in two or more teams and make it a competition – more ideas will be created and can be merged at the end.

What you need

You need paper and marker pens to draw your storyboard. Make sure you catch every idea on paper during the game – even if the idea is the most fleeting thought with seemingly no relevance, write it down or draw it out.

Have your four quest items at the ready:

- **Research Objectives map;**
- **Broader Themes log;**
- **Participant Profile(s);**
- **Concept Board.**

Print these out and have them in front of you. This will help you stay focused on the problem you are solving and discourage you in designing for 'design's sake'. As you begin your design keep asking yourself: how is this goal, feedback, narrative, use of avatars, environment etc relevant to the study? Anything irrelevant should be removed. Every part of your design must have a function.

Your goal as the designer is multipurpose

This is where the knowledge from all the previous chapters comes together:

- Heed the knowledge from the ethics chapter, the vocabulary of play (where relevant) and the 10 tips for building the right design foundations from Chapters 13, 14 and 15 respectively.
- Think about emotion and experience: is it necessary to, and can you, construct a design to simulate emotive and experiential environments?

- Ensure the payoff for the participants (the reward) is reflective of their efforts.

- Ensure that the design allows for self- and creative expression.

- Keep internal consistency with the gameplay and narrative.

- Evoke the six vital states – think about how you are going to inspire the participants, motivate them to begin, intrinsically engage them and encourage play and induce flow, while providing an enjoyable research experience.

Six rules of the 20 for 20 game

Categorize your research objectives and business needs for level development. For example, in a study about creating a new product, Level 1 can be focused on questions about preferences, Level 2 can be focused on idea-generation and Level 3 can be focused on pricing and so on. Categorizing the questions and translating these questions as levels will help your narrative flow and ensure the participants can focus on one subject area at a time. In traditional surveys, this is often known as 'chunking'. This process will also help you design achievements or rewards that are related to the level content. For example, if the participant has completed a level regarding idea-generation for product names, you may wish to design an achievement that reflects his or her efforts in that area so that the rewards are narratologically relevant and relevant to the research questions.

- **Adhere to the four game ingredients.** Goals, autonomy opportunities, rules and feedback. Tick them off as you include these ingredients in your design.

- **Only spend time designing for a strict 20 minutes.** This will discourage over-deliberation and encourage more 'raw' design thinking.

- **No cheating!** If you are playing this game competitively, move away from the other person or team so you don't even get to peak at their drawings or overhear them talking. You want to make sure you have *more* than one set of original ideas, and there is no point playing competitively if your ideas cross over through cheating. More interesting ideas will arise if different people are working on the same project separately and can combine ideas together afterwards.

- **The game-based survey you design should only take a participant 20 minutes to fill out.** This is why the game is called 20 for 20, because you're going to restrict yourself to design what would be a 20-minute game-based survey, in just 20 minutes.

- **Think of a name for your team if you're designing in a group with others or competitively.** This will make sure the creative juices start to flow.

PLAY 20 FOR 20:
DESIGN YOUR 20-MINUTE GAME-BASED RESEARCH
IN 20 MINUTES!

Fill out this worksheet to help prompt your thinking and your design. If you are using a narrative, then start with an appropriate and relevant story and link the game ingredients with the story. If you are not using a narrative, ignore the 'story' box.

GAME NAME:_____

Narrative

Goal(s)	Autonomy opportunities

Rules	Feedback

START YOUR 20-MINUTE COUNTDOWN NOW.
If you have everything ready, start your stopwatch for a 20-minute countdown now.

STOP THE CLOCK AFTER 20 MINUTES.
How did you do?

Playing this game goes to show how even in as little time as 20 minutes (which you could steal away before work or during a lunch break), you can create an engaging, effective design by following the guidelines of the game ingredients, components and elements and thinking about the four game values.

However, no matter how well-designed your game-based survey might be, you won't know about its effectiveness until it is built and out 'in the field'. But before that day comes, there are opportunities and limitations to consider, not just in your specific design of a game-based survey, but the general opportunities and drawbacks of the methodologies.

Advantages and drawbacks

Every time I play 20 for 20 in a guest lecture or workshop, I see the enthused faces of delegates; happy that they have been able to create what they think is an engaging, effective design. But, their faces seem to drop at the reality that their design might never get off the ground because of some of the preconceived notions about games and gamification that their team members, or clients, might have (to which I say, send them a copy of Chapter 3 'Debunking common misconceptions'), and because of things like the amount of time it will take to build, the concerns about costs and so on.

It is likely that your list of pros and cons is the same as everyone who has played this game. Table 18.2 is an amalgamation of the feedback from a few hundred people who have played 20 for 20 over the years. Note that the perceived disadvantages in the chart are not my own, but an accumulation from players of 20 for 20 over the years to illustrate that you have the same concerns as your peers, but we'll look at how to dispel those perceived disadvantages. The perceived advantages and disadvantages of their designs are more often than not the same among the different groups I play this game with.

This comparison shows that ultimately, it is a lack of time and money that are the immediate drawbacks. But with researchers able to save time and money through increased engagement, and through that increased

Table 18.2   20 for 20 players' feedback

Advantages	Disadvantages
Engaging design can lead to better response rates and completion rates	Researchers might not have time to fully design a game-based survey (with graphic development and programming etc)
Where response and completion rates are higher, this could save the time in field	More money required to develop the game-based design than a traditional survey
Saving time in field can equate to money saved and larger profit margins per project	Would need to run a pilot study to make sure the design is effective and 'works', which can cost time and money
Participants would enjoy the experience and likely come back for more in the future	Lack of human resources skilled and/or available to design and build a game-based survey
Could also improve continuation rates across multiple touch-point studies	The game-based survey design could induce participant bias
Could gain better data quality as participants are more engaged	Role-play might mean people 'forget' to answer about themselves and be too immersed in their character.
Could gain untapped insights through observational approaches and passive data collection	If an Avatar Creator Tool is included in the design, this can take weeks to develop
This could lead to better evidenced and sound business decisions for research clients through better data quality and untapped insights	If music is used, it can take time and money to source and edit for the game-based survey

completion rates, the drawbacks of time and money will eventually become obsolete.

Yes, the initial investment of time and budget is a must – but the benefits of clients gaining better quality responses and participants becoming engaged for fruitful ongoing relationships with both parties is invaluable. As we explore in Part Three, there are many ways in which to upcycle content and create a game-based survey design architecture to increase your return on investment, as you can use things like Avatar Creator Tools, virtual environments, even some reward graphics, time and time again for future studies. Creating a library – a 'game-based survey engine' (much like digital games for entertainment are built using game engines like Steam or Unity) will allow you to develop research-games and gamified surveys using the same process as how we use existing survey software to quickly build surveys.

For concerns about participant bias, the response is twofold:

1 Game-based research designers (like myself) spend more time researching the audience and trying to understand them and their existing
relationship with the research content than those scripting traditional
online surveys. This is so we can ensure we are asking the right questions
and/or creating the most appropriate game environments to engage the
participants and immerse them in the research subject, stimulate their
memory, evoke the relevant emotions and so on. As several 20 for 20
players have noted in the past, 'We should build Participant Profiles and
do this much upfront research *for every research study*!'

2 With straightlining, button-mashing and lack of participant engagement
so commonplace with traditional surveys, bias doesn't even come into
play when we consider that some responses are completely inaccurate
or useless anyway. When a participant is straightlining through a survey
because of lack of engagement, who is worried about bias when the
results can't even be used?

In addition, we have already explored how games can immerse people
emotionally in different contexts, so bias can be *reduced* by using games
techniques.

In terms of people being carried away with role-play, we have already
explored that reminders of the realism in the fantasy can be useful. In short,
the way we design the game-based survey can be instrumental at negating
this perceived drawback.

Finally, what I would ask is this: is it sustainable to *keep* making the same
traditional online surveys that spur low engagement? No. Isn't it time to
invest in real change? Yes. Therefore, we must invest our time, money, skill
and take some risks to future-proof our research using games.

ACTIVITIES

- **Play 20 for 20 to create more game-based survey designs with different
  research projects.** Try to work on a range of research subjects with
  different audiences.

- **Play 20 for 20 with others.** Share your ideas afterwards and merge them
  to create new storyboards.

Notes

1 Crawford, C (2003) *Chris Crawford on Game Design*, New Riders Publishing, Indiana

2 Kanani, Rahim (2014) [accessed 22 May 2018] The transformative power of play and its link to creativity, *Forbes* [Online] www.forbes.com/sites/rahimkanani/2014/01/25/the-transformative-power-of-play-and-its-link-to-creativity/#54cfa373115c

3 Fox News (2012) [accessed 25 May 2018] Work hard, play harder: Fun at work boosts creativity, productivity [Online] www.foxnews.com/health/2012/09/13/work-hard-play-harder-fun-at-work-boosts-creativity-productivity.html

4 Hammon, Darell (2010) [accessed 22 May 2018] How to boost creativity, productivity and morale in the workplace: Let your employees play, *Huffington Post*, Updated 6 December 2017 [Online] www.huffingtonpost.com/darell-hammond/how-to-boost-creativity-p_b_523069.html

5 Vaughan, Christopher and Brown, Dr Stuart (2010) *Play: How it shapes the brain, opens the imagination, and invigorates the soul*, Avery

6 Williams, C (2015) writing in *The Human Brain, New Scientist: The Collection*, 2 (1), Chapter 9, p 119 (magazine) published 5 March

7 Nelson, Debra L and Simons, Bret L (2003) [accessed 27 May 2018] Eustress: An elusive construct, an engaging pursuit, *Research in Occupational Stress and Well Being* [Online] https://www.emeraldinsight.com/doi/pdfplus/10.1016/S1479-3555%2803%2903007-5

8 O'Sullivan, Geraldine (2011) [accessed 22 May 2018] The relationship between hope, eustress, self-efficacy, and life satisfaction among undergraduates, *Social Indicators Research*, 101 (155), Springer [Online] https://doi.org/10.1007/s11205-010-9662-z

9 Gottschall, J (2013) *Storytelling Animal: How stories make us human*, Mariner Books, New York

10 Suits, B (1978) *The Grasshopper: Games, life and utopia*, University of Toronto Press, Toronto

PART THREE
World of
Making – overview

Building your design and seeing it 'come to life' is one of the most rewarding things about the game-based research process. But how do you go from a design, like the one you created in the 20 for 20 game in Part Two, to a fully-fledged and working game-based survey?

First, you must prepare the necessary documentation. In this world you will explore the documentation to prepare for the building process – from storyboards to 'data maps' so you can onboard not just your client, but your own team. From there, you need to assess whether your game-based survey is built for a one-off, ad-hoc study or if it should be used long-term for increased ROI and sustainability. We will also question the benefits and drawbacks of 'tailor-made' versus 'ready-made' game-based surveys, but also the middle ground of 'customizable off-the-shelf' game-based surveys.

Once you have chosen the path that suits your needs best, it's time to build; this is the programming and playtesting stage. Part Three: World of Making takes you on a step-by-step journey from 'design on a piece of paper' to a live, working game-based survey.

Stakeholder onboarding and preparing to build your game-based survey design

19

This chapter explores:

- evolving your game-based survey design from the 20 for 20 game: seven materials you will need to articulate your game or gamification idea and engage key stakeholders;

- using these seven materials as a blueprint to guide the build stage, where the game-based survey is programmed and playtested. These materials will form your Design Proposal and Storyboard (DPS).

Preparing the materials you need for build mode, and for client and team onboarding: your DPS

In Part Two: World of Design, you designed a game-based survey by playing '20 for 20'. Next, you will want to articulate the research-game or gamified survey idea and design for three audiences:

- your colleagues;
- the research buyer;
- the programming team (who will code the game-based survey from your design).

A Design Proposal and Storyboard (DPS) describes the collection of documents to help you communicate your design idea to these stakeholders. The DPS also communicates things like the data outputs, user flow, survey logic, where passive data is collected and other information. A programmer, as much as a research buyer, would need this information.

You will need these materials in preparation for Chapters 20 and 21, when you are assessing whether or not to create a tailor-made or re-useable game-based survey architecture, and for 'build mode' (programming the research-game or gamified survey). Note: the materials in this chapter are not exclusive to game-based research methods. As a researcher, these are the kinds of materials you should use and actions that should be undertaken when you adopt any unexplored methodology.

When I first started Research Through Gaming, there were no rules, handbooks or design guidelines on what kinds of material and documentation to prepare. I developed and evolved these as time went on, from feedback to new iteration, to develop the most effective collection of materials that includes everything you and your stakeholders need to gain approval to build the game-based survey.

The documents are noted in sequential order; for example, you would be unable to create the Storyboard without the graphics, and you would be unable to generate the Why Guide without the research brief.

1 Research brief

This document should cover everything the research buyer has described as the research objectives and business needs. To prepare this document, there are key questions to ask to ensure the study is as focused as possible, for example:

- Why this research, and why now?
- What do we already know about this area of study/brand/audience?
- What is the budget?
- Who are the target audience?

A full list of relevant questions to ask the research buyer in order to prepare a focused Research Brief can be found in any good market research book.

2 Why Guide

When you have generated the idea for the research-game or gamified survey design, you will need to document the reasons for choosing some of the styles of aesthetic, narratives, question wording and so on. As covered in Part Two: World of Design, this is part of the SIMC process – where every design aspect needs to be functional. Your Why Guide will include research that evidences your design choices, information that you might want to share with the client so they can truly understand the reasons behind every decision made, and how it comes back to upholding their research objectives and gathering effective insight. A Why Guide helps the client see the design from your point of view, and is a great tool for onboarding the client. You can explain anything from why specific fonts were chosen, to why certain background music was selected, to why certain rewards are designed the way they are.

3 Graphics

The digital graphics for your game-based survey must be made so the research buyer can fully understand the design and see what the participant will see. No matter how great a text-based description may be of your idea, or even how detailed hand-drawings may be to show off the design, the nuances of digital design will better capture your ideas for the aesthetic and user flow. Once the graphics are complete, you will use them to create the storyboard.

4 Storyboard

A series of PSDs (Photoshop files) or other picture files aren't going to give the research buyer, your team, or your programming team any idea about your design, therefore the graphics need to be displayed in the user flow order in a storyboard. You can use PowerPoint, Keynote or other software you find appropriate to show your team every screen of the research-game or gamified survey in sequential order, from the first screen the participant will see to the last (Figure 19.1).

5 Screen by Screen script

The storyboard on its own provides a visual walk-through of the game-based survey, but won't have the level of description or instruction required to show the research buyer or programmer what is expected to happen in each screen, level or simulation. That's where the Screen by Screen script helps. This document should be both descriptive and instructive of what is happening in each screen of the storyboard, for example: 'Once the participant presses "start" on the countdown timer, a 30-second countdown will

Figure 19.1   A hand-drawn Storyboard forming part of a Digital Information Pack

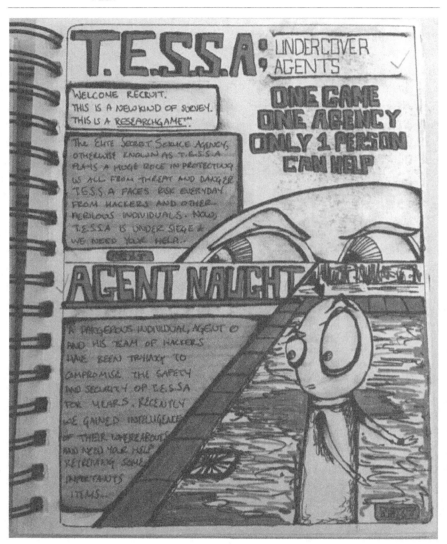

SOURCE © Research Through Gaming Ltd

begin' or 'Data will be collected on how long the participant has taken to complete this activity' or 'If the participant guesses incorrectly, he or she "loses a life" but will have two more opportunities to find the right answer'. Screen by Screen scripts have been valuable to the programming teams I've worked with, not just to understand the ways participant interaction is expected, but what should happen when *unexpected* interactions take place. For instance, another instruction in your script could be 'If the 30-second timer runs out, the participant should have another opportunity to start the activity again'.

6 Data map

Just like coding a traditional online survey, we need to know where the redirects will be, what the character limitations are (if any) to an open-end question, if a series of answer options are single response, multi-response, numerical response or otherwise. The data map is the 'Word document' version of your game-based survey, outlining each question/activity in chronological order.

7 Price and timeline proposal

Only once you have all the above items in place can you create a price and timeline proposal where, as the name suggests, you will outline:

- the internal cost for the game-based survey design and build;
- the fee to charge the research buyer;
- the time required to build the game-based survey;
- other services that the researcher buyer might need such as data analysis, insight reporting etc;
- how long the development and playtesting process will take – it's worth creating a timetable to add to this document (more on playtesting is covered in Chapter 21).

Other points to consider: What if the client decides to change aspects of the game-based survey later on, will you charge for that? If so, what are your rates? What will your fees be for language translation, for rerunning the game-based survey in the future, for more completes etc? By thinking of all eventualities, and pricing them accordingly internally and/or externally to clients, you can make sure the execution of the design is financially viable.

You've prepared these materials, now what?

You will need these materials for Chapters 20 and 21. The materials will help you understand whether or not to create a tailor-made or re-useable game-based survey architecture, and for programming the research-game or gamified survey.

Tailor-made versus ready-made game-based surveys 20

Differences, benefits and drawbacks

This chapter explores:

- the differences, drawbacks and benefits of tailor-made and ready-made digital game-based surveys;
- editable templates: creating a game-based survey architecture to re-use for multiple research studies.

There are pros and cons to both creating a pre-made game-based survey that you can use for a variety of research subjects and wide-ranging groups of participants compared with creating a tailor-made game-based survey, specific to a client or demographic of participants.

Exploring the tailor-made approach

Research buyers and suppliers shouldn't be put off by how long it takes to develop tailor-made game-based surveys. The time needed to develop the initial idea, design the graphics, programme it, playtest it and launch it is actually a shorter time-period compared with the digital games industry. As game designer Chris Crawford notes, in the games industry the duration of building is so long it can grind away at creativity: 'such is the time from inspiration to product'.[1] If you asked an indie game developer to create a game that collected specific data, developed with the ethics guidelines and professional market research codes of conduct in mind, it's likely that this process could take over a year. We are living in a day and age where a team of hundreds of people could labour for several years to bring a commercial game to market.[2] By contrast, the longest time my programming team has needed to build a tailor-made ResearchGame has been around seven weeks for a 40–45 minute ResearchGame with *all* the bells and whistles, including but not limited to music and sound effects and a bespoke Avatar Maker. This is a much faster development time by comparison to the entertainment games industry – but only because I've created and streamlined the processes and build stages – something which you should also consider.

For anyone embarking on game-based research for the first time, you should allow yourself three months from the initial design stages through to launch, to accommodate the time you will need to develop the required skills, acquire the right human resources, prepare the right documentation, and other parts of the process.

Tailor-made approach advantages

It's unique

Creating a tailor-made research-game or gamified survey means it will be completely unique to your client. You would be surprised how much a research buyer will value that they have a research approach that is completely their own and unlike anything that a competitor is using. This is a value-add that doesn't cost anything extra, as the high value perception and uniqueness is a by-product of something being bespoke.

It's specific

Even the same research topics, like researching the frequency of use for laundry detergents, will have different target consumers and specific needs from different clients. Consider, for example, the customer feedback survey. The way you approach your game-based survey design for a customer feedback survey to parents for a toy store would be completely different from, say, a customer feedback survey for C-level executives about the purchase of a software product. As such, being specific via the bespoke approach means designing your game-based survey in such a way that you are working to truly engage a distinct group of people for a specific product or brand. The more honed-in you are on such detailed elements, the more you can engage and be relevant to an audience, and through that, gain better data quality.

Cost

'Budgets for games have risen from about US $25,000 in 1980 to several million dollars today, a hundred fold increase' notes game designer Chris

Crawford (2003).[3] A research buyer can expect to pay around the price of a 1980s game for a game-based survey today.

In the book *Market Research in Practice* (2016), the authors note a research project can cost the equivalent of a medium-sized saloon car.[4] A quick internet search shows that a middle-of-the-range brand, medium-sized saloon car is between £27,845 and £33,915. By contrast, a tailor-made game-based survey can be less expensive, or at least similar in price. The authors of *Market Research in Practice* also show a 10-week timetable from the initial commissioning meeting through to the presentation of research results. This is a similar length of time to the time required for a tailor-made game-based survey. In fact, my most speedy development time has been less, at eight weeks from initial design to fully implemented research-game.

Tailor-made approach drawbacks

Scalability issues

Imagine you have created your bespoke game-based survey for a client. You have invested weeks from the commissioning conversations through to design, development and launch. You want to get the most out of that investment of time. But, because you have designed your game-based survey so specifically for your client, their needs and the audience, you can't really re-use the research-game or gamified survey anywhere else. As such, this represents scalability issues and can limit your ability to benefit further financially.

Time

Like the tailor who crafts away at a suit for weeks or months, you can pour your time into a product only to receive a one-time fee. Of course, this is a completely different set-up from those who mass-produce suits and may sell them cheaper, benefiting from economies of scale. Although the same time is needed for the tailor-made game-based survey approach and the traditional online survey approach as we read about above, more time is needed initially to learn more about game-based methodologies, acquire new skills and hire the right human resources.

Exploring the ready-made approach

Ready-made game-based surveys – advantages

The advantages of ready-made are pretty straightforward:

- Upfront investment in the product means your team can focus on sales, and your programming team can focus on developing other products.

- Buy-in from research buyers takes less time: they don't have to wait to get a game-based product specially made for them.

- Because the buying cycle is faster, and more straightforward, this can increase quantity of sales (which has its own benefits, naturally).

Ready-made game-based surveys – drawbacks

Ready-made game-based surveys would still need customization; a research buyer might want to alter the questions and/or game scenarios to suit his or her own needs, and may want to do things like put the client's logo on the survey and so on. However, these levels of customization for ready-made survey products don't usually go beyond those sorts of simple changes, which can be restrictive. Ready-made game-based survey products assume that 'one size fits all'. There is little to no wiggle room to do things like change the vocabulary to cater for different ages of audience, or perhaps if you are using audio, change the music and sound effects to harmonize with different research content. As such, the ready-made game-based survey product isn't as engaging as it can be and isn't as fully catered for the target audience.

Exploring the middle ground: building re-useable game-based survey architecture

I went into a hardware store to buy paint and asked a member of staff if they had a specific shade of turquoise. He pointed me to the Valspar brand section of the store, a brand that had an in-store wall of what looked like a million colour swatches, each colour ready to be made as paint in less than 10 minutes, in any size container. Customers could also hand over almost any piece of material that had the colour they liked, and the Valspar technology could match the colour and mix up the paint right then and there. Their computer told the paint-mixing machine exactly how much of the primary colours to mix for the quantity of paint the customer wanted. Human involvement was needed to do things like put the pre-prepared containers of paint in the 'shake machine' (a machine that clamped and shook the paint container until all colours were mixed) and they quality-checked that the final colour and consistency of the paint was satisfactory for the customer. This was automated and product-driven customization. It was making the bespoke into a product that could be mass-produced. Game-based survey architecture can be developed like the tailor-made Valspar paint.

As long as you invest the time upfront to create the process and the foundations of the 'basic' product, your research-game or gamified survey can be customized to deliver something specific and unique while ensuring you benefit from scalability and make your valued time go further. This approach is arguably more commercially sound as both the supplier and buyer can have a higher return on investment. Budding game-based survey designers are encouraged to follow this route where relevant. While you might want to start with a tailor-made approach to get an idea of what types of clients are mostly interested in game-based research, think about what types of research studies you mostly carry out (for example, voice of the customer or product preference testing) and what groups of participants you are mostly asked to speak to. From there you can think about developing a game-based survey design architecture that fits, say, voice of the customer among mums, but with areas of customization to suit different clients. Therefore, you get a semi-tailor-made and semi-ready-made approach that can still be specific to an audience, but general enough that it can be re-used in the future.

ACTIVITY

Think about the participants you mostly need to communicate with, and what types of research you typically conduct. Play 20 for 20 again and design a customizable game-based survey architecture that could suit many different types of clients for the same or similar research content. This way, you'll end up with a collection of different research-games or gamified surveys that answer different research needs.

Notes

1 Crawford, C (2003) *Chris Crawford on Game Design*, New Riders Publishing, Indiana

2 Crawford, C (2003) *Chris Crawford on Game Design*, New Riders Publishing, Indiana

3 Crawford, C (2003) *Chris Crawford on Game Design*, New Riders Publishing, Indiana

4 Hague, P, Cupman, J, Harrison, M and Truman, O (2016) *Market Research in Practice*, 3rd edn, Kogan Page, London

Build mode 21

Create, playtest, maintain and launch your game-based survey

This chapter explores:

- the human resources required to build your digital game-based survey;
- options to upskill – learn how to become a graphic designer or programmer;
- playtesting – key aspects of your game-based survey to analyse and test;
- launching your game-based survey – soft launching, analysis and full-launch.

You have understood the power and relevance of game-based research in World 1, you have created a game-based survey design in World 2, and now you are ready to make your game-based survey come to life. This is the most technical part of the process. If you are not a 'techy' that's okay, because you will probably need to hire technical support to build your game-based survey but it is still important to understand and implement good playtesting and execution procedures.

Being involved with the making of your first research-game or gamified survey design is a huge learning curve, and rewarding. Watching the levels come to life, where you can playtest them after only seeing your designs as graphics files for weeks is exciting, and exciting for the client. Every one of my clients has always been delighted to get involved in the playtesting process because for them it is also the first time they see the design come to life, and see what the experience will be like for the participant.

The most important advice is to **always add buffer time to your development schedule**, especially when you are working on your first game-based survey design. Even the most experienced programming team can't predict the myriad of things that could hinder progress, like the Amazon Web Server (AWS) going 'down' (which actually happened in 2017, and disrupted operations for many businesses) or a browser carrying out an impromptu update. These are both extreme examples, but if you speak to people working in digital media development, they will tell you to add in buffer time so make sure you do, no matter how tight timelines are.

With good project management and working with good programmers and graphics designers (and adding in the all-important buffer time), the 'making' process should be a relatively stress-free and exciting experience.

Finding a good graphic designer, or becoming a graphic designer

There are thousands of great graphic designers. However, being a self-taught graphic designer, I couldn't imagine anyone else creating the graphics for the ResearchGames I design. I am aware that no one will be able to understand the audience as I have done, who will understand the clients' research and business needs as I have done, and therefore couldn't create the ResearchGame graphics with the same nuances as I do. Also, and perhaps more crucially, the DIY approach saves a lot of time; by the time I articulate to a graphic designer that some text should be moved up a few pixels, a shade of blue changed, or the contrast of a product image darkened, I could have done it myself.

My recommendation is to use Adobe Photoshop to begin with; this is one of the more complex graphic design programs compared with free programs available, but will teach you how to create graphics that developers can work with. There are lots of online free trials and tutorial videos to get you started.

If learning this new skill is not an option, you could look within your own company or team for a graphic designer. You never know if the person sitting a few desks away from you is a wizard with Photoshop. If no one in your network can help, hire a freelance designer. Check out his or her portfolio. Good designers will typically have examples and case studies on their websites.

Finding a team of programmers, or learning how to code yourself

My choice is to go for the former, not the latter. What I could learn about programming even in a year of intense training couldn't match the years of knowledge accumulated by a qualified and experienced program-mer. Your programmer or programming team should be able to produce device-agnostic platforms and have experience in platforms that also collect data. As with the graphic designer, you will want to see a portfolio of work.

You've got your dream team together – now what?

It is now time for you to take on the role of project managing the development stage, making sure the graphics are correct and tidy for the programmers to use, and ensure that your team are developing to the milestones/schedule you have agreed. This is where the materials in the Design Proposal and Storyboard (DPS) from Chapter 19 are needed. These materials will articulate the user flow, interactions, data to be collected, survey logic and other important elements.

Playtest and review

With any luck, your development progress is going well, and now it's time for you to playtest your game-based survey *before* going live. This version of your game-based survey is known as the alpha version. If you have spotted something that doesn't look as you intended aesthetically, or something isn't working, create a detailed playtesting report:

- **Highlight the exact location of the error and the error type:** be it a typo or instructions for a different font size. Where relevant, note the level, screen number, and get a screengrab. Make sure your playtesting report is clear on whether the problem is technical (for instance, one of the screens is not loading) or something which developers might call 'superficial'. In programming terms, superficial means something aesthetic-based that is easy to fix, like changing font size, the positioning of an image, and other 'look and feel' aspects. As such, your playtesting report should be clearly sectioned into feedback on technical issues and aesthetic/superficial aspects.

- **Note what device, device version, browser and browser version you were using at the time of playtesting.** This will help your programmers replicate the problem to pinpoint what's going wrong and find solutions. For instance, 'I'm using my MacBook Pro, macOS Sierra, version 10.12 with Chrome, version 58.0.3029.81.'

- **Make suggestions on solutions and be specific.** In reporting superficial errors, make it clear to the programming team and/or graphic designers what should change. If you want a button to be 'more blue' be helpful by selecting the shade yourself or finding the shade HEX code.

Once the playtesting report is completed, share it with your programming team and ask how long it may take for the issues to be resolved. Bear in mind that some technical errors may not have a clear duration of time to be fixed, as it may be something a developer needs to investigate first, then figure out how the problem was caused so the team can implement a solution. Once all items are resolved, you can move on to the beta stage, where you will need to playtest the next iterations of the game-based survey design. It may be that further issues are spotted, or if all goes well, you can move on to the soft launch of your game-based survey.

Launching your game-based survey

Hurrah! Reaching this stage means your research-game or gamified survey is ready and has been given the stamp of approval for launch by your client. But just like any other research project, follow best practices by conducting a soft launch first.

A soft launch gives your team and your client time to review the data coming through. A soft launch is usually when a survey is completed by a percentage of the entire quantity of target completes – usually between 2 per cent and 5 per cent. This process lets you know if participants are experiencing any issues, and if they are, you will want to make sure they have a way of telling you. Including a 'help' button in your game-based survey is useful, or a contact email address in the e-invitation. With any luck, your extensive playtesting means there are zero issues, but even the most experienced website, games and app programmers often face issues illustrated by users that they couldn't have predicted. Once issues are resolved, you are ready to fully launch your game-based survey.

ACTIVITIES

- Put a call out to your team: who already has some of the skills and experience discussed in this chapter, that you could harness to build game-based surveys?

- If no one in your team or company has these skills, seek out quotations and advice from practitioners in the relevant fields.

- Prefer to upskill? Check out Chapter 23: Building a career in game-based research.

Analysing the quality of game-based research designs

This chapter explores:

- methods to analyse the quality of game-based research, including the assessment of participant engagement and identification of engagement gaps;
- the three facets of design success: participant engagement, client satisfaction and research impact;
- the iterative design of one of my own ResearchGames, as an example;
- five key ways to improve game-based research design.

To analyse the quality of game-based research designs, a variety of aspects must be considered including but not limited to data quality, completion rates, drop-out rates and whether the design addresses the research questions. Pilot testing for design weaknesses is essential. As with any research methodology, the quality of game-based research designs must be tested not only before launching the study, but also during and after the study has finished. Because game-based surveys can include things like narrative, music, avatars etc, this means there are more moving parts, and potentially more opportunities for design weaknesses compared to traditional questionnaires.

The process of seeking out design weaknesses should be interpreted as a gift of knowledge. Each time you identify weaknesses and implement solutions, you grow as a game-based researcher. Along the way, take detailed records of what went wrong and why, and carry that knowledge into your next design. There is as much to learn from what was ineffective, as well as what was effective.

What constitutes design weaknesses and how to detect them

Design weaknesses are any elements of the research, for instance weaknesses in accessibility or aesthetics, which are ineffective. This could include a design component that unintentionally creates user confusion or user error. Ideally, weaknesses should be spotted before the research goes live. There are two approaches to detecting design weaknesses: solicit feedback during the design stage; and measure these three facets of design success: participant engagement, client happiness and research impact.

Solicit feedback during the design stage

Before programming the game-based survey, solicit feedback from stakeholders, including the client. These people are your 'concept testers' who will evaluate the game idea and Storyboard. Their feedback on three main elements is essential:

- **Clarity of instructions:** Do the concept testers understand what they are expected to do during the game-based survey? Can the legibility of text and images be improved? Can the comprehension of any audio or visual materials be improved? What aspects of the activities are confusing?

- **Consistency of content:** Do the design, narrative and visuals match the research topic? Where are there disconnects? For example, do concept testers feel that the narrative drives their immersion in the research content, or do aspects of the narrative and direction feel 'shoe-horned in'?

- **Research impact:** Most importantly, is it clear how the results will answer the research objectives and support the business needs of the research buyer?

Early feedback from concept testers will reveal where design improvements can be made. And, it is easier and less time-consuming to amend images, audio and video during the storyboarding phase rather than in a live study. Plan to solicit feedback before the 'build' stage in order to incorporate improvements into the next design iteration.

Keep in mind that some design weaknesses cannot be detected during the storyboarding phase. For example, issues such as accessibility, unexpected screen layouts on different devices and slow loading times won't be revealed until a study is programmed and playtested as an alpha or beta version.

Measure these three facets of design success: participant engagement, client satisfaction and research impact

Monitor the three facets of design success while the study is live as well as after it has closed. If an activity within your research-game or gamified survey is identified as not user-friendly, or the background music is distracting, or the narrative is convoluted, this will influence engagement, results and impact. Monitor the three facets throughout the process to ensure you have a successful study.

Participant engagement, client satisfaction and research impact are inherently connected. When participants are engaged, they will provide quality research results, which will in turn satisfy client needs for insight. The opposite is also true. Participants who have been button-mashing (or barely responding at all) are likely to be disengaged, won't provide quality data and there will be little chance for insight or impact. The process of understanding why participants become disengaged will reveal design weaknesses.

Let's look more closely at the three facets of design success and how to analyse the quality of the research design.

Facet of success #1: Participant engagement

In Chapter 8, we explored the 12 signs of player engagement and learned that intrinsically engaged users are creative and collaborative. These 12 signs are an excellent way to measure participant engagement. For example, did participants go 'over and above' the call of duty? Did they conduct any voluntary actions? Did they try to take part in the study a second or third time (the replay effect)?

In addition, consider:

- Response rates: high response rates are good measures of interest in the topic.
- Completion rates: high completion rates are good measures of participant engagement and satisfaction.
- Drop-out: high drop-out rates are indications of a problem within the research. Look for the spot where most people drop out and try to make improvements there.
- Data quality: issues with data quality can point you to sections of the research that might be confusing, boring or have high cognitive load.

To help you understand participant engagement further, be sure to also:

- Include a space for participant feedback near the end of the study. Watch for key words such as 'enjoyed', 'engaged', 'fun' and 'thank you'. If you don't see these types of descriptions, your design might need further iterations.

- Take note of whether participants voluntarily ask to participate in more research like this in the future.

- Approach the design like an engineer when you discover negative participant feedback. Document the issues and implement solutions.

- Ask participants if they would like to take part in game-based research again in the future. This will help you understand if there is a continuation desire, which is an outcome of intrinsic engagement and play.

- Record the duration of participant interaction from start to finish. This will help you understand if satisficing, or taking the easy way out, has taken place.

Facet of success #2: Client satisfaction

Client satisfaction with the resulting insights is usually evaluated after a study has closed. However, the usefulness of data can be evaluated while the research is still in field. Ask your client (and yourself):

- Does the client feel that their research questions will be answered via the research?

- Is it clear how the results can be used? Will the results be actionable?

- Will the results answer the questions of the original research objectives?

- Are participant responses rich and detailed, or full of blank and nonsense responses?

If there are concerns while the study is live, revisit the design around those problematic data points.

Facet of success #3: Research impact

No matter how conceptual or straightforward the research topic is, all types of research results can be quantified and compared to benchmark data sets to permit some sort of 'pre and post' or 'before and after' view of a situation. Ideally, your research buyer has a set of benchmarks that allows them to measure any improvements in data quality and impact of the results in their business.

Similarly, research suppliers should also have a set of key benchmarks. Once these are identified, a number of questions can be addressed:

- Are the data and results as expected? Or do they challenge expectations?
- Do the data directly address the research questions and allow the research buyer to make valid and reliable decisions?
- Can the research buyer show tangible examples linking insight to impact (eg before and after comparative information)?
- How is the research helping the client's business in other ways?

CASE STUDY Dissecting a ResearchGame

Title of ResearchGame: *What Kind of Student Are You?*
Research buyer: University of Surrey, United Kingdom
Audience: Prospective university students from around the world aged 18 to 22 years old

Purpose

Through previous research, the University of Surrey had segmented students into six types. The purpose of the research was to understand how many prospective students fell into each of the six segments, and understand their different interests and values in relation to university and university life.

The information derived from this study would help the university evolve their:

- understanding of the changing landscape of prospective student segments who are interested in studying at their university, and;
- marketing communications to engage the different segments.

Context

Based on previous research, 10 university interests and values accompanied each of the six student segments. For instance, the 'safety conscious' student profile type had 'security' as one of their interests and values. The 'socially driven' student profile type had 'nightlife' as one of their interests and values. Thus, across six profiles, there were 60 interests and values.

The ResearchGame went through three design iterations. The first user flow was as follows:

Step 1: Each prospective student (participant) answered four demographic and 17 'golden' questions. These questions determined the participant's segment and profile result.

Step 2: The profile result appeared on the screen with a visual and text-based description that students could download and share.

Step 3: Participants were then shown a list of 10 interests and values relating to their expectations and desires for university and university life, and were invited to adjust the list as well as create a 'hashtag' to identify other important elements of university life that were not already on the list.

Step 4: The study was complete. However, as a form of intrinsic incentive, participants could then review other profiles, download their own profile, provide feedback about the ResearchGame or visit the university's Instagram profile.

The 'interest and values' and 'tag' questions (pictured in Figure 22.1) were designed so students could add a hashtag, as is commonly used on social networks like Twitter, to identify additional topics that were important to them. These questions were specifically designed to gain insight into how the interests and values for each student profile might change over time. The data from these questions would support the research purpose: to enable the evolution of marketing communications so that they could engage more effectively with the six different student types not just in the present day, but also in the future.

Problems

Few participants answered the 'interests and values' and 'tag' questions, despite being engaged in the previous questions and gaining their profile result. The small amount of responses we did get were revealing and important (eg #MakeNewFriends, #LGBT and #FieldTrips), but there were too few to conduct any type of thematic analysis or to identify patterns and segment responses.

Why did so few participants answer these questions? Was it an issue with the vocabulary, the layout of the questions, the instructions, or something else? What did I do wrong?

Two external reviewers were brought in to offer a fresh-eyes approach to the user experience. Their feedback was quick and surprising. Neither playtester realized there was a step after receiving their profile result. They simply did not notice the 'NEXT' button at the bottom of the screen. This instantly explained why so few people completed those questions, and the need for the first design iteration was immediately obvious.

Figure 22.1   A close-up from Version 1 (original) design of the ResearchGame showing the 'interests and values' and 'tag' questions. The NEXT button, although large, was easily missed

SOURCE © Research Through Gaming Ltd and University of Surrey

Design change 1

Looking back, it was easy to see how the 'NEXT' button could have been missed – the button was transparent. The second design iteration employed a larger 'NEXT' button and changed the colour from transparent to green to make it more pronounced.

Unfortunately, this still did not resolve the problem as a further pilot test revealed that people still didn't answer the two questions. This time, we hypothesized that perhaps participants were not motivated to answer further questions because they had already received their profile result – they reached their goal. A second design change was necessary to test this hypothesis.

Design change 2

The 10 interests and values and tag questions were moved to appear before the profile result screen. In addition, the question wording was revised (Figure 22.2). The process would be slightly longer for participants now because they would have to answer those two questions before their profile was revealed, but we were confident that this move would be effective. We had already seen that 97 per cent of participants who began the 17 golden questions went on to complete them and receive their profile so we knew the profile was valuable enough to participants to consider answering two more questions before they received it.

The result? The percentage of participants who left a tag after receiving their profile increased from 1 per cent to 4 per cent. Unfortunately, quadrupling the number of responses was still insufficient to develop a detailed thematic analysis. Another design iteration would be necessary.

Design change 3

Interests and values activity

In this third iteration, the question was revised such that participants were asked to select their top three interests and values from the 10-point list rather than deselect the items they weren't interested in. The difference in the wording can be seen in Figures 22.2 and 22.3. We hypothesized that people were better at identifying what was more relevant as opposed to identifying what was less relevant.

Figure 22.2   BEFORE – Version 2 of the design showing the interests and values and tag questions

Thanks!

Now let's look at things that might be interesting or valuable to you as part of university and university life. We guessed 10 different things.

Did we get it right? What did we miss?
Tell us so we can determine your result!

Here are 10 items we guessed.
Take away the items that are *not* priorities or of interest, and only leave the things that are important to you.

Social atmosphere	Campus environment
Enjoyable subject	Social facilities
Meeting people	Nightlife
A town I like	Having fun
Sports facilities	Moving from home

What else is important to you?
Add tags to tell us what would add to your university experience.

#AddATagHere #DescribeYourValues

FIND OUT WHAT KIND
OF STUDENT YOU ARE!

SOURCE © Research Through Gaming Ltd and University of Surrey

Figure 22.3   AFTER – Version 3 showing the interests and values and tag
questions. This was the final design used in the live ResearchGame

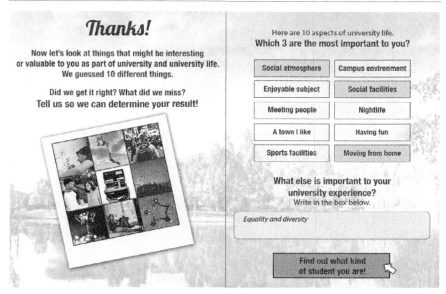

SOURCE © Research Through Gaming Ltd and University of Surrey

Tag activity

As you can see in Figure 22.1, participants were asked to 'create tags' not
'create a hashtag'. We hypothesized that the word 'tag' was being misinterpreted
to mean naming someone as they might do with a social media image or status
update using the '@' symbol (like when you tag '@' a friend in a photo). Further,
we hypothesized that some participants might not have known how to generate
the '#' (hashtag) symbol on their device.

Thus, in this final design iteration, the term 'tag' was completely removed.
Instead, rather than encouraging concise answers with a hashtag, the length
of the response was left undefined. Participants were offered a more familiar
comment box to provide their answer.

Positive (and unexpected) results!

The percentage of participants who completed the golden questions and
received a profile result decreased from 97 per cent to 91 per cent. However,
responses to the interest and values and tag questions increased: 9 per cent
of participants responded to the 'tag/comment box' question, and 28 per cent
responded to the interests and values question. We now had sufficient data for
themes and patterns to emerge.

Participants were engaged and enjoyed the research as a 'self-discovery' experience

Though obvious now, at the time of designing the ResearchGame, I hadn't thought of it as a tool to help students assess what they were truly looking for from university life. By including a feedback question in the study we learned that students found the research to be helpful:

- 'It was really helpful and interesting. This quiz helped me to rethink myself and what it feels like to join a big university. Thank u.'
- 'It was a very fun quiz and made me asks question I didn't think of asking before, a great idea for undergraduate students in my opinion.'
- 'Really useful and informative.'
- 'I like the insight it has given me.'
- 'I really liked the quiz and think that it is a brilliant thing to help students with confidence and know a little bit about where they will fit in at university.'

Self-discovery can be a valuable tool to engage participants, even for people who are notoriously hard to engage in traditional online surveys, like students.

The ResearchGame became a marketing tool in itself

My clients often distribute their ResearchGames in different ways compared to traditional online surveys. They might place the ResearchGame on their company website or promote the study on social media. For this particular project, the *What Kind of Student Are You?* ResearchGame was shared on social media, displayed on the university's website homepage, and promoted on a variety of print and digital marketing assets. Creating a better research experience was something the client was happy to share, and students were happy to see a university take more care in developing better and useful research experiences.

The iterative design changes made a marked difference and eventually resulted in the insight tool the client needed. By assessing the quality of the research design through iterations, the degree of interaction with non-mandatory questions improved.

As a final step, the issues were documented and lessons for future improvement were learned. These five key learnings will help you in creating effective game-based survey designs.

Five key learnings to improve game-based survey designs

Be open to having the design challenged

The 'fresh-eyed' playtesters challenged what was thought to be a coherent user flow – it wasn't! Be open and actively listen to constructive criticism.

Don't get attached to the design

Being open to having the design challenged means you can't get attached to it. Research must perform a function for the research buyer and participants. If a design element is not effective, then change it or lose it.

Be willing to admit the design has weaknesses, and take the time to make improvements

Be transparent with clients about design weaknesses and share ideas for how to improve the design. Create a communication environment in which the client can share ideas too. Clients will appreciate your dedication to design improvements and they will be collaborative and appreciative if you are transparent. Remember, design weaknesses are rampant in all types of quantitative and qualitative marketing research, not just research-games and gamified surveys. Give yourself a break, take a breath, and keep improving.

Get some fresh eyes on the case

As the game-based survey designer, you will be biased. With potentially hundreds of hours invested in the research project, you cannot test it with fresh eyes. You have probably playtested the same level dozens if not hundreds of times, so some of the most important components of the study can become 'invisible' to you. It is essential that you hire fresh-eyed playtesters who have never heard anything about the research to review it.

Sometimes the design flaw isn't related to the game or gamification design

Sometimes, participant engagement issues aren't related to the game-based survey design, but rather the question wording or something technical. By deliberately looking at the three facets of design success, problems linked to, or not linked to the design (again, such as unforeseen technical issues) can be speedily identified and improvements/solutions implemented.

PART FOUR
A New Market Research World – overview

While exploring game-based research, it may seem as if the prospect of research-games and gamified surveys is futuristic, but it isn't. The real future lies in how game-based research evolves with technologies already inherent in the games industry: virtual reality (VR), augmented reality (AR), automation, artificial intelligence (AI), motion sensing technologies and more.

The full powerful potential of game-based research can be realized in combination with these technologies, not just using these technologies in isolation for market research. For example, VR is already being used for research, but not in combination with games. But how long before participants tire of VR research? Before they get bored with walking through virtual spaces and answering questions? That's why games must be used in combination with these technologies because play and intrinsic engagement, as we have already explored, are key to ensuring successful market research with increased participant productivity, problem-solving, focus, creativity and collaboration, among other benefits.

While some predictions of the future in this world may sound far-fetched, the reality is that the technology to do these things is already happening. It is impossible to pick up a copy of any technology- or business-focused publication without seeing examples of this; articles exploring combinations of game theory, Serious Games, game technologies, engagement and data collection feature in every publication I have bought for the last decade. In some examples, we see how VR games are already used to engage, motivate and collect data to diagnose and improve mental and physical health,[1] and how *Pokémon Go*, the AR game, became one of 2016's most talked-about hits.

The future is undoubtedly here, but it's our ability to imagine what game-based research can do that will flick the switch from doing business as usual in market research to working with what are currently unusual (but will soon become the 'new normal') affective methods of engaging participants, collecting data and gathering insight. Indeed, the future of our world and the role of games within it, in combination with technologies like VR, AR, AI, automation and motion sensing technology, have already been imagined. Fiction, such as *Ready Player One* (the book by Ernest Cline and Steven Spielberg's movie adaptation), *Westworld, Black Mirror* and *Star Trek the Next Generation*, shows us worlds where these technologies are used synonymously and harmoniously with data collection.

What scope do these not-so-unreal visions have for market research? This world explores what we should expect in the next 5 to 10 years, including new careers and new skills for market researchers.

Note

1 Armstrong, S (2018) Gaming is shaking up mental health, *Wired*, UK edn (May)

Building a career in game-based research 23

This chapter will explore:

- advice on building a career in game-based research;
- relevant skills that will help you become a well-rounded game-based research methodology practitioner;
- future careers in game-based research.

If you are ready for exploring new territory and rewarding challenges, then a career in GbRM is for you. What's more, building *a* career in game-based research builds *careers* in game-based research. The more people involved, the better for everyone. Now is the perfect time to get involved and push boundaries.

The moving landscapes of the games, data collection and insight industries opens many avenues for professional growth and the growth of game-based methodologies beyond the digital and analog research-games and gamified research we see today. As we explore in Chapter 24, there are exciting opportunities for GbRM with VR, AR, AI and more. Take advantage of these opportunities. We are in mostly unchartered territory so making your mark, however large or small, with some hard work, will be a fruitful opportunity.

Already there is promise from talented and bright young people who are eager to dive in. After my guest lectures at universities, common questions from students are: Which companies are using GbRM? How can I start a career in this area? And even whether my company has any vacancies. These are students who (as I have been told by their professors) didn't show much enthusiasm for traditional market research before.

Observing some 500 students design their own research-games over the course of many years gives me great confidence in their abilities; their designs never fail to fascinate. They totally 'get it'. Some students are already exploring GbRM through their own volition. One student from MICA University in India made research-games the subject of her dissertation. Another student had written about gamified surveys as part of a final module essay. Other students get in touch with me to show their experiments with different designs. RTG frequently receives résumés, without having advertised vacancies, from graduates who want a career in the area. Several years of observing this kind of energy from students indicates clearly that they are interested in data collection and insight, but it is GbRM that is going to engage the next generation of researchers.

This energy to join market research and explore GbRM is contrasted by the reality. Not only are there not enough, if any, careers available in this area but the market research industry as a whole struggles to recruit and retain young talent, according to an article by Hasson Associates[1] – a market research recruitment company. This situation must change for market research to survive and thrive because when graduates opt for roles in firms like Google, Amazon and Facebook, market research loses out.

But, with more research individuals and companies using and progressing GbRM, we can heighten the chance that future generations of researchers will want to join and stay. Clearly there is an appetite for it. Game-based research can create more jobs, and more exciting jobs, involving technology, design, analysis and engineering.

For the situation to improve, two things must happen. To entice future researchers, we need to attract them with the right environment – market research needs to be 'GbRM career ready'. To do that, we need more researcher buyers and suppliers adopting the methodologies. So, we need more GbRM experts *today*.

How to develop a career in game-based methods – five tips

1 Start today – design and experiment

Design analog-based research-games, VR-based research-games, avatar tools, experiment with audio in surveys, design questions as mini-games – get it wrong, get it right, but experiment, experiment, experiment. Create hand-drawn stick-people storyboards and get to grips with graphic design software. Keep notes of your design processes, what techniques have worked better than others, the participant feedback and results, response rates, completion rates etc. Prepare to get things wrong and learn. If you are on a budget, see if you can collaborate with a survey software supplier and/or panel supplier who may offer discounted rates if you offer to write a paper or conference presentation to share the results, and highlight their brand's involvement. In my very early research into the readiness of games as research instruments,[2] a sample provider developed my questions and provided the participant sample free of charge in exchange for being credited in the paper and presentation. Not every sample company may want to do that, but it doesn't hurt to ask.

2 Share knowledge

We know little of what we could know about the true scope of GbRM, so *any and all* knowledge is progress. While there are many people sharing knowledge now, this is often done in silos as any results or insight become commercial currency. The truth is: we need to pool our knowledge together and not just the success stories, but also which game-based survey designs *didn't* achieve desired results. The LinkedIn group 'Game-based Research Methods – GbRM' (request to join if interested) is one such place where researchers can share information and ask questions. Here are two ideas on what kinds of content to share:

Every client case study is gold – the successes and the 'failures'

As practitioners and academics, researchers are at once bound by client confidentiality as they are by a desire to share their knowledge on what case studies have shown. But, both things *can* happen. Approximately 40 per cent of Research Through Gaming clients have provided permissions to share our work publicly in various forums. But it's not just success stories we should share; there are key learnings in the failures too. What design tactics didn't work? Which groups did not seem as engaged as others? In my experience, audiences are more receptive when you share the pitfalls and the good results.

Content that helps you will help someone else

Did you read a paper on semiotics that can help other practitioners with GbRM design? Did you read a game design article that inspired your work in making a gamified survey? Did you watch a video on new mixed reality software that has promise for game-based research? Try to share inspiring and helpful content with other game-based research practitioners. Academia.edu, ResearchGate and a variety of other online social sites like the 'Game-based Research Methods – GbRM' LinkedIn group I've started (as part of the launch of this book) are great places to share such content and get connected with like-minded people.

3 Connect and collaborate

In developing game-based research designs, it can be easy not to notice the amazing work being achieved in the wider game-based research community (however sparse it currently is) or in the indie games industry, or indeed all the other disciplines relating to games for research such as developments in semiotics, heuristics and more. Check out who is doing interesting things and see if a skill or knowledge swap is possible. Achievement is nothing without collaboration.

And don't be shy to connect with people! There is nothing to lose. In my own experience, requesting expert interviews with leading figures in games and gamification has: a) been much easier than I thought, especially considering how time pressed the interviewees are; and b) fast-tracked my knowledge by providing an understanding of the nuances/arguments of the wider conversations around games, gamification and data collection that no book or article could have provided with the same detail. You will probably find most 'pracademics' open to connect as I did, but avoid brain-picking. Many of the key figures in these industries work as consultants and trade on their knowledge (ie writing papers, contributing to journals, providing keynote presentations etc) so their time is money. As such, explore ways you can give back – collaborate.

4 Learn new skills

Whether you are interested in digital research-games or gamified survey design, or using board games in focus groups, start to identify the skills you need for those jobs. Skills like coding or graphic design are not just useful for making game-based surveys, but also useful as transferable skills to do things like make infographics and improving insight-reporting presentations. Indeed, learning more about games and gamification will be transferable skills too; you can think about how to gamify internal training sessions, your next conference talk, and even use gamification in promoting your business.

The tips below are starting-off points in developing these skills to help kick-start your career as a GbRM designer. Readers are encouraged to conduct further research pertaining to their specific interests and view courses/workshops/webinars and so on in their region.

Graphic design

If you are on a budget, learning how to use graphic design software means you can do this work for the cost of your time, instead of hiring graphic designers – although hiring an experienced graphic designer is always recommended. What's more, if you do hire a designer, your experience in using graphic design software (however briefly) will help you to be a better communicator of ideas with the experts. It's all about learning the vocabulary as well as the skill. As a graphic designer of some 15 years, I still benefit from collaboration with other designers, especially with so many changes in trends and software updates; there is always something new to learn. An online search will quickly show how-to guides for packages like Adobe Photoshop, Illustrator, Sketch and so on – there is lots of content to help you get started.

Adobe Photoshop and Illustrator offer free trials, with a licence fee to the 'creative cloud' to be paid thereafter. If you are going to do serious digital design work, you will want the paid packages. For just learning the ropes, free graphic design programs like Gimp and Sketch are a good start. Your local training centre, college or university may also offer courses.

Coding

Learning how to code is not just a skill but also a mindset, and takes a huge amount of patience and time. Learning how to code properly can take years, but for those who want to make a start, *Codecademy*, the online (and gamified) programming education site is free and well reviewed. Seven programming languages are available including JavaScript, Ruby and Python (if these mean nothing to you, don't worry, *Codecademy* is great at introducing the uses and applications of these languages). Alternatively, your local training centre, college or university may offer courses. Again, nothing will beat hiring an expert programmer or programming team but learning how to code, even the basics, will again help you to communicate ideas better with the professionals.

Note: if your organization already licenses survey software, get in touch with the providers and ask if their developers can help you realize your designs. If they have the capacity, they may be able to help. You should expect to pay a fee.

Another alternative is using a game engine. Game engines include all the tools non-coders and coding beginners need to make a game, as Wordpress does for building websites. Game engines such as Unity, Game Salad and Amazon's Lumberyard offer non-coders the ability to make games, using their in-built game architecture. These are three of many different types of game engines. Some specialize in 3D games, some in 2D, VR games or all of them. This list from *Slant* recommends the top game engines for beginners: www.slant.co/topics/1907/~game-engines-for-beginners-and-non-programmers.

Microsoft's Azure is less game-focused and more about building general applications. The only issue with these platforms are limitations in data collection and exporting that data in a fashion fit for market research purposes. But using these platforms as a strategy to get you thinking about the design, the general user experience, the participant interactions and so on is a good place to start.

Game and gamification design

While there are fantastic 'how to' videos on game and gamification design online, attending a course is going to be more useful as you will have the freedom to experiment, fail and improve in a cushioned environment. You will also get to understand game and gamification design principles more holistically, and apply that knowledge to GbRM.

For game design, check out the best games courses at colleges and universities in your local area, or check out the 2018 *Princeton Review* list of the top 25 postgraduate courses in the world: www.princetonreview.com/college-rankings/game-design/top-25-game-design-grad. The *Game Designing* site also lists their top 75 courses globally: www.gamedesigning.org/video-game-design-schools. (Both of these lists are mainly US centric.)

For gamification design, this *Udemy* page lists online and offline courses: www.udemy.com/topic/gamification.

Learning these skills will take more of your time; university and/or college courses can take two or three years. Crash courses like this one at Nottingham Trent University in the United Kingdom (www.ntu.ac.uk/study-and-courses/courses/find-your-course/confetti/computer-games-design) are two to four weeks and probably more feasible. Again, check out your local area for short courses.

Research Through Gaming offers a two-day workshop through the Market Research Society specifically on learning game-based research theory and design, where you will create a design based on a genuine research project of your own. More details can be found on the MRS website: www.mrs.org.uk (search "Game-based research methods" or "Betty Adamou").

For conferences in this area, the following are great places to start:

- Game Developers conference (based in the United States): www.gdconf.com

- Future Games Summit (based in the United Kingdom): www.nbmevents.uk/futuregamessummit

- GWC conference (a conference based on using gamification for engagement, based in the United Kingdom): www.gwc-conference.com

5 *Learn job-specific skills to get you 'future ready'*

According to the Misk Global Forum, 65 per cent of children today will end up in careers that don't even exist yet.[3] The 'future careers' list below shows more than 25 potential jobs we can expect to see in the near future in GbRM. For whichever job titles grab your attention, find relevant courses, people and publications in those areas (for example, in sound or virtual environment design) and refer to the above tips – start experimenting in these specific areas, share your work, connect and collaborate.

Future careers in and/or related to game-based research methods

- Participant experience managers
- Sound engineers
- Music editors
- Music composers
- Research-game SFX specialists
- Concept artists
- Storyboard artists
- Graphic designers
- Playtesters
- Virtual reality environment designers
- 2D and 3D virtual environment designers
- Voiceover actors
- Research-game programmers
- Avatar clothing designers
- Avatar accessory designers

- 3D human modelling experts
- 3D product modelling experts
- Badge and reward designers
- Narratologists and scriptwriters
- Specialist project managers
- Specialist data analysts
- UX design specialists
- Heuristics specialists
- Videographers and photographers
- Research-game actors (people hired to play roles in research-games)
- Research-game models (people hired to pose for photographs so their image is used to portray a character in a research-game)
- Augmented reality gamified survey designers

This list encapsulates many of the roles I undertake myself: concept art, simulation design, 2D graphic design, music and sound effects editing. When you start out, you may also find that you also wear many hats until you find a specialism and develop a team of appropriate human resources.

Some of these roles are not as far-fetched as they sound. Indeed, many of these jobs already exist in the traditional games industry so it makes sense that these sorts of jobs, like 3D modelling, should exist in game-based research.

In a time where the market research industry has 'client success managers' it makes sense to have 'participant experience managers'. After all, the engagement of *both* audiences is crucial for market research to prosper.

Research-game actors and models will also become important because stock images of people won't always portray the expressions you want for the 'characters' in your game-based surveys. In the screengrab from ResearchGame *TESSA Undercover Agents* (Figure 23.1) we see the character Agent Naught played by my friend Carl, who was gracious enough to pose for the photoshoot. In the same ResearchGame, our client, Professor Liesbet van Zoonen, had a cameo role as someone administering a personality test. Sometimes creating your own footage is better than stock images but will take more time. For those who have more time constraints and need copyright- and royalty-free images, www.pexels.com searches through several sites and is free to download most images as long as the artist/photographer is credited.

Figure 23.1   My friend, Carl, plays the role of Agent Naught in the
ResearchGame *TESSA Undercover Agents*

SOURCE © Research Through Gaming Ltd. Image used with kind permission

Figure 23.2 The beginning of a living room concept my college made with Google Sketch

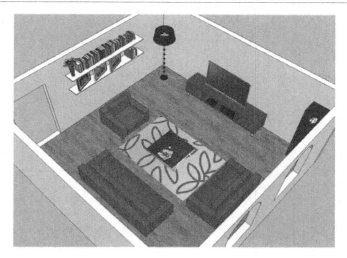

SOURCE © Research Through Gaming Ltd

Figure 23.3 Google Sketch allows users to create virtual environments and 'tour' through them as 3D spaces. You can use it to make 3D environments even if your research-game or gamified survey only requires 2D images, because you can take a screengrab of your virtual environment from any angle and you will have 'true perspective', like in this kitchen environment my college created. This might be faster than trying to create 2D images of 3D environments in a program like Photoshop or Illustrator

SOURCE © Research Through Gaming Ltd

Figure 23.4 Editing music to coincide with the different scenes in one of RTG's ResearchGames: I first record my screen as I play the ResearchGame, then place the recording with the music in an editing suite. As I go through the recording, I can see where the music and sound effects should change to coincide with the different scenes

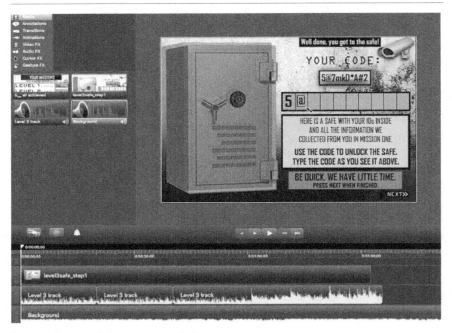

SOURCE © Research Through Gaming Ltd

There are many more job titles yet to be envisaged. Only with new technologies and experimentation can we begin to understand the breadth of new careers. Time will tell, but what we do know is that game-based research offers exciting prospects for young talent, can offer new pathways for veteran researchers, can completely change the way we interact with participants, and offers new levels of insight previously unavailable through traditional techniques.

Summary

- A career in GbRM can be rich and rewarding, and there are many opportunities to make your mark, but you will need to learn new skills and develop an understanding about related disciplines.

- There are many kinds of GbRM jobs to expect in the future – the earlier you get started in carving out these careers, the better your head start.

- Building your career and knowledge in GbRM will help others, as long as you collaborate, share your work and most importantly **experiment!**

ACTIVITIES

- Request to join the Game-based Research Methods – GbRM LinkedIn group and share content. Share your case studies as webinars, talks and other publications. As long as you contribute to collective knowledge of GbRM, you will make a difference in growing this part of the market research industry. This is *your* knowledge value and transcendent purpose!

- Select three job titles from the 'future jobs' list that interest you and investigate the skills you might need for those roles. This is your self-discovery purpose!

- Connect and collaborate with relevant people/organizations in the related fields (ie in AR, UX design etc). This is your feedback system and relatedness!

Notes

1 Hasson, Sinead (2015) [accessed 25 May 2018] It's time for MR to design a workplace for the future [Online] http://hassonassociates.com/2015/07/15/its-time-for-mr-to-design-a-workplace-for-the-future/

2 Adamou, B (2011) [accessed 25 May 2018] The future of research through gaming, Proceedings of CASRO Online conference, Las Vegas, 3 March [Online] www.academia.edu/9487174/The_Future_of_Research_Through_Gaming

3 Misk Global Forum (no date) [accessed 22 May 2018] Tomorrow's Job, Today [Online] http://miskglobalforum.com/tomorrows-jobs/

The future of game-based research

24

This chapter explores:

- predictions of how market research, influenced by games and game technologies, will evolve in 5 to 10 years with virtual reality (VR), augmented reality (AR), automation, artificial intelligence (AI) and motion sensing technology.

The market research industry is obsessed with innovation. Research buyers want it, and research suppliers want to be the face of it.

Fortunately, the games industry is not just one of the most innovative industries in the world, it is one of the most inventive. It is because of the games industry that many innovations in computer science have come to fruition. Thanks to the games industry, we can discuss the uses of AR and VR in the market research field. As Frank Lantz, director of the New York University Games Centre, writes in the foreword of *Rules of Play: Game design fundamentals*, 'there is a sense of boundless potential... that games could succeed film as the defining form of popular culture for the new century'.[1]

Games are the future of art and entertainment. They push the boundaries not just in hardware and software but also in human understanding, play, artistic expression, graphic design, AI, programming, sound, storytelling and data storage.

With games at the forefront of innovation and being the most engaging medium of all time (more than film and music combined),[2] is it any wonder that the homes of young adults have Xboxes and PlayStations to play games, access the internet and watch TV? Ten years ago, would anyone have guessed that a game console would be the multi-functional hub of your living room? Probably not.

So if it's innovation we seek, and researchers are already keen to borrow from the games industry (VR most recently), then games can provide market research with the innovation it wants. Game developers advance the technologies that researchers get excited about. In fact, so much of what researchers want to do with AI, automation and VR, like gain in-the-moment data, simulate experiences and understand behaviours in context, has already been done in the games industry. While the market research industry catches up, researchers also need to keep an eye on the horizon. Technology and games are evolving at such a rapid pace that by the time the market research community catches up, it will be time to move on again. As such, researchers need to think today about the future requirements of research buyers and suppliers, and game-based research will need to evolve to meet those ever-changing needs.

Research suppliers will increasingly support businesses that want to use an evidence-based approach to design decisions. This is already happening in the fashion industry, where one of my ResearchGames helped a sports brand with a new line of clothing.[3] Research buyers will continue to try to understand consumer current needs and desires as well as possible. But once they understand their consumers to the nth degree – what's next? **Predicting the future**. Becoming reliable trendwatchers. Pre-empting new trends to be 'event ready'. Research suppliers will need to behave more like oracles – using data to predict the future.

Market researchers are beginning to harness what is labelled 'System 3'[4] thinking to encourage participants to imagine hypothetical situations. The hope is that researchers can use these techniques to gain insight into consumer desires for future developments. SciFutures, a company that uses science fiction to help brands shape their business growth, uses their capabilities to 'rehearse the future'.[5] Research buyers want to know anything that will help them gain a profitable edge. Companies that can provide those services will become more commonplace.

With this in mind, the definition of what constitutes market research a decade from now will be unrecognizable. When games and other technologies are combined, researchers won't just be able to improve participant engagement, data quality, techniques or processes but *re-invent* what these things mean.

Here are 19 predictions of what game-based research methods (GbRM) combined with AI, VR, AR, automation, motion sensing and motion capture technologies might look like in 5 to 10 years.

Artificial intelligence and game-based research

AI is spurring excitement in the market research industry. It is forecast to disrupt and bring innovations to everything from survey design to field management.[6]

Like the other emerging technologies, AI has an ongoing relationship with games. AI learns by *playing* games.[7] As AI systems play games, problem-solving skills increase and 'intuitive thinking' grows. Alpha Go, the AI system from Google DeepMind, is now the world's best *Go* player. Human *Go* masters say the game requires intuition, which in turn requires creative thinking. If true, AI now displays human-like intuition and even curiosity[8] that has allowed it to top the leaderboard.[9]

AI is already prevalent in digital games. It is used to create intelligent non-player characters (NPCs) that interact with human players, mimicking human behaviours and conversations. As AI helps NPCs become more realistic, the emotional connection between player and game grows, helping to create what feels like genuine relationships in many game environments. As such, AI is a key component in creating engaging videogames. In a video interview with Peter Molyneux, creator of Project Natal (the codename for the early versions of development for the Xbox Kinect), we see just how real NPCs can feel. Molyneux talks about Milo, a virtual boy, who is said to feel so real that when he throws an item for the player to catch, people actually bend down to catch it because they feel 'so connected to Milo's world'.[10]

This AI technology can provide market researchers with a variety of benefits, which brings us to our first two predictions.

Prediction 1:
AI will create intelligent and emotive NPCs (non-*participant* characters) that will be used in digital research-games to encourage more natural 'conversations' with real participants; conversations that researchers can observe in context.

Prediction 2:
Human-like NPCs will be used as game-based survey moderators and 'survey guides', helping participants through VR- and AR-based research-game worlds.

When these predictions come to fruition, researchers can focus more on the design, data analysis and insight gathering process while gaining more accurate insight. 'Survey guides' and in-game moderators will help participants through virtual or mixed-reality environments, helping participants make fewer mistakes and feel more comfortable with the techniques. This will be particularly important since AR and VR technologies are relatively novel.

Where AI can be used to create in-game characters, researchers can gain more accurate insight by observing participant interactions with 'other people'. What kind of truths would participants share with an intelligent virtual doctor that they might feel too self-conscious to share with a human doctor, let alone a researcher, in real life? What things could we understand about brand perceptions by 'listening in', with consent, to conversations between friends, even if one of those friends is virtual? The development of intelligent NPCs would have huge benefits for data accuracy and gaining untapped insights otherwise unavailable through traditional online survey methods. They would bring qualitative research into the digital space with quantitative-scale insight.

In the entertainment games industry, AI will respond to player gaming habits and behaviours by evolving the game to suit their style. *Tech Radar,* in January 2018, notes: 'If AI was able to collect data on players and understand their preferred style of play, we could end up with game worlds that are more reactive to individual players in-game.'[11] If such capabilities become available, AI could impact GbRM in two further ways:

Prediction 3:
AI will be used with game-based research to collect data on participants and their preferences for products, services, brands etc, and create research-game worlds and experiences that react to individual participants in real time, in game.
Rather than use a one-size fits all research-game, AI will evolve the research-game experience to cater for different participants.

Prediction 4:
AI will use data from participant interactions in research-games to forecast future trends and predict consumer needs.

Why is it important that a digital research-game world caters for individual participants? We all have different circumstances, personalities, budgets, time to spare, and things we do in our leisure time. We all have different expectations of the clothes, food, products and services that we purchase. In that sense, there are billions of parallel worlds, with each individual in his or her own world. **Research-games can make those worlds digital and literal.**

If a research platform can understand our behaviours and habits, and can cater to a 'world' that better replicates our own experiences, then AI can learn (with great detail) what stimuli, nudges, promotions and marketing affect each participant. It can focus on things they find important, test things that are relevant and remove things that are not integral to their real life. AI could even replicate consumer homes in the digital world for research purposes. **Digital versions of our worlds could become gameplay environments for market research.**

Earlier in this book, we explored using long-term, re-useable simulation-based research-games that collect trend data over time. AI systems can be embedded in such research-games for predictive modelling. Research buyers can derive data from participants to run algorithms determining how consumers will react to anything from changes to product packaging to logo design, and more. What's more, this use of AI will help research buyers prepare for consumer trends and events that are not yet being considered. While AI forecasting is currently rudimentary, it is useful. Google AI predicts trends in fashion and even produces a fashion trend report.[12] Other AI systems predict delivery and transportation demands.[13]

In the games industry, AI is designing new videogames and even merging ideas to create entirely new game genres.[14] This brings us to our next prediction:

Prediction 5:
**AI will design, and help researchers design
engaging and effective research-games.**

AI could aggregate paradata and metadata across previous research-games to recommend more engaging designs or content for certain groups of participants. Researchers will have an evidence-based and automated approach to designing new research-games.

But what if a research-game is aimed at a new target audience that hasn't previously been researched before? AI would simply aggregate information from across the internet to make research-game design recommendations to you that would engage the target market. In short, AI could create the participant profiles, concept boards and storyboards for research-games in the future.

As well as using AI systems to design new games for entertainment, AI is also helping to design an array of products from spinal implants[15] to home furnishings.[16] AI is becoming creative through evolutionary computation.[17] Thus, AI aiding design for traditional and even game-based market research is at our fingertips.

Virtual reality and game-based research

Like AI, VR has a history, present and future with games and is another technology igniting interest in the market research industry. In 1983, a Japanese company called Takara Tomy Co. Ltd created the TomyTronic – a small handheld machine that looked like a pair of binoculars. The TomyTronic included simple games, and is arguably the first example of a head-mounted VR machine specific for gaming (and certainly the first one I ever experienced as a child. I had the red TomyTronic).

It wasn't until 1987 that the term 'virtual reality' became popular as a term to encompass what previous machines and head-mounted displays really did. Jaron Lanier, one of the 'founding fathers' of VR, first coined the term. He worked at Atari, the producer of the first gaming console, and later went on to co-create the first company to sell VR goggles and gloves.

Leap to 1991 and VR progressed again with the introduction of Virtuality Group arcade machines, which allowed people to play VR games while seated and wearing a head-mounted set. Since then, VR has been most closely associated with games.

In 1993, SEGA released their VR glasses. In 1995, the Nintendo Virtual Boy came to market. Now we are spoiled for choice when it comes to VR gaming. We can choose from PlayStation VR, HTC Vive, Oculus Rift, Google Daydream, Google Cardboard and Samsung Gear, and more are on the horizon. By 2025, the VR gaming market is predicted to be worth more than US $45 billion.[18]

VR-based Serious Games (Serious Games is a genre of games used for serious and/or commercial purposes, such as games for helping people in healthcare, employee training and other non-entertainment areas) may not be included in that dollar figure but it is a fast-growing and important market. In the book *Advanced Computational Intelligence Paradigms in Healthcare 6: Virtual reality in psychotherapy, rehabilitation, and assessment* (2011)[19] the authors list multiple uses of VR Serious Games in healthcare including helping people who have dementia, other mental health issues and physical challenges. At Sheffield Hallam University in the United Kingdom, VR games are used to help burns victims by placing them in alternative digital realities so they feel less pain;[20] such is the immersive power of well-designed VR games.

In the context of game-based research, VR can help us explore HR: Hidden Realities. What behaviours do people display in virtual worlds, and what do they pay attention to, that researchers can measure in VR but not in traditional research? Researchers can uncover what have been previously hidden truths about what people think, feel and what they will do. But why stop there? There is so much potential with VR and GbRM than virtual supermarket shelves.

Prediction 6:
Researchers will build multi-sensory VR homes, villages, towns and entire worlds, ready for consumer interaction at any time.

Such a capability would allow researchers to understand multiple layers of context when it comes to participant behaviours and choices. While ready-made virtual worlds on this scale would require significant investment, such products can be re-used time and again across a variety of studies. This means that:

Prediction 7:
Researchers will take advantage of the virtual reality (and 3D and 4D) rendering software used by the games industry.

Whether virtual homes, towns or worlds are built in VR or for flat screens, this will mean that researchers will need to harness the software commonly used by game developers to build such worlds. These systems allow game developers to build 3D, 4D and VR spaces, and have characters interact with them, like we see in many videogames such as *Call of Duty* (Activision) or *Gears of War* (Epic Games).[21] In the future, researchers could use game engines like Unity or Unreal Engine (used by game developers) or even build their own research-game engines, like my team did.

Augmented reality and game-based research

Augmented reality, the mixed reality software, has already been harnessed in dozens of fields. Basic forms of AR allow tangible physical glossy maga- zines to 'come to life' with digital overlays, like this example from *Esquire* magazine featuring the celebrity Robert Downey Jr: https://tinyurl.com/ y7cfbyun. But AR with AI does more; make-up company Rimmel London's app allows users to see their face made-up with the favourite looks, *IKEA Place* lets customers view virtual furniture in their homes, and the learn- ing app *Mondly*[22] helps people learn new languages in real time and on the move. We have also seen, and waved goodbye to, Google Glass. But, augmented reality in the games industry is on a different level.

Pokémon Go, the popular AR app game, should be a source of inspira- tion for market researchers. Players hunt for virtual Pokémon (characters who have different abilities – with some characters more rare than others) in the physical world. The possibilities this kind of AR game has for market research are endless: we can create engaging qual/quant experiences by overlaying digital components in the real world, helping participants do things like see products in different colours, shapes and patterns and select their preferences, or answer questions overlaid on their realities while on the move. Participants can use AR research-games to recognize and comment on anything they see and could even co-create urban development. *Blippar,* one of the first AR apps, is not only using this technology with great success but merging it with wearable technology, AI, and geo-location technology,[23] which paves a big road of opportunity for research. Participants could play AR-based research-games without having to answer questions at all, but data can still be collected accurately about the participants' movements and choices. This is already being made possible as Google is opening up Google Maps for game developers to make 'the next *Pokémon Go*'.[24] This brings us four more predictions:

Prediction 8:
Augmented reality will help research-games become forms of creative expression.

Prediction 9:
Researchers will use augmented board games in focus groups.

Prediction 10:
Researchers will use AR with wearable, motion sensing technology and location mapping.

Prediction 11:
Researchers will use audio-only AR research-games with location mapping.

At the moment, AR allows people to use digital interfaces to manipulate physical things – we can overlay different patterns on crockery, furniture and so on. But as AR and AI advance, it will become possible for participants to completely reimagine and manipulate the world around them, allowing AR-based research-games to become tools for invention and creative expression.

In terms of augmented board games for focus groups, we are already seeing how board games have evolved in this way in the entertainment sector.[25] With board games already being used in research, a digital component can help grow the focus group experience in other ways, allowing participants to imagine the future and see it digitally overlaid on reality while never having to leave the viewing facility. We could even have AR pop-ups from paper surveys.

In terms of audio-only AR, the research experience could be used by people who have visual impairments or don't want digital interfaces overlaid on reality. Imagine participants walking down the street. Their geo-location-enabled devices determine they are in the vicinity of a poster from a brand's new marketing campaign. An AI voice assistant, triggered by geo co-ordinates, asks participants if they have noticed the ad and, if so, what they thought of it. Rather than expecting participants to remember to fill in a survey at a later time, audio AR can overlay sound on reality to prompt thinking and act as a reminder. But why even be prompted? Participants could simply call a name, like 'Siri', to share their opinions with a market research company or a brand whenever they feel like it. Indeed, a whole new genre of 'hearables'[26] is becoming prominent already.[27]

Motion sensing and motion capture (mocap) technology, and AI, automation, and game-based research

The Xbox Kinect has 3D motion sensing, face and voice recognition, and has a lot of potential in research.[28] The technology uses dialogue, and represents an opportunity for researchers to use voice recognition to capture participant data. The technology also demonstrates people flicking through virtual clothes on a TV to 'try on' outfits without going to a store. This brings us to our next two predictions:

Prediction 12:
Researchers will use Kinect-like technologies with voice recognition and projectors to create fully immersive research-game experiences from the participant's own home.

Prediction 13:
Motion capture software with voice recognition will allow moderators to facilitate focus groups and other types of qualitative research from different locations.

Not only is motion sensing technology available and evolving, it is also combined with image projectors to convert our rooms into extended virtual environments. RoomAlive[29] (previously named *IllumiRoom*) projects game environments and characters around a room to extend the gameplay from the flat screen into four dimensions. Researchers could use this technology to bring the outside inside for participants wherever they are in the world. Indeed, they could bring a room from anywhere into a participant's home.

But how can motion capture and AI be used once data is collected? This brings us to:

Prediction 14:
Interactive insight: we will use motion capture technology
with AI and automation
to build realistic digital insight agents.

Brands want to understand consumers, and while qualitative research allows brand managers to watch consumers behind one-way glass, they rarely communicate with participants directly. Instead, the researcher is the 'middle person', translating his or her understanding of the consumer to the brand stakeholders.

But what if you could plug all the data you have harnessed about your consumers and allow a digital agent to play out the role of different consumers? Brand managers could ask questions and interact with a digital 'person' who could answer questions in a way their consumers would. While this won't (and shouldn't) replace research, it is an automated and efficient way to store market research data and make it 'come to life'. What better way than to visualize your data and insight than to actually communicate with it?

While thinking about a digital agent might bring to mind rudimentary chatbots and Siri-like systems, interactive, realistic human-like digital agents could be reality. The software exists to make this possible in the games and film industries[30] and AI has already been used to simulate many complex human behaviours.

In the games industry, AI systems are used for playtesting games, replacing real humans. AI systems use 'human player data to emulate human game play' including 'human-like imprecisions, limited reaction time, and choosing incorrect actions'.[31] If AI can simulate human behaviours in these complex ways, then it is possible to create AI systems that simulate consumer behaviours as well in the style of an insight agent.

Prediction 15:
Researchers will use motion capture technology with AI to allow
participants to build, grow and maintain their avatars.

While Avatar Creator Tools exist in research, these are currently 2D avatars that may have interactivity within a traditional or game-based survey environment. Our use of avatars will grow to become more intelligent.

AI will help to create more realistic non-player characters, but it could also be used to create a 'digital self'– an avatar – for participants. Facial mapping software can do this, like the software that is used for social media filters that overlay decorations onto selfies. A participant's avatar could be used in multiple game-based research experiences where rewards for participation could be avatar-related. Finished a short survey? Choose one of these three smartphones for your avatar! Finished an online diary study? Choose one of these three branded sweatshirts for your avatar! Not only can these rewards engage participants and help their avatars evolve, the data gathered on the choice of rewards can offer an additional layer of insight into preferences. Why stop there? Why not allow participants to design the clothing, gadgets and more for their avatars as rewards for survey completion?

Further predictions on the future of game-based research and market research in general

> Prediction 16:
> **Participants will demand more engaging research experiences.**

As researchers collect more data from participants, from multiple sources, the higher participant expectations will be. They will want market research to provide them with safe, ethical and engaging research experiences. As our day-to-day interactions with digital content evolve, participants (especially younger participants) are unlikely to put up with cumbersome and boring traditional data collection techniques. People will expect their research experiences to be like their other digital experiences.

> Prediction 17:
> **Brands will have more influence on the consumer research experience.**

Brands have used games as sources of consumer engagement and brand promotion for decades. As companies understand more that their research programmes are an extension of their brand, they will want the research experience to be viewed favourably by consumers – even if their brand isn't revealed in the process. The push for more innovation and engagement in research will continue to come from the research buyer.

Prediction 18:
We will make 'Insight Games' for research buyers.

Harnessing the intrinsic engagement and play that comes with games has multiple benefits for focus, collaboration, creativity and problem-solving for participants. We can also harness these advantages for research clients by using games to report insight and research results.

What I call Insight Games can help researchers distribute insight in immersive ways for maximum engagement, memory retention and to build empathy. An Insight Game can do anything from test knowledge and provide quizzes to guess correctly about different research results, to 'guess who' style games to retain information on consumer segmentation, and to allow the research buyer to be immersed in the participants' world to understand them better. Insight Games could immerse research buyers in engaging, emotive and experiential simulations to understand consumers better than ever before.

The more engaged and understanding research buyers are of research findings, the more likely those findings will translate into action. At the very least, an Insight Game would be more enjoyable than sitting through long presentations. **The future of client relationships is in serious play.**

These predictions show how the future of game-based research, or market research in general, is not far off. Not only are game-based approaches the future of market research, but market research needs to stay very close to the games industry if it wants to stay attuned to technology trends and be innovative.

When these predictions are realized, there will be more opportunities for the market research community to *invent* hardware and software systems specific to market research games, gamified experiences and data collection. Market research will need to employ game designers and game developers to do much of this work, or upskill existing researchers, who will need to use the software systems used for entertainment games as research-games. When that happens, the lines may very well begin to blur between what is a game and what is research.

Which brings us to the final prediction:

Prediction 19:
**The market research industry
and the games industry will merge.**

Notes

1 Salen, K and Zimmerman, E (2004) *Rules of Play: Game design fundamentals*, MIT Press, Cambridge, MA

2 Mobile games accounted for more revenue than any other form of entertainment in 2017, generating US $40.6 billion worldwide, according to *Statista* (www.statista.com/topics/1906/mobile-gaming/) and people spend more money on games than they do on movies and music combined (at an estimated revenue of US $92 billion in 2017) according to *Huffington Post* (www.huffingtonpost.co.uk/george-taylor/why-is-gaming-more-popular-than-music-and-film_b_10095376.html)

3 Adamou, Betty (2017) [accessed 22 May 2018] Data the new little black dress in fashion, *Research Live* [Online] www.research-live.com/article/opinion/data–the-new-little-black-dress-in-fashion/id/5026582

4 Caldwell, Leigh (2018) [accessed 22 May 2018] Introducing System 3: How we use our imagination to make choices [Blog] [Online] www.knowingandmaking.com/2018/04/introducing-system-3-how-we-use-our.html

5 *SciFutures* website: www.scifutures.com

6 Sackman, David (2016) [accessed 22 May 2018] Predictions 2017: Take the long view [Blog] *GreenBook* [Online] http://greenbookblog.org/2016/12/20/predictions-2017-take-the-long-view/

7 Gibney, Elizabeth (2016) [accessed 22 May 2018] Game-playing software holds lessons for neuroscience, *Nature*, 25 February [Online] www.nature.com/news/game-playing-software-holds-lessons-for-neuroscience-1.16979

8 Pavlus, John (2017) [accessed 22 May 2018] Clever machines learn how to be curious, *Quanta Magazine*, 19 September [Online] www.quantamagazine.org/clever-machines-learn-how-to-be-curious-20170919/

9 BBC (2016) [accessed 22 May 2018] Google's AI beats world Go champion in first of five matches [Online] www.bbc.co.uk/news/technology-35761246

10 Edwards, Andru (2009) [accessed 22 May 2018] *E3 2009: Project Natal Milo Demo*, uploaded 2 June [Online] www.youtube.com/watch?v=CPIbGnBQcJY

11 Boyle, Emma (2018) [accessed 22 May 2018] Game on! How AI is transforming video games forever, *TechRadar* [Online] www.techradar.com/news/game-on-how-ai-is-transforming-video-games-forever

12 The Economist (2017) [accessed 22 May 2018] Can data predict fashion trends? *The Economist*, 27 July [Online] www.economist.com/news/business/21725599-technology-may-be-disrupting-peculiar-business-can-data-predict-fashion-trends

13 Triskele Logistics (2018) [accessed 22 May 2018] Using Artificial Intelligence to Predict and Forecast Distribution and Transportation Demands [Blog] [Online] https://tinyurl.com/y7c8msd9

14 Parkin, Simon (2017) [accessed 9 May 2018] AI is dreaming up new kinds of video games, *MIT Technology Review*, 29 November [Online] www.technologyreview.com/s/609482/ai-is-dreaming-up-new-kinds-of-video-games/

15 Christian, Bonnie (2018) Want an original design? Better ask a machine, *Wired*, UK edn (May)

16 Holland, Oscar (2017) [accessed 9 May 2018] How Artificial Intelligence and Robots Can Change Your Living Spaces [Online] https://edition.cnn.com/style/article/joris-laarman-smithsonian-digital-design/index.html

17 Miikkulainen, Risto (2018) [accessed 30 May 2018] Evolutionary computation will drive the future of creative AI, *VentureBeat* [Online] https://venturebeat.com/2018/05/17/evolutionary-computation-will-drive-the-future-of-creative-ai/

18 Grand View Research (2017) [accessed 30 May 2018] Virtual Reality (VR) in Gaming Market Size Worth $45.09 Billion by 2025 [Report] [Online] www.grandviewresearch.com/press-release/global-virtual-reality-in-gaming-market

19 Ma, Minhua and Zheng, Huiru (2011) Virtual reality and serious games in healthcare, in *Advanced Computational Intelligence Paradigms in Healthcare 6: Virtual Reality in Psychotherapy, Rehabilitation, and Assessment*, ed S Brahnam and LC Jain, Chapter 9, Springer [Online] https://link.springer.com/chapter/10.1007/978-3-642-17824-5_9

20 Author unknown (2018) [accessed 30 May 2018] Virtual reality game helps ease pain for burns victims, *BBC News*, 18 April [Online] www.bbc.co.uk/news/uk-england-south-yorkshire-43744009

21 *Gears of War* game: https://gearsofwar.com/

22 *Mondly* game: www.mondly.com/ar

23 Blippar (2018) [accessed 30 May 2018] *The power of Augmented Reality & Computer Vision – Blippar's latest tech breakthroughs* [Video] [Online] https://youtu.be/yWYn5xvqsQI

24 Webster, Andrew (2018) [accessed 30 May 2018] Google is opening
    up Maps so game developers can create the next Pokémon Go, *The
    Verge*, 14 March [Online] www.theverge.com/2018/3/14/17114494/
    google-maps-location-games-jurassic-world-walking-dead

25 Peitz, Johan, Eriksson, Daniel and Björk, Staffan (2005) [accessed 30 May
    2018] Augmented Board Games – Enhancing board games with electronics,
    Proceedings of DiGRA 2005 Conference: Changing Views – World in Play
    [Online] www.digra.org/wp-content/uploads/digital-library/06278.47142.pdf

26 Hunn, Nick (2014) [accessed 30 May 2018] Hearables – the new Wearables
    [Blog] [Online] www.nickhunn.com/hearables-the-new-wearables

27 Robertson, Adi (2018) [accessed 30 May 2018] Bose's
    augmented reality glasses use sound instead of sight, *The Verge*,
    12 March [Online] www.theverge.com/2018/3/12/17106688/
    bose-ar-audio-augmented-reality-glasses-demo-sxsw-2018

28 An early demonstration of Xbox Kinect technology can be viewed here:
    https://tinyurl.com/yc77bobr

29 Dent, Steve (2014) [accessed 30 May 2018] Microsoft's RoomAlive turns
    your den into a video game level, *Engadget*, 10 May [Online] www.engadget.
    com/2014/10/05/microsoft-roomalive-illumiroom

30 Crecente, Brian (2018) [accessed 30 May 2018] Watch Digital Andy
    Serkis Perform 'Macbeth'. And then watch him perform it as an alien,
    Rolling Stone, 21 March [Online] www.rollingstone.com/glixel/news/
    digital-andy-serkis-shows-potential-of-digital-actors-w518178

31 Roohi, Shaghayegh, Takatalo, Jari, Guckelsberger, Christian and Hamalainen,
    Pertty (2018) [accessed 30 May 2018] Review of Intrinsic Motivation in
    Simulation-based Game Testing, Proceedings of the CHI [Online]
    https://tinyurl.com/yd6gm3x7

Final words

Researchers can't afford to ignore the power of games for research and keep doing 'business as usual'. We have seen that this is not sustainable, and could eventually render the market research industry obsolete. Ultimately, the more we give as researchers, the more we get from participants. The more researchers invest in better survey design and experiences, the more they will get back from participants in effort, collaboration and creative ideas.

Take heed of the 50+ years of research on the creative, problem-solving, focus-inducing benefits of play and intrinsic engagement. Take advantage of the way play fosters empathy, allows people to express their individuality, express their core truths, and even enjoy the passing of time in what is otherwise the mostly boring activity that is traditional online research. Commercially benefit from the ways play and intrinsic engagement encourage collaboration and a desire for continuation. Learn from how games and play are already being used to collect data and insight on a global scale. Take advantage of the self-fulfilment and personal growth that will come with providing valuable, enjoyable experiences for participants and mastering the skills you will learn in becoming a game-based survey designer.

Games, gamification and playful research are the future of market research. It is our insurance policy, allowing researchers to embrace and perpetuate invention, innovation, data quality and insight to improve the world around us. Game-based research will help us *thrive*.

INDEX